Rock Climbing for Instructors

Rock Climbing for Instructors

Alun Richardson

First published in 2001 by
The Crowood Press Ltd
Ramsbury, Marlborough
Wiltshire SN8 2HR

www.crowood.com

This impression 2007

British Library Cataloguing-in-Publication Data
A catalogue record for this book is available from the British Library.

ISBN 978 1 86126 422 0

Line illustrations by Chris Wheeler
Photographs by the author
Front cover photograph: climber Lucy Archer

Typeset by Jean Cussons Typesetting, Diss, Norfolk

Printed and bound in Great Britain by Bell & Bain Ltd., Glasgow

CONTENTS

ACKNOWLEDGEMENTS

Sir Isaac Newton said, 'If I see farther than others, it is because I stood on the shoulders of giants'. I am deeply grateful to all the talented instructors who freely shared their wealth of knowledge and experience with me.

Thanks must go to Pat Horscroft (who helped to turn an early version into something readable), John Taylor, Andy Long, S. Quinton, Stefan Doerr, Jim Beynon, Nick Clements, Peter Gilliver, Lorna Marsden, Guido Kostermeyer, Eluned Roberts, Shaun McCann, Steve Long, Tim Jepson, Dave Williams, Johnny Dawes, Roger Wild, Professor David Hopkins, Danny Brown, Mark Bridgeman-Smith (Wild Country) and Frank Bennet (Lyon Equipment) who gave very useful comments on the manuscript. A special thanks must go to Steve Richardson, Suresh Paul, Dave Turnbull, Jane Worsley, Clive Hebblethwaite, Phil Poole, Robb Spencer, Jean Paul Eatock and Adrian Berry for their contributions. I must also thank John Matthews and Don Mabbs (The Dukes Barn Adventure Centre) and Simon Cloney (Calvert Trust Kielder) for their assistance with the 'Climbing for All' section.

I would like to give a particular thanks to Lucy Archer, Clive Hebblethwaite, Mike 'Twid' Turner, Louise Thomas, John Brailsford and Nick Banks who spent much of their valuable time reading and advising on the final copy.

I am also deeply in debt to Chris Wheeler for his superb illustrations.

Thanks must also go to the UKMLTB for allowing me to use its information on awards for instructors.

The photography was made easier due to support from Lyon Equipment, Beal Ropes, DMM, Lowe, Wild Country, Stone Monkey clothing, 5.10 and Scarpa. I would also like to pay special tribute to Trevor Massiah, Babs Jongman, Gareth and Rhiannon Richardson and a whole host of other climbers and instructors who suffered my artistic side and posed for the photographs.

Any of the opinions expressed in this book are mine and should not be associated with any of the above people, companies or organizations.

Finally a special thanks to my wife Liz who has given me the freedom and support to pursue every goal I have ever wanted; Gareth and Rhiannon who put up with me during the book's long gestation period; Alex and Pam Hayter for their support, and my mum and dad for bringing me up to be determined.

INTRODUCTION

In 1886, Walter Parry Haskett Smith, a gentleman lawyer, made an audacious solo climb of Napes Needle in the Lake District. This is regarded by many climbers as the start of the sport of rock climbing, not because it was the first ascent of a rock route (which it was not), but because he climbed it for the sheer fun and love of climbing. Since Haskett Smith's ascent, rock climbing has evolved from a simple facet of mountaineering into a complex game with many sub-divisions and specialities. There are now climbers who never get very far off the ground, preferring to search for the ultimate technical problem on boulders, and climbers who never set foot on real rock, being happy to climb on man-made indoor walls. There are safe, bolted sport routes and adventure climbs, equipment is stronger, lighter and more versatile, and the amount of information available today is far greater than during my initiation many years ago. This means that learning to climb is no longer the straightforward matter it once was.

Like Haskett Smith, I believe that there are few things more satisfying than the simple pleasure of moving over rock and teaching others how to do it. This book is written for those climbers starting out on their instructing career, covering many of the ideas and much of the information that would have smoothed my path into the world of instructing and guiding. It is the first book on climbing that looks at not only *what* to teach, but also *how* to teach. It contains an introduction to some important subjects such as the theory of learning and the teaching of movement: both are at the front of the book to reflect their importance. Other important topics such as anatomy, navigation, history, weather and the structure of mountains have been left for others to describe elsewhere. The chapter on rope techniques and skills is an attempt to answer the multitude of questions I have been asked on my climbing courses; they are not rules and regulations (there are seldom right and wrong answers in instructing). You can select

the ideas from this book that suit your style of instructing, but do not be surprised if you are told something different - everyone has a justification for using a different knot or rope-work technique. I have chosen the ones that have worked for me.

The sections on scrambling and coasteering are placed at the rear of the book to reflect the amount of experience required to make the judgements necessary for safe instructing.

But why have I put my head above the parapet and written a book about instructing rock climbing? The view exists that instructors merely provide novices with a grounding in safety techniques and that subsequent technical improvement only comes about if the students take responsibility for it themselves. I believe that instructors can do much more than this; they can improve their student's efficiency of movement and ability to train effectively, but in particular they can influence their student's attitude towards climbing, their awareness of danger, their self-belief and their confidence.

There is, however, a fear among some climbers that the above developments and the integration of training methods and coaching techniques from other sports will sanitize climbing. I hope that this book helps to alleviate their worries. Climbing will never become like other sports because there are no rules or referees, the difficulty can be changed to suit the level of the participants, and, most importantly, it is full of anti-establishment eccentrics. However, rock climbing has moved on, and the closer analysis of movement, the development of indoor climbing walls and improved training methods have explained the mystical brilliance of past masters. These new developments can help those climbers who teach climbing to be more effective.

Finally, and probably most importantly, we have the privilege of working and playing in some of the most diverse and beautiful yet fragile landscapes in the world. But privilege bears a heavy responsibility. There is a hugely increased pressure on our cliffs and crags from a wide spectrum of users, and there is an equal pressure to reduce the burden. Ideally, we should try to work within the all-encompassing framework of environmental sensitivity, within which should sit the framework of safety and within that the framework of teaching. We should also keep in mind, however, that the effects of climbing on the environment pale into insignificance when compared to the effects of overpopulation, farming, quarrying, transport and industrial pollution. Climbers and instructors are organized in readily defined areas and are therefore easy targets for those with power to yield. If we do not act in a manner that preserves our cliff environment for future generations, some less understanding body will do it for us.

I would welcome comments and views, tips and techniques missed to be emailed to me on alunrichardson@hotmail.com or alunrichardson@cs.com.

There is no doubt that wearing a helmet reduces the chances of head injuries, especially on lower grade routes, where a fall is more likely to end on a ledge. The climbing world is slow to embrace the helmet and although some of the photographs show climbers without a helmet, the advice given here is always to wear one.

Alun Richardson

CHAPTER 1

TOWARDS EFFECTIVE INSTRUCTING

Experience is not what happens to you.
Experience is what you do with what happens to you.
Aldous Huxley

There is the belief among many climbers that all instructors who take students climbing are teaching them how to climb. This is as misguided as the belief held by some instructors and centre managers that climbing has an inherent capacity to teach their students how to be better people or superior team players. The ability to educate young people about life skills/teamwork lies with the instructor, not with climbing. This book is written primarily for instructors who teach climbing, but it does have information useful to the outdoor educationalist.

Climbing instructors can be put into three broad categories:

- Those that give groups, mostly youngsters, a taste of climbing, such as Scout leaders and schoolteachers. They have a great responsi-

Success and a smiling face is reward enough.

bility to portray climbing as a fun and exciting adventure, and to lay down the foundations for efficient movement, because bad movement patterns cannot be lost.
- Those that teach climbing to serious novices and climbers progressing with their climbing.
- Guides who may not focus on instruction, but concentrate on sharing a climb with their students, allowing them to see the mountains through new eyes.

Many rock climbing courses focus on the use of climbing ropes, gear and abseiling because that is what students expect, and because it is easier for the instructor to teach than the more sophisticated, physically demanding movement skills. There is, however, much more to being a climbing instructor than the ability to lead a simple climb and teach the fundamentals of safe ropework. An instructor should be a good role model and, most importantly, inspire confidence by moving well on difficult ground. Unfortunately, the training available to budding instructors is limited and the quality of rock climbing courses is left to the individual instructor.

This chapter looks closely at the attributes and knowledge needed to help you become an effective instructor. However, effective instructing cannot be learned from this book: you must be willing to apply what you read and learn from your mistakes. Only then will you learn the most important skills of instructing: judgement, the ability to make a decision based on previous experience.

THE EFFECTIVE INSTRUCTOR

You can probably remember the teachers from your school days who had that extra sparkle and whose lessons held your attention right to the end or maybe you can remember the talented instructor who put you on the road to climbing success. They may have been born with the skill to keep you spellbound, but for most instructors and teachers the magic did not come easily.

So what separates the effective instructor from the average amateur? The effective climbing instructor understands how students learn and is able to assess whether someone has learned by reviewing a coaching session or if they are lucky by other types of longer term assessment (it is debatable whether someone can be as effective over the short term as someone who works with students over the longer term). The effective instructor plans and prepares their instructing and is able to organize students to improve their chances of acquiring new skills, attitudes, techniques and information. To do this effectively, the instructor takes into account clarity of voice, body language and environmental conditions, such as how hot it is and where the sun is coming from. They consider their style of delivery – is it going to be 'chalk and talk', student-led or instructor-led learning? They work to their strengths and within the limits of any weaknesses. They are interested in their students, have an empathy with them and a caring attitude towards them. Most importantly, they possess a passion for climbing, combined with a wealth of experience.

Before you take your first steps into the world of instructing there are three issues that should be considered.

ACCEPTING RESPONSIBILITY

If you accept the role of instructor, even as an unpaid volunteer, you cannot avoid the responsibility that goes with it. An instructor's responsibilities are on a par with those of a nurse or a teacher, and at the higher echelons with those of a medical doctor or head teacher. You will certainly have to make life or death decisions based upon your experience and training.

Your students will instantly and unflinchingly believe that you are the person who is going to keep them safe, give them a good time and educate them. This trust should not be taken lightly, and accepting this responsibility is an important step towards becoming a talented instructor. It takes maturity, training and experience to exercise that responsibility with integrity.

The Effective Instructor

- Accepts responsibility and appreciates what the law expects from them.
- Has an aim for their climbing session.
- Has a variety of teaching methods, reviewing and feedback skills to measure the effectiveness of their teaching.
- Evaluates their teaching, searching for different and fascinating ways to engage the interest of their students.
- Enjoys teaching and the company of others above self-achievement.
- Is interested in the students and has a caring attitude towards them.
- Is persuasive/encouraging, has sound judgement and is able to make clear decisions even when under stress.
- Is passionate about rock climbing and can present it as a stimulating and exciting adventure.
- Understands the importance of learning good movement at the start of a climbing career.
- Can provide advice on training, injury avoidance and equipment.
- When necessary they understands the underlying philosophies behind outdoor education and team building.
- Has empathy with access and conservation issues and is able to communicate this to the students.
- Has an awareness of objective danger.
- Is a good role model and inspires confidence.

Can Instructors be Called Professionals?

Society and, unfortunately, the 'outdoor world' do not regard instructing as a profession. However, to be viewed as a professional does not depend upon schemes of training and assessment. Rather, it is an approach to instructing and is hinged on the manner in which we conduct ourselves and the attitude we have towards our students. Instructors may teach or guide part-time, some may dabble in it for fun and others may make a full-time career out of it, but they can all adopt a professional approach to their instructing.

SAFE INSTRUCTING

Your primary role as an instructor is to make learning effective, exciting, enjoyable and interesting while keeping risk at an acceptable level. But what is acceptable?

Acceptable risk is not easily defined and is dependent on a variety of social and personal factors. Perceptions of risk also differ – for example, a student may perceive abseiling as

> **Coach or Instructor?**
>
> One definition of an instructor is 'someone who teaches, informs and directs others'. In reality, instructing is about the way in which these things are done, rather than what is done. The team 'coach' is probably more appropriate because it describes unlocking someone's potential to maximize their performance – coaching them to learn rather than instructing them to do.

dangerous and a slippery slope as safe, whereas from your viewpoint the opposite may well be true.

Society would like to wrap everyone in cotton wool and create rules and regulations to remove the risk totally from climbing, but this is a mistake that would change climbing's unique character. In fact, when any outdoor activity is developed with safety rather than the development of the students in mind it is likely to be boring. The Royal Society for the Prevention of Accidents (RoSPA) has shown that children's playgrounds that have no risk are less likely to be used, because young people will find excitement and adventure elsewhere.

Reducing risk by helping students learn good judgement and how to cope with real hazards is ultimately safer than avoiding them or sanitising adventure. You can play a vital role in a student's learning of safety judgement by exposing them to the dangers inherent in the outdoors, providing them with the skills and knowledge to tackle the dangers in as safe a manner as possible, and allowing them to make errors while maintaining adequate safety margins. Demonstrating safety skills and techniques on real climbs, in real situations where your judgement will be on view is an effective way of doing this. The problem with this method is that it takes years of experience to do it well.

When taking students into adventurous situations, remember that the conditions we find challenging may frighten the 'living daylights' out of them. You cannot rely on your students to react competently in situations where they are under stress, therefore be careful when putting yourself in a position where safety depends totally on the student's actions and reactions.

Risk is frequently thought of in terms of physical injury, but we should also consider the psychological effects of what we do. If outdoor activities can be character building, they can also be character destroying. Psychological damage can be inflicted in many ways, for example, by forcing the students to do things they do not want to do; by making fun of them for the things they cannot do; by forcing them to climb by using peer group pressure, such as 'we are not leaving here until you have all climbed'; or by placing pressure on someone to lead before they are ready for it. Respect your students' ability to say 'no'; having the courage to say 'no' can actually be braver than saying 'yes'. This is a good argument for having optional involvement into and out of activities.

Part of the ability to manage risk is that instructors must put aside their personal ambitions. Their desire to climb comes secondary to the needs, desires and safety of their students. However, it is also important that the personal ambitions of the students are secondary to safety. The process of learning to be safe

Risk is a subjective thing – Mike 'Twid' Turner on 'Voyage to the bottom of the sea' E5 6a.

involves the transition from recreational climber to instructor/guide and depends on training and experience, but most importantly on self-analysis. Where were we at greatest risk? Could we have done something different?

Safe instructing is a matter of judgement; of being aware of danger, but also being aware that what worked well in a given place at a given time may not be appropriate in the same place at a different time. Judging the situation by protocol or rules invites disaster. Instructing in a safe manner means considering the consequences of everything we do – asking the question 'What if?', and learning from our experiences. There are many youngsters who are not gaining the real benefit of being in the outdoors because rules and regulations only limit the experiences that a talented instructor can provide for them. The skill of an experienced instructor is knowing to do the right thing at the right time. This may seem a simple concept but it often takes courage and experience to do it well e.g. 'bailing out' of a situation and having to justify why the group did not complete the trip or session.

While we are on the subject of safety let's look at what are the legal risks to instructors, and what can negate that risk.

LEGAL CONSIDERATIONS

(Adrian Berry)

It is easy to forget that the law applies to every action made whilst instructing – there is no situation where the relationship between an instructor and a student is above the scrutiny of the law.

The most typical situation an instructor is likely to deal with is where a mishap occurs, a student is injured and they want compensation for their injuries. To obtain damages they will be relying on civil law. The two branches of civil law of concern here are contract law and the law of tort (or delict in Scotland).

Contract

This is a legally binding agreement between two persons. Each party promises to do something for something in return. In the context of instructing, an instructor may offer to take a student on an activity in return for payment. Once the student has accepted the offer, there is a contract and each party is obliged to fulfil their obligations. It is immaterial whether a contract is made in writing, using the telephone, via the Internet, or over a pint of beer, but having a clear written list of the terms is good practice, as each party then knows what is expected, and what to expect. A signature is evidence that the party has agreed to the terms. Where an aspect of an agreement is not expressly agreed, then the law will imply certain things, such as that the instructor must perform their service with 'reasonable skill and care'.

Damages

If the student does not pay the agreed fee, or the instructor provides less than was promised, then the courts may be called upon to award damages that will restore the aggrieved party to where they would have been had the contract been fulfilled. So, for example, if an instructor were to fail to deliver their services with 'reasonable skill and care', resulting in an accident, then they would be liable to compensate the student not only for their injury, but also for the disappointment caused by the failure to deliver an enjoyable activity.

Tort/Delict

This is the branch of civil law that holds persons responsible for their actions, regardless of whether they are already governed by a contract. Instructors will often have no contract with their students; they may be employees of a company that holds the contract. The most relevant aspect of this is the tort of negligence.

What is 'Duty of Care'?

A person owes a duty of care to others who are so closely and directly affected by their actions that the person ought reasonably to have them in mind as being affected by those actions. So an instructor owes a duty of care to their students because they are so closely and directly affected by ythe instructor's actions that it is quite reasonable to have them in mind. For a person to be liable, they have to breach a duty of care that they owe to the victim, and the damage must result from that breach of duty of care.

An instructor is not liable for injuries caused by the inherent risks associated with the activity. An example you may be familiar with is the BMC Participation Statement. It is often seen in the vicinity of climbing walls as if a talisman against lawsuits. It goes like this:

The BMC recognizes that climbing and mountaineering are activities with a danger of personal injury or death. Participants in these activities should be aware of and accept these risks and be responsible for their own actions and involvement.

It is, of course, important to inform complete novices that they are going to be participating in a sport that has certain risks. These risks are what you might call just accidents; they are nobody's fault. A climber pulling off a hold which hits their belayer is just one of those things.

The Standard of Care

The crucial part of all this is what that standard of care will be. The issue is what a reasonably careful and competent instructor should be expected to do in any given situation. There are certain factors which influence the standard of care.

Experience and Professionalism
The standard of care will be higher for the more experienced person. In other words, the standard of care that a trained instructor owes to a novice will be greater than that owed to an equally experienced peer. A professional qualification will raise the standards expected of the holder.

Age of Students
When one is instructing children, the standard is at least that which would be taken by a *reasonably prudent parent*, a definition worth considering carefully. The standard of care of an instructor is in fact likely to go further than that of a parent or teacher where there is specialist knowledge of the particular dangers associated with an activity.

Danger
Obviously a more dangerous activity requires a higher level of care, and conversely a less dangerous activity would not require such a high degree of control.

Foreseeability of Danger
Some dangers may not be foreseeable, and instructors cannot be expected to have a sixth sense. However, if a danger becomes apparent, through experience or research, then instructors will be expected to modify their approach to ensure that their students are protected from it.

Risk-cost Ratio
Instructors are not expected to remove minor risks where to do so would be extremely costly.

Generally Accepted Safety Procedures
The law does not present a body of rules that can easily be referred to. Different circumstances require a different approach. The judge in any case will refer to 'universally recognized good practice' and 'generally accepted safety procedures'. So what is the universally recognized good practice for an instructor? In addition, where are these generally accepted safety procedures? The courts have various ways to find the answer to these questions, essentially trying to discover what is the 'norm'. The court may well ask some 'reasonably careful and competent' instructors to act as expert witnesses, or it may refer to what has been written in manuals. It is up to each ide to find an experienced, accomplished and respected professional to be their expert. Preferably, their expert will be sympathetic to their cause.

Who is at Risk? Vicarious Liability

Where an individual is an employee of another person (a company or individual), then the employer will be vicariously liable for the actions of the employee *in the course of their employment*. The employee will still be responsible, but in contract to the employer. Not all contractual relationships between an instructor and the other party generate vicarious liability. Where an instructor is a self-employed freelancer, they will be responsible for their actions directly to the student. In determining whether a relationship is that of employment or freelance, the law takes into account the regularity of the work, holiday arrangements and the payment of tax.

Avoiding or Reducing Liability

Exclusion notices
Informing students that you do not accept liability for death or injury is a nice try, but legally ineffective. However, informing them (or their parents) in advance that the activities you

provide are not free from risk is a positive step towards fulfilling the required duty of care.

Contributory Negligence

Where a student has acted in a way that contributed to the injury, then the amount of damages paid out is reduced in accordance with the extent of their contribution. This is known as contributory negligence.

Volenti

The courts are very reluctant to find that a person has freely consented to a particular risk. This defence, known as volenti, is not available at all where there is negligence or where the risk is not usually associated with the particular activity that causes the injury.

Insurance

Being insured means that your insurance company can take over a lawsuit against you, and will pay up if you are sued. However, they are not obliged to defend you if your actions are of a degree of gross negligence such that it would have been obvious to any reasonable persons that serious injury or death would have resulted from your actions. An employee is at little risk of being sued where there is a solvent or insured employer to chase. However, failing that, action for negligence could be taken.

The freelance instructor is potentially liable for acts of negligence, and will wish to take appropriate cover and reflect this in their fees. Where a freelancer is working for another person, it is possible to agree an arrangement whereby the person 'employing' extends their insurance to cover the contractor, and to indemnify them against legal action.

Clearly, an outdoor activity centre is open to a significant risk of legal action for the actions of its employees. It is not just for accidents during activities that an employer may be sued. There is a duty of care to be exercised whilst selecting instructional staff to ensure that they are competent to run activity sessions safely.

Often it will be cheaper for an insurance company to pay out than to fight a case, and so an insured person makes a much better target than a non-insured person. However, a well-advised victim of an accident will always go where the money is, whether covered by insurance or not. That means private companies and local authorities are in need of the most protec-tion, and are most likely to cover themselves with insurance.

THE INSTRUCTOR – FIRST IMPRESSIONS

However politically correct we are, it is an unfortunate fact of life that your physique, attractiveness, height, weight and body odours can all have an effect on how the students think of you.

Research suggests that many of us judge someone within two minutes of meeting them. Personal appearance is a matter of individual taste, but what we wear and how we look after ourselves reflect the image we portray e.g. an instructor extolling the virtues of keeping fit, yet smoking, may not communicate the correct message. Dirty clothes are fine for a dirty activity, but to present an acceptable face to the students try to be clean and tidy when you meet them. This is not a question of fashion, suits and uniforms create anonymity, but unwashed clothes with tears in them suggest a lack of professionalism and care.

Your initial contact with students sends important messages both about your intended role and also the standards you expect from them.

A clean and tidy instructor, with a pleasant manner, will instil confidence in their students.

When you first meet the students, introduce yourself and greet each one to make them feel welcome. Find out as many names as possible, as people tend to respond better when you use their name. Act in a confident manner because this reflects knowledge, authority and experience. However, do not confuse confidence as an instructor with self-confidence. Confidence with your instructing comes from understanding what you want the students to learn and is often determined by how well-prepared you are, not what you think of yourself.

DEVELOPING A GOOD RAPPORT

A major factor that makes someone an effective instructor is their ability to form a good relationship with their students and to gain their respect. Developing a good rapport and gaining control of your students' actions will allow you to teach in a relaxed manner and when safety issues are involved it will ensure that they listen to you. How much control is needed will depends on the age of the students, their experience, the situation and the level of risk.

Some of the factors that can lead to a loss of control are boredom, too much mental effort, climbing at a level that is too hard, lack of self-confidence, behavioural problems and lack of communication skills on the part of the instructor. To maintain control the talented instructor picks up subtle cues from the students and if the group is bored or the task is too difficult, the instructor changes it. There are also, however, those students who find misbehaving exciting or attention-grabbing, and these may ultimately be beyond your control and the session should be ended.

Here are some eclectic suggestions that may help to improve your relationship with your students and to manage and control them. They are particularly pertinent to instructors working with young students.

- Just because you find learning exciting does not mean everyone does. If you want your students to be excited by your instructing, smile, be positive and above all instruct with enthusiasm.
- Teach by example. Be as good as your word and communicate with consistency (see Communication Skills below). For example,

telling students that climbing is all about confidence and then destroying their feelings of self-worth by shouting at them for their errors, or telling students off for being late and turning up late yourself may eventually destroy their trust and respect for you.
- Admit your mistakes and anything you do not know straight away; do not try to bluff it out, or be afraid to say sorry. The students may put you on a pedestal but you are still human.
- The most talented instructors are not domineering or authoritarian. Be fair, firm and friendly. Be positive and reward good behaviour. Say 'thank you' and 'well done' (in measured doses), and praise when someone has performed well.
- The quickest way to make students switch off is to use sarcasm, patronize or embarrass them. Jokes and humour at the expense of a student are only acceptable once a good rapport has been developed.
- Patience comes through understanding and a compassion for others. It is perfectly normal to feel frustrated when a student is taking an inordinately long time over a simple task, but it is all too easy to forget how difficult your first knots or climbs were. If you find this aspect difficult, try to regain the experience of what it is like to be a beginner by learning something technical that you are not good at.
- Pitch your instructing at the correct level. Set your students' expectations at a challenging but achievable level so that they never feel inadequate because of their poor performance. Success breeds confidence and self-esteem, so build on the students' successes by praising the smallest efforts at easy tasks to make them feel worthwhile, giving encouragement even after a mistake or failure. Try to give failing students an 'opt out' such as 'Never mind, that route/move is very hard.' Competition is neither good nor bad; it is simply a way of measuring one performance against another but winning should not be stressed above the benefits of taking part.
- Instructors are a role model and should therefore try to set an example by helping all the students, not just the more likeable ones. Students who are easier to teach are not necessarily the ones who need your help. Have confidence in all the students' abilities to learn something (don't judge

them too quickly); if you expect good things of them, good things tend to happen. Mix stronger and weaker students – you could ask the stronger ones to help the weaker ones.

- Do not ignore students or put them down. Give everyone the chance to speak and treat everyone as equals regardless of age, sex, ethnic origin, religion or political persuasion. This does not, however, mean that you treat all people the same – for example, a large, fit person is capable of carrying more than a small person or the same route may not be suitable for everyone.

- It is useful to continually assess your students, but simply asking them how they are feeling may not be enough. Try to gauge your students not from their spoken response but through evaluation of the nature of the response, assessment of the overall situation, the students performance and experience. Just asking 'are you all okay' is not enough because students are often un-willing to admit discomfort for a variety of reasons, therefore try to look for clues about the true nature of their condition even when they say they are fine. If one student is cold and uncomfortable the chances are the rest may be.

- Do not intentionally make climbing fright-ening. While this may prove funny for a few confident students, it could seriously affect the ones who are waiting to climb.

- Identify appropriate and acceptable behav-iour and explain why any restrictions/controls are being applied. By being forewarned students, will then expect control when they overstep the mark.

- Deal immediately with anything unaccept-able in a firm manner and with confidence.

- Do not communicate the solution, communi-cate the problem. It is better if the student can see the solution themselves.

- If you do have to be firm with someone it may be better to take them aside than to chastise them in front of the other students.

- Control can be more effective if you move into the student's personal space because they may then assume that you are not scared of them. However, you should consider the consequences if you are a small person and the student acts unpredictably.

- Have the courage to abandon a session if you lose control of the students.

Teach by example! If you do have to be firm it is better to take the student aside than to do it in front of the others.

Coping in a Crisis

The ultimate test of your management and control is when there is a crisis. Even routine days do not always run smoothly – for example, the minibus is late, the storeroom is locked, helmets have been forgotten or you have arrived at the base of a mountain crag and forgotten your rock boots. A calm and relaxed approach is best even when everything around you is collapsing. Coping in a crisis can be an onerous responsibility and it is definitely worth practising for 'crisis management'. A plan of action that can be put into play may prove vital when things go wrong. Think about how you would like to see yourself coping during a crisis. Play through the scenario of an accident or situation and how you see yourself acting. It can reduce your stress levels when something really happens.

COMMUNICATION SKILLS

The way you communicate can affect how the students view you, their respect for what you are teaching and therefore the success of your teaching. Good communication takes practice and planning and it is worthwhile taking the

> **Tips for Better Communication**
>
> - Capture the students' attention.
> - Check that the pitch, tone and level of your voice are comfortable and interesting.
> - Match non-verbal messages with verbal messages.
> - Improve your listening skills.
> - Use language that is appropriate for the students.

time to measure the response you get with differing ways of communicating. Video yourself working or get a friend to watch you and comment on the communication skills used.

An important skill that can help your instructing, or any aspect of life for that matter, is to communicate with a positive approach. A *positive* approach emphasizes praise and reward; it can affect the students' view of themselves, their motivation and their abilty to learn. So when they are performing poorly do not be negative – emphasize the positive things in their performance and acknowledge contributions from the group by giving praise and positive responses. Explain where they have gone wrong, but do not labour the point.

A *negative* approach uses criticism and punishment to eliminate undesirable habits. It is rarely successful. It may work with self-confident students, but when used frequently it ruins the learning process by creating negative emotions that result in caution, defensiveness and a reluctance to try things in case of failure.

Active Listening

Communication is not just about an instructor's ability to speak; it is also about their ability to listen effectively. Most untrained listeners hear less than 20 per cent of what is said to them. A positive correlation has been shown between those instructors who are poor listeners and those who fail to develop a good rapport with and have less control over their students. Listening is so much harder than talking. Some instructors are so busy teaching that they never give others the chance to speak, or when they do speak and receive a different answer to the one expected, or even no answer at all, they blindly carry on. Being a good listener will show that you have time for your students, respect them and care about how they feel.

The jargon for this is 'active listening'. It provides the talker with the proof that you have understood what they have said. For example, a student just starting to learn to lead asks, 'What's the worst fall you have seen'? The instructor replies 'I once saw someone fall sixty feet, rip six runners out and land on the shoulder of the person belaying them. '

In fact, before answering, the instructor should have considered why the question was asked and responded positively:

Student: 'What's the worst fall you have ever seen?'
Instructor: 'I've not seen too many big falls. Are you worried about falling off?'
Student: 'Yes it looks very steep.'
Instructor: 'Well, the rock is good, this route is well protected and you will have the rope above you so focus on the climbing and do not worry about falling off.'

> **Improving Listening Skills**
>
> - Recognize the need to listen.
> - Concentrate on listening.
> - Search for the meaning of the message rather than details.
> - Avoid interrupting students.
> - Do not anticipate what students are going to say or put word into their mouths.
> - Respect their views.
> - Respond constructively.

Elements of Speech

The way that we talk can also influence the effectiveness of our teaching. What would you rather listen to, a voice that sings or a monotone one? Young people switch off from a 'teacher's voice' quite easily and it can be more effective to adopt a conversational tone from the start. There are certain elements of speech that important to effective communication.

Tone of Voice
Tone of voice can convey anger, joy or boredom. Varying it can add clarity to what is said and may help to maintain the interest and attention of the students. Listen to the radio and examine how some presenters make their voices sing by raising and lowering the tone.

Pitch of Voice

Try not to shout or whisper. Rather, pitch your voice at a level that obliges the students to listen. Do not be afraid to raise or lower your voice for effect.

Emphasis

Placing emphasis on certain things you want to stress is important. By emphasizing certain words, you may help the listener to understand the message.

Speed of Speech

Students tend to listen more attentively if the speed of speech is varied. Increasing the speed will create anticipation in the listener, but do not be afraid to pause, especially when things are new to the group. It may seem like hours to you, but it will only feel like seconds to the listener, who may welcome a rest and the chance to absorb new information. Avoid filling the pauses with unnecessary 'uhms' and avoid repeating the same phrase repeatedly, such as 'okay' or 'all right', because after a while no one will take anything you say seriously.

Pronunciation

Most newsreaders pronounce words correctly because they have practised them. The constant mispronunciation of words or names can become annoying.

Content

You will be more effective if the students can understand the meaning of the words you use. Think carefully abut the content of what you say.

Figurative Language

Figurative speech that uses metaphor, simile, and hyperbole can make what you are saying interesting, but be careful not to offend anyone, and make sure the listener understands when you are exaggerating.

Humour

Talented instructors use humour to maintain attention and interest. A smile and a pleasant manner work wonders, but for some instructors trying to be funny is very difficult and can result in a loss of credibility as their attempts at humour fall flat. The key to being witty is to judge the tone of the conversation and the relationship that has been built with the students.

Body Language

Just as an instructor or student can communicate thoughts using words, they can also communicate positively and negatively through their body language. The faces they pull, the amount of eye contact they make and the gestures made with their body can all have a profound effect on the success of their instructing. It has been estimated that 70 per cent of our total communication is non-verbal. If you doubt this, try adopting different body languages to see the effect they have on people and watch other instructors for the responses they are getting from their students.

Remember, however, that although your body language has a profound affect, a student's manner or their distress might be caused by someone or something else other than you. The student's body language also needs to be put into the context of the session. They may be about to embark on their first lead and be nervous, or they may simply have had a row with someone. In addition, do not assume that you can be as familiar with the same person as another instructor has just been – they may have met the student many times before and have a closer relationship with them. There are six main individual elements of body language to take into consideration when instructing.

Facial Expressions

The face is a spontaneous communicator, often when an instructor least wants it to be. Facial expressions can communicate likes and dislikes, and emotions such as despair and frustration. Ensure that your facial expressions reflect what you are saying and do not give a contradictory message. Above all, look alert, awake and happy … even if you are not!

Eye Contact

Do not be afraid of eye contact, but try not to focus on one person. On the other hand, do not go to the other extreme and look at the floor. Looking into a student's eyes shows that you are being attentive and concentrating on what is being said. Shifting your eyes around may mean you fail to inspire trust, while the opposite, a piercing stare, might be valued as a sign of aggression. The only time to avoid direct eye contact is when you are reprimanding someone, as this could be interpreted as a challenge. Instead look between their eyes. There is also the

The successful instructor has a variety of ways to teach a given task. Photo: Mike 'Twid' Turner.

possibility that too much eye contact may make the student think you are attracted to them.

Posture

How you move, sit or stand and position your limbs may reflect your attitude to someone. Sitting with your hands between your legs is a defensive posture and putting hands on hips may be seen as an aggressive stance. Leaning towards someone or sitting with legs apart and arms unfolded displays warmth. Students may clearly display dislike by turning away, arms folded and legs crossed. An erect posture and a purposeful walk may be interpreted as confident and self-assured, while a stiff, tense or rigid posture may express anger. Keep moving; it keeps the students' eyes moving and helps them to concentrate, although you should try to avoid distracting body movements. Students who stare at the ground may be showing they are scared or intimidated.

Gestures

Certain gestures can replace the need for words, possibly totally if the student does not speak English. For example, a wave acknowledges someone's presence, and a fist beaten on a table shows you are anxious or angry. Try to avoid continual subconscious gestures that can be distracting, such as scratching your face or stroking your hair.

Proximity

Being close to a student may inform them how you feel about them and how you view them. Proximity is often affected by how formal the session is. When barriers and distance are reduced an instructor will often be able to communicate more effectively, so get into the group. There are certain situations, however, where personal distance may need to be maintained. A female student may feel threatened if a male instructor gets too close, or you may want to stay behind the desk if reprimanding someone. It may be useful to bring yourself down to the height of the students by sitting or kneeling.

Touch

It is very rare that you will have to touch someone. Be aware that some people may be naturally reserved. A pat on the back or a brief handshake is acceptable to most people, but an over-intimate touch such as a hug may threaten or cause someone to distrust the relationship. Be careful about touching any child, even when helping them to put on a harness and especially when alone. Ask their permission first and if possible have another adult present. However, do not be too paranoid to give a hug to a child if it is needed, unless of course you have been given a reason not to.

Here are some of the common signs of body language that people express and what they may mean:

- **Students willing to listen**: rub hands together, lean forwards, rest chin on hands, look at the instructor and nod in agreement.

- **Students showing friendliness**: smile, make eye contact, are still, use non-threatening gestures such as handshakes or a pat on the back, initiate conversation, use humour in their speech, are polite and courteous.
- **Anxious students**: place their hands on your arm, fidget with themselves, look intently at you, shift their posture all the time and talk to their neighbour.
- **Frustrated or rejected students**: use aggressive downward movements, tighten their clothing, raise the tone of their voice and withdraw from conversation.
- **Threatened or confused students**: fold their arms, frown, withdraw eye contact, become verbally aggressive and stand their ground.

HOW STUDENTS LEARN

Because effective instructing is about providing the best conditions for learning, it is a good idea to have an understanding of how your students learn. The way we learn movement is looked at in more detail in Chapter 2.

Presenting the same session in the same manner to every student is not effective instructing. All of us have our own way of learning, we take in information through our different senses and as we grow up, our genes, the environment, peer group pressure and parents will push us towards the learning methods we find easiest and often to our future vocation. Those students who are theoretical and analytical learn best by thinking about things (theorists), those who are physical and active learn best by doing (activists) and those who are artistic or enjoy visual things learn by watching (watchers). We are not solely one or the other and we learn most effectiely by using different strategies in different situations, nevertheless one strategy is likely to be dominant. The reality of instructing, however, is that you will have to accommodate all of these learning strategies in one go. This is sometimes referred to as the 'shotgun approach' where we scatter information at the students in a variety of forms. There is a lot of wastage but that is unavoidable. Most instructors subconsciously use an appropriate approach through trial and error. If explanations do not work give a demonstration or use both. However, the advantage of understanding the preferences is that you can more often identify those students with partic-

ular learning preferences, minimizing the wastage of the shotgun approach.

To match your instructing to your students learning strategy means that you may have to use a variety of styles of teaching. Style is your philosophy of instructing – the way you like to work. Style is a tool that can be broadly divided into 'directive' or 'student-centred' instructing. These instructing styles can be further subdivided for academic interest, but in reality they are a progression from one style to the other. The style you adopt depends entirely on you, the subject matter and the expertise of the students, but as a rule of thumb use a style that provides what the student cannot provide for themselves and gives the learner success.

It is said that people absorb 10 per cent of what they read, 15 per cent of what they hear and 25 per cent of what they do. Therefore, ensure your instructing is appropriate, aim for 15–20% from the instuctor and 80% from the student. When teaching facts use hearing and seeing and when instructing skills do not just talk about them. Simply say 'I am now going to demonstrate how to put a harness on' then do it.

Activity not talk

We hear half of what is said.   (50%)
We listen to half of that.   (25%)
We understand half of that.   (12%)
We believe half of that.   (6%)
And we remember half of that.   (3%)

Some instructrs talk too much. Place the emplasis on doing. The students will remember more of what the see and most of what they do.

Maintain the group's attention by changing the sensory channels they are using: listen, look, listen, look, touch, listen, and talk. Pass things around to break up the session. Try to accommodate all the learning strategies by starting with a lecture then a discussion and note taking, follow this with a practical session and then maybe a video.

Adventure is an activity for which success is not predetermined and you can share in the unpredictable nature of it with your students especially mature ones. Once you are at ease with instructing it pays to be innovative, because experimenting can keep you stimulated and help to make your sessions lively and fresh. Some of your experiments will be successful and some may not come up to your usual high standards, but your students will probably not realize it. Try not to work in isolation; it helps to network ideas and discuss views with other instructors even if they are novices, as they may have a different way of looking at things that you had not considered. If you are working with other instructors make sure you coordinate with each other and teach compatible things. It is usually best if you are working in a group for one instructor to assume leadership and take charge of coordinating the day.

Directive Instructing

Directive/autocratic instructing places the emphasis on the instructor. Techniques taught most effectively by a directive approach are those where there is a defined correct and incorrect way of performing the skill. It may be that an incorrect action could lead to injury and the skill is often better mastered in a safe environment before moving to a realistic one. It may be something specific that has to be done to avoid a hazard, such as belaying. Time pressures can also impose the need for a directive style of instructing. Demonstration and mnemonics like IDEAS or EDICT, which describe methods of teaching (see the way we learn movement Chapter 2) are all examples of directive teaching.

Student-Centred Instructing

Student-centred instructing places greater emphasis on the student and is not just dependent on what the instructor is telling them. It is concerned with learning by experience. The content, pace and rate of learning are dictated by the students' needs. This style lends itself to teaching principles and theories like judgement or movement rather than hard facts and figures. Students are taught in an environment where exploration and discovery are encouraged and they can compare and think about what they are doing.

This style, however, does require the instructor to have a broad knowledge of climbing and a deep understanding of what they are teaching. It is also heavily dependent on

quality feedback between instructor and student. It often takes longer and is harder for the instructor, but it does create a wider knowledge base for the student to work from. It is best used where safety does not depend on the students' decisions or performance unless they are experienced enough to deal with the consequences.

REVIEWING AND FEEDBACK

Reviewing and feedback skills are one of the most important attribute an instructor can have, because the one thing a student cannot get from a book is a review of the day and immediate feedback on their performance. Reviewing and feedback can also allow you to change your strategy should your students not understand you. It can also be used to motivate your students. Its effectiveness, however, does depend on your ability to observe, analyse and communicate effectively.

Feedback

For students to improve, practice usually needs to be accompanied by feedback. Every fault has a cause and an effect, therefore it is very useful to recognize the cause as well as the effect. Be selective, however, as giving too much feedback can also be a problem. It has been established that a person is most receptive to feedback/instruction 8 seconds after physical activity, so wait a few seconds before launching into your feedback and avoid the temptation of talking while the student is concentrating.

With expert students it is sometimes difficult to decide whether the student has failed to perform a movement skill because they have not yet developed the motor programme, or because of a performance error, that is, failure to make a movement which is within the student's capabilities. This can only be decided by the instructor having an understanding of how climbers move and what effect changing the movement will have on the outcome.

Try to ensure that the feedback tells the student more than the result has alreadyshown them; do not state the obvious without providing the solution. First tell the student what they are doing well and then be precise about what they can do to improve, or, better still, ask them what they personally feel they need to do to improve. Do not give feedback about anything that is not immediately rectifiable. For example, an error caused by lack of strength is not easily remedied. Keep feedback simple with young climbers especially, and make sure they understand you.

Here is an example of poor feedback (a) and an example of good feedback (b):

(a) 'That was awful. You fell off then because your feet slipped. You must use your feet.'
(b) 'Good try. You were pushing hard with your legs, but next time try to place your feet with more precision to give you a better platform to push from. Show me what I mean. That's it, now try again.'

Try not to use leading questions. These tend to indicate the attitude of the instructor and invite the reply they want to hear. Leading questions often end with 'did you?'; 'were you?', or 'could you?'. In addition, they often contain judgemental words, for example, bad, good, successful. It is better to encourage the students to analyse why they failed. 'What would have happened if you had leaned the other way when you made that move?' Give responsibility to the students for their learning by asking rather than telling.

Reviewing

Reviewing is a time during which the students can reflect, describe, analyse and communicate their experiences. It is important with young people because they have fewer experiences to which to they can relate what they have learned. Reviewing is more than asking, 'Did you enjoy the activity' or 'What was your high point, low point, best or worst bits?'. When coaching climbers, a lot of information may have been given and the students may need to reflect on what they have achieved. More importantly, you have no other way of knowing whether the students have achieved their objectives. Have they remembered and understood what was taught (summarize)? Can they use the information (have they internalized it)? Knowledge without understanding is useless.

Reviewing can be done continually during the day, but if it is not possible at the climbing venue be prepared to meet for a review soon afterwards. A video recorder and sometimes a tape recorder can be a useful tool for recalling points during the day. With young people a post activity test can help them to focus on what they have learned.

Reviewing can take 5 minutes or 2 hours, but whatever the duration practise it at every opportunity. If you have trouble structuring the questions try following the sequence which follows:

- **Recall/remember:** do you remember an example where you did not use your feet precisely?
- **Cause/effect:** what did you feel when you were asked to move like a ballerina?
- **Summary:** what did it tell you?
- **Application:** how does this relate to real climbing/affect your climbing?
- **Commitment:** how will this improve your climbing after the course?

An important aspect of reviewing and feedback is your ability to listen. Your facial expressions, posture and gestures all reflect whether you are listening. Learn to paraphrase what the student has said to see if your understanding is correct. Indicate frequently that you are listening by nodding or saying 'I see.' Do not be afraid to invite the student to expand, but be careful to focus on the issue and not just debate.

Questions

An *open* question indicates the area of interest, but allows a variety of replies. It will provide you will more information.

A *closed* question allows a short, defined answer, for example, yes or no, and little information.

A *leading* question leads the student towards a particular answer.

Be careful not to give premature advice; build an understanding first. Learn to focus on what the student wants to know and is ready to accept. Advice that may work for you may be inappropriate for the student. Being brutally honest too soon in a session about what a student needs to do to improve may leave the student focusing on what you have said, not on what you trying to teach.

Try not to be judgemental; avoid statements such as 'Surely you must have realized that route was too hard for you?'. Respect everyone's views, give encouragement and praise effort even when the result is failure. Encourage the language of success, rather than the language of failure – I haven't succeeded on that route yet' rather than 'I have failed on that route'. Involve everyone in the reviewing process and do not put people down or judge them. Use open-ended questions and do not be preoccupied with the next one. Do not dominate the session; listen actively, be open and receptive.

Avoid questions that allow the students a one-word answer, such as 'Did you look for the hold above you'?. 'Do you understand?'. The student can only answer 'yes' or 'no' and the information received is limited. The instructor then has no way of evaluating whether the students have understood the question. Open-ended questions almost always begin with how and why, such as 'How do you know?'. Closed questions often begin with who, what or where, or phrases like how many or how long, or words such as did or was?

THE TOOLS OF INSTRUCTING

In addition to the manner in which you conduct yourself, the way you communicate and your style of instructing, the tools you use to teach can have an effect on the success of your teaching.

Planning and Preparation

It takes a very experienced instructor to teach 'off the top of their head'. A successful session, no matter what the subject or where the setting is, will benefit from having been planned and prepared.

> The six Ps – Prior Planning and Preparation Prevent a Poor Performance – a useful philosophy to live by.

You may not always be on top form, so create lists of equipment needed, points to be covered and so on. Plan to be flexible – it may rain, only half the students may turn up or double the number may arrive!

The first thing to decide is what the lesson's objective or goal should be. For learning to occur, try to make the students aware of the objectives of the day and help them to see these as useful and relevant. The objective for a

> ### A Structure
>
> Whatever the objective is, the session should have a distinct structure. This can be applied to the whole day and the individual parts:
>
> - A *beginning* where the instructor explains what is to be taught and why.
> - A *middle* where the instructor teaches in stages and gives feedback.
> - An *end* that involves a practice and revision session where the instructor assesses whether the students have learnt and understood the session.

coaching session may be that the students appreciate the importance of good footwork. A climbing session with a group of young people may have as its objective that they are inspired by climbing. Identify the minimum young students need to know and what additional information would be useful. Is there time to teach the mechanics or do they simply need to know the underlying principles?

The next step is to work out how you are going to achieve the objective. The student may need to build confidence, so a long day in the hills doing an easy multi-pitch climb may be appropriate. A session on footwork may involve looking at centre of balance and using exercises to focus on the importance of footwork. An introductory session with a group of children may involve some bouldering to introduce movement and some ropework to raise the issue of safety, ending up with a roped climbing session. You may simply shadow a group to improve their judgement skills.

In planning a climbing session try to remember that most students can only pay attention to one thing at a time. Attempting to cover everything just makes life difficult. Asking a novice to absorb names, movement skills, ropework, how to tie knots, place runners, and put a harness on all while they are nervous is an impossible task. Try not to spend too much time explaining and too little practising. You may have days where you feel that you have given the students little, but to them it will have been highly informative.

Is the environment and the conditions correct for teaching? A cold, wet student may not learn as effectively as a warm, dry comfortable one, and it is important to remember that adrenalin is a great block to effective learning. It may be better to scramble, do a big easy route or even visit a climbing wall than to run a performance coaching session when it is cold, windy and raining. On the other hand why be indoors when it is sunny! Try to ensure that you have everyone's attention and that they can all see and hear. Is the sun in their eyes? Are there any distracting noises or activities? Climbing walls have many interesting diversions so keep talk to a minimum. Students do not generally listen if they are absorbed in a person abseiling behind the instructor.

Lectures and Resources

There are theoretical elements to any climbing course that may need to be taught before the students can practise them, and although unremitting verbal explanation is a bad way of teaching, a stimulating lecture can be superb. It may be a lecture to one's peers or to a group of students, it may be indoors or outdoors. It may last a few minutes or an hour. Whatever the audience, wherever and how long it is, there are a number of ways in which an instructor can make the presentation more effective.

The best lectures are those that are prepared, planned and rehearsed. To start with, establish why you are teaching through this medium and then set clear objectives by considering what the audience wants to learn. Consider what you want from the session. Do you want to increase the audience's knowledge, persuade them of a new point of view, or improve their under-standing? Once you have considered the purpose and set objectives, consider the size of the audience. With a small audience, it is easier to include them in the lecture. Do you know them? What do they already know?

Try to make the content interesting, concise, clearly understandable and presentable in the time available to achieve the objectives. Start by welcoming the audience, identify yourself and what you hope to achieve and why. If they have been with you the day before or in an earlier session recap on what they have already done. Provide an outline of the session and what is expected of them and give them the opportunity to ask questions. The introduction can be bold, simple or take the form of a question, but never apologetic. Do not overload the audience; follow a sequence where each point builds upon the last. Vary the format whenever you are speaking to the same students. Frequently review what you have said during the lecture. If you find the audience starts yawning, get them to do something related to your lecture or pose a question and split them into groups to discuss the answer. If the lecture is on fitness, get them out for a short run in the fresh air to measure heart-rate changes.

Late arrivals, projectors breaking down or even people fainting are things you may have to deal with. Remember with all of these events, you are in control. It is your responsibility to manage things carefully. Do not speak through a temporary disturbance such as a plane, wait for it to pass.

Unremitting verbal explanation is a bad way of teaching but a stimulating lecture can be superb.

There is a variety of resources available to the instructor to help to bring the lecture to life. The use of resources can enliven the talk, making it more enjoyable, particularly in the formal training of climbers. Visual aids and handouts can provide structure. They can also help you to remember things, clarify things to the students, speed up the grasp of complex problems and hold the attention of the students. Remember the instructor can also be the actual visual aids.

Direct Aids

Direct aids are items that can be directly written on such as whiteboards, blackboards and flip charts. They are useful for displaying data, key words and phrases, and summarizing and recording points raised by the students. Their usefulness, however, is limited by the size, legibility and organization of your writing. Keep the design simple and focus on key information rather than sentences.

Projected Aids

These include overhead projectors (OHP) and slide projectors. The advantages of projected aids are that they enlarge the images and can be used repeatedly. A well-prepared slide or overhead can add a strong visual impact to any presentation. When preparing any visual aids keep them simple, use coordinated colours to add to their appeal, and keep them neat and legible. Most importantly, write in large letters and do not overload them with too much information. Only display the visual aid when referring to it. Speak to the audience, not the visual aid, and point to the transparency rather than the screen when drawing their attention to the information. Do not stand in front of the image. Visual aids can be used to support the presentation, but not vice versa. Overuse of visual aids is very monotonous and counterproductive.

An OHP uses acetate sheets that are written on and then projected onto a screen. They have the advantage over a board that you face the audience more often. They can also be prepared by photocopying or via a computer printer using special sheets. They can be structured so that they can be laid on top of each other to create a final image or sections can be hidden and revealed slowly. They are superior to writing and when used with a computer the spelling is more likely to be correct.

Slides are a visual aid that can be made from images on computers, but if you are photographing them yourself make sure they are well lit and use a tripod to keep the image sharp. One problem of a slide projector is that it is more difficult to backtrack quickly to an earlier slide.

Videos

It has long been recognized that the standard of public tennis improves during the Wimbledon championships because of the impact of television. Videos of top climbers are just as effective in illustrating how top climbers move. However, it is bad practice to show hours of tape to emphasize a single point or simply to entertain. Switch off between unnecessary bits, and pose questions before and after the video. Practise any techniques shown as soon as is possible.

A video recorder can also be used to allow the students to analyse themselves as many times as they like and in slow motion. It cannot, however, do the coaching for you. Simply filming a student climbing may not teach you or them anything. Do not use zoom lenses because the more you zoom the steadier the camera needs to be. Carry a lens cloth and tripod or monopod. Turn the microphone off to prevent embarrassing comments being captured. You can always commentate later.

Handouts

Handouts can be used to communicate technical information or to remind the audience of essential points. Typed ones, bearing only the essential points and attractively presented, are more likely to be read. It is important to consider when to use them. Handouts given before a talk can act as a guide, but the listener may then ignore what is said. Given at the end, they may not be read at all. A compromise is to hand them out during the talk, but forewarn the audience that this is going to happen. Reiterate the key points before distributing the handout and then allow some time for it to be read. It may be better to put the handouts away before continuing. They can also be used to write notes on.

WORKING WITH YOUNG PEOPLE

The ideas and information in this chapter are applicable to any age group, but there are certain additional factors that must also be considered if you are working with young people.

Harassment/Abuse

The number of instances of children being abused is unfortunately growing and you would be complacent if you thought that you could not be accused of any impropriety. You will often find yourself in a unique position with young people and you will have to develop the judgement necessary so that children and adults feel secure in your company.

Being alone with a child is sometimes unavoidable, but try to ensure that it occurs with the full knowledge of the parents or teacher. Try to keep swearing to a minimum and avoid making sexual innuendoes. It is worthwhile breaking up abusive youth peer activities such as bullying before they get out of hand. It is very tempting to get involved in physical games with young people where there is a high degree of contact, but be aware that others may misinterpret your friendly gestures in another way. On no account should you enter changing rooms of the opposite sex or take children to your home. Avoid taking children alone in a car on journeys, however short. You will often be asked to help a student put a harness on or zip up a jacket, do take great care that your actions are not misinterpreted. It may be safer to get one of their friends to do it for you.

In addition to protecting yourself you are also in a position to recognize the physical and behavioural signs of abuse. Abuse can take many forms:

- **Physical:** intentionally injured or made to do excessive exercises or punishment.
- **Sexual:** where a child is exposed to inappropriate sexual contact, activity or behaviour.
- **Emotional:** where a child is made fun of, criticized, discriminated against or put under unrealistic pressure to perform.
- **Neglect:** where a child is not provided an appropriate level of care or supervision.

Look out for things such as:

- unexplained bruising, cuts or burns, particularly if they are on parts of the body not normally injured;

Counselling

Some young people will see you as an ally and you may become close. If a student confides a problem to you, do not forget that there is no continuity after the student has left the course. Most instructors are not trained/qualified in counselling skills and difficult problems should always be passed to an accompanying member of staff, who may already know that the problem exists.

The best counselling you can offer, is to listen with unconditional positive regard for the person (you can disapprove of their actions but not them as a person). Check that you understand what has been said by asking questions and paraphrasing. Most people just want to talk and express their feelings. Have empathy with the person (see the problem through their eyes). If asked for, offer sound advice, although usually the student can work out what they want to do.

You may be at risk legally if you offer incorrect advice.

- changes in behaviour, such as a child becoming quiet, tearful or aggressive;
- loss of weight and eating problems;
- aparticularly dirty or unkempt child;
- sexually explicit behaviour inappropriate for the child's age, or a child describing an abusive act involving him/herself;
- running away or self-inflicted injuries;
- a lack of trust in adults. Disturbed sleep and nightmares.

Abuse of a physical or sexual nature should always be reported to the accompanying member of staff, higher authorities in your workplace, the NSPCC or the police.

CLIMBING FOR ALL

(by Suresh Paul [Design for Life Centre])

The appeal of climbing and mountain sports compels the climber to perform regardless of disability or impairment.

In the past three or four years there has been an increase in the number of disabled people participating in outdoor and adventure activities in a meaningful way. Much work and development has been undertaken in canoeing, sailing and water sports and opportunities are now being extended into land-based and mountain sports.

Outdoor Education
John Palmer, Warden of Bryntisilio Outdoor Education Centre

Outdoor and Adventurous Activities (OAA) is not simply giving an experience of climbing to a group and letting them draw their own conclusions. That is like giving an art class paints and letting them discover how to paint without guidance. OAA is an approach to learning rather than a subject. It is a medium to educate people. It involves teaching and learning strategies that are capable of reinforcing and enriching all subjects.

For example, some experiences in the outdoors require the acquisition of some mathematical skill in their planning and execution where the consequences of an error would be more serious than a cross in their book e.g. working out tides or estimating time across a hillside. Conversely, some activities require calculation and measurement of scale, which can give real meaning to mathematical concepts. Similarly, respect for and an understanding of safety principles can be reached and natural phenomena observed. Through OAA, young people learn a skill; they develop personally and socially and can develop leisure time interests. OAA promotes cognitive development, an understanding of the natural world, aesthetic awareness, and sensitivity towards the natural environment.

OAA offers unique opportunities for physical and intellectual challenge, in real life situations, where discipline, self-reliance, self-awareness and self-confidence can be developed. The discovery of personal strengths and limitations can lead to a heightened awareness and an understanding of the strengths and weaknesses of others, promoting valuable opportunities for developing aspects of leadership, tolerance, co-operation and decision making.

It is not an easy job if it is be done well. If you wish to be paid to go climbing, outdoor education is not the job to do. In fact, it would be the worst job in the world. Many young people are not motivated and those who are will soon be turned off by an inappropriate approach. It may be the tenth introductory session for the instructor in as many weeks, but for the group members on that day it has to be the most rewarding day that they have ever had. This demands enthusiasm and the ability to make an immediate connection with the members of the group.

Technical skills are essential but only to the instructor. National Governing Body awards are as important as the driving licence that enables the instructor to drive the group to the venue. Competence in the activity frees the instructor to concentrate on the educative process without having to focus on what knot to tie. You must have respect for the people you are working with and an unshakeable faith in their potential. The way we do things has far more effect than what we say and it is my belief that the role model we present teaches as much if not more than what we teach.

The Adventure Designs project launched at the Royal Geographical Society (with the Institute of British Geographers) in 1995 has driven back the technical and equipment barriers faced by disabled people seeking full and meaningful participation in adventure sport and expeditions. New developments in equipment, for example the KITE climbing harness, have made it possible for many disabled people to participate in a greater range of adventure activities.

The aim of this section is to help you to incorporate many of the principles outlined in this book into instructional and coaching techniques so as to include everyone regardless of ability. The need is to overcome prejudices and involve disabled people in the widest range of activities possible.

In the UK the Disability Discrimination Act 1995 has given legal back-up to the use of positive action to provide accessible services and remove inhibiting barriers. Part M Building Regulations, now in its fourth impression, provides a basic standard for buildings.

The reorganization of 'disability sport' at a national level has placed the emphasis on integration. A number of organizations including the National Coaching Foundation and the Central Council for Physical Recreation have produced a range of generic support guides and materials for instructors and sports coaches to help ensure that those who deliver day-to-day activities have the support that they require to provide sporting opportunities for everyone. People with disabilities are aware that a climbing club is working to produce access. They will have greater confidence in developing their connections with the club.

Barriers to Participation

In broad terms the barriers disabled people face when seeking full inclusion in society can be considered under the following headings:

- Environmental – physical and sensory access to the urban, rural or wilderness environments.
- Negative attitudes.
- Legal.
- Cultural.
- Institutional.

The Cycle of Oppression

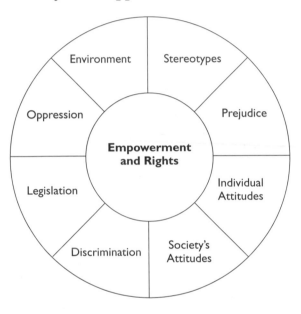

Barriers can be considered in a cumulative or cyclic manner. The 'Cycle of Oppression' describes what, if it is not challenged, can be an ongoing negative experience for the individual as well as society as a whole. The need is to challenge the process in whatever manner is possible, either through the use of positive language, or through pragmatic approaches that encourage participation at a range of levels. The wheel often turns slowly, but with good management and goal setting the process of positive change can occur.

Models of Disability

In the past, disabled people were all too often considered to be a problem requiring a medical solution. Individual personalities and achievments were hidden. The social model of disability was developed mainly by disabled people as a reaction to the medical model of disability. The social model of disability describes the life experience of the person as a whole, placing the emphasis on the removal of barriers. In the social model it is the environment which creates the disability, not the individual.

The Functional Model

What is described below is an overview of a functional model which it is hoped will facilitate a partnership approach to access, where the solutions are owned by all involved. The barriers faced by disabled people wishing to participate in climbing can largely be overcome by a positive attitude, good organization and simple physical modifications.

The functional model of disability accepts that barriers to participation are created largely by the structure of society. The aim is to understand a person's needs in a practical manner in order to ensure that positive actions can be taken to create new and progressive opportunities for all. Developing an understanding of a person's needs can be partly achieved by training and reading, but there is nothing like the real thing. By taking a partnership approach, it is possible to develop the practical empathy that will help everyone to develop their awareness of how to improve the opportunities for disabled climbers.

The barriers faced by disabled people can largely be overcome by a positive attitude. Chris Bannister abseiling with a student. Photo: Chris Bannister collection.

Terminology

There are many words associated with the field of disability, which if used positively can promote understanding of what can often seem complex and daunting. An accurate use of words can do much to make a situation positive.

- **Impairment:** the functional limitation within the individual caused by physical, mental or sensory impairment.
- **Disability:** the loss or limitation of opportunities to take part in the normal life of the community on equal level with others due to physical or social barriers.

Disability Groupings

In broad terms, disability can be broken down into the following areas:

- learning disabilities;
- educational and emotional disabilities;
- sensory impairments;
- communication disabilities.

Adaptive Physical Activity

It is generally possible to break down an activity into the following components, which can be modified or balanced to ensure that your activities are both inclusive and meaningful:

- aims and objectives;
- planning and preparation;
- complexity;
- risk assessment;
- environment;
- duration and intensity;
- number of participants;
- ability and skills mix of participants;
- the individual;
- grouping and buddying;
- equipment;
- communication.

There are many benefits to inclusive climbing practice. These include:

- it is more fun;
- increases the knowledge of the team and individuals;
- creating a cross-disciplinary approach;
- alternative challenges;
- breaking down social barriers;
- increasing level of participation;
- promoting access to science;
- inclusive role models and mentoring;
- more fun.

By promoting an accessible and equitable climbing environment your sessions will enjoy:

- an opportunity to bring climbing to an increased market segment;
- more meaningful representation of all areas of society in the committees and structures of the clubs and organizations, leading to a better understanding of the needs of the climbers in your area;
- accessible services, which are sensitive to the needs of customers, members and climbers;
- access to an increased pool of administrators' leaders, coaches, supporters and managers;
- increased numbers of potential élite performers;
- improved public image as a credible, responsibly organized, forward-thinking climbing club mindful of community considerations and global awareness.

Your Approach is Vital

Your open-minded, positive attitude as a coach or instructor will do as much for the development of possibilities as will any enabling equipment or specialist technique or rope system. In essence, the need is to work on ability rather than disability. There are a number of key tools which can help make a practical difference to your teaching.

- **Consultation:** approach your coaching by offering opportunities for people to perform, ensuring that you continue to ask individuals what they want and what they feel that goals should be.
- **Work on ability not disability:** start with considering and exploring the possible.
- **Never assume:** if in doubt ask, even the obvious common-sense question asked in a polite manner will make an individual feel as though you value their opinion. Create the time in your session plans to make it possible for you to develop your skills and confidence in a way which ensures that you are able to explore the basics before you move on to the more complex. Consider the possibility of one-to-one sessions if you feel that you need to explore issues in confidence or without the pressures of the rest of the group.

- **Gather the necessary information:** check your understanding of this information with the disabled person so that you agree on the objectives and needs. Carers and personal assistants may often have additional information; however, your main working relationship needs to be focused on the performer, so use your information gathering to reinforce this.
- **Don't make assumptions:** individuals with a particular need will not automatically have other specific needs – each individual is different. Whether coaching disabled or non-disabled climbers remember to coach the performer, not the sport.
- **Body centred learning:** it is possible to look at the human body as a simple mechanical system, which can be broken down into a number of component parts. These can be assessed individually to ensure that you are able to work on the strengths of the individual rather than the weaknesses.
- **Communication:** by keeping things simple and succinct and by using a range of formats, your instructing can be made accessible to everyone, regardless of whether the individual has a learning disability or sensory impairment. Different communication pathways include; visual, verbal or auditory, tactile or kinaesthetic use of a combination of different communication techniques can help to make your work with multi-disability groups more effective.

We are all different, with our own specific needs; each of us is disabled in some way. We can all benefit from a positive and open environment which promotes integration and participation. Although this section contains an array of technical and practical information, it is essential to remember that the key to integration, equality and access for all is responsibility: integration is a process, not an end result.

The needs of disabled climbers should be taken into account at all levels of the provision of climbing opportunities. The development of climbing opportunities for all should be made possible for all clubs and organizations regardless of size, resources or geographical location. The provision of accessible opportunities requires an imaginative and sensitive attitude; when approached logically and systematically, amenities built in at an early stage, or even added to an established site, need not be costly or complex. In the twenty-first century, the provision of facilities for all should be given. Instructors should not be limiting their support to the able-bodied or technically expert few; they should be mindful of the benefits climbing offers and enable all to have the pleasures and delights of getting onto the rock.

Specific Medical Conditions

One of the commonest misconceptions about 'disability' is that it brings with it a vast array of additional medical requirements, meaning that meaningful participation is restricted. The reality is that most medical situations which may arise can be dealt with using standard first-aid procedures. If you are in doubt, then ask the individual. The following headings are intended to provide a starting point:

- **Skin care:** discuss the implications of bumps and bruises, especially to areas where sensation may be lacking or intermittent.
- **Personal hygiene requirements:** be aware that people may need extra time and privacy to maintain their independence; also be mindful of adjusting harnesses so as not to restrict any catheters or sensitive areas in the groin or pelvis – ask.
- **Dietary requirements:** be mindful of specific needs; consider also the timing and quantities of food required throughout the session or day.
- **Medication:** make sure that any medication which an individual may require throughout the day is in a suitable place so that it is accessible to the individual in the same manner as it would be in their daily life. Use your consent forms as a reference should you need to pass on information to medical personnel in the advent of an emergency. Your aim here should be to ensure that the individual as far as possible maintains control of their own needs in what may be a new and challenging environment.
- **Keeping warm:** for people with mobility disabilities the need to stay warm can be of even greater importance, so consider the timing and duration of outdoor sessions in particular.

Making Your Equipment Work for You

You can use your equipment in ways that will assist your instructing:

- Choose the colour of your ropes to make communication simpler, and differentiate between the background and the ropes.
- Use colour coding of the handholds and footholds to help you to explain the proposed route.
- Using colour can help you to use non-verbal communication or simple signs.
- Consider and notice the texture of the equipment that you are using and make it part of your communication, especially with people with visual impairments or low vision.

Creative rope work can be used to help support the specific needs of a disabled climber. Many of the principles are similar to those used in climbing and mountaineering, but may have been mixed with some components more commonly associated with caving or rescue.

- Use pulley systems to help overcome strength problems – consider the nature of the rope being used to maximize the efficiency of the system and to obtain the best climbing experience.
- Use tramlines as non-load-bearing guides for people with sensory impairments to reduce the level of communication required during the actual climb.
- Create tyroleans that allow students to ascend; this will ensure that the 'flying fox' experience can be won as well as provided.
- Consider the use of ground anchors and the range of movement available to an individual to ensure that they are able to belay even if they cannot participate in another manner.

- Use skateboarding pads for elbow and knee protection and shinpads to protect areas which may be without sensation for mobility-disabled climbers.
- Use appropriate safety equipment which does not make the climber feel out of the ordinary (XXXL climbing belts and leg loops are available).
- Use the KITE harness where appropriate.
- Larger helmets make it easier to fit people with larger heads. Consider the weight as some people with enlarged heads may also have slightly weaker necks.
- Consider clothing so that the midriff does not become exposed, during prolonged sessions.
- Use spreader bars or anchor plates on chest or full body harnesses to prevent pressure on the chest.

Sources of Information and Support

In the Outdoor World
Adventure for All.

Disability Organizations
Many organizations exist which offer support and advice on specific disability or impairment issues. Often it is possible to gain the most up-to-date information and discuss your concerns with regard to the involvement of an individual in confidence with an advisor or support worker. Lists of disability-specific organizationx can be obtained from the following:

- Disability Information Trust.
- Disabled Living Foundation.
- RADAR.

CHAPTER 2

MOVEMENT SKILLS

Climbing skill is not a gift bestowed on the chosen few; it is a learned art.
Michael Loughman, *Learning to Rock Climb*

What is it that allows some climbers to float up an E4, whereas others wobble with the coordination of a flip flop on a VS? Is it just fitness and mental control, or can an instructor help a student with more than simply supplying safety skills?

To understand how students can be helped to move more effectively, it is first necessary to understand what climbers who operate at the highest standards have in common:

● They are highly motivated individuals.
● They make the fewest movement errors because they possess a wide repertoire of movements and automatically select the most efficient one for the job.
● They are able to focus and climb to the best of their physical capabilities, even in demanding situations.
● They find marginal rests in order to recover physically and mentally.
● They understand safety so they do not have to waste valuable energy and time thinking what to do or how to do it.
● They are not recklessly bold, but are simply confident in their abilities to do the climb.

But how have they achieved this? Is being a good climber in our genes or can everyone become a better climber? While we all have a biological predisposition created by our genes, ability is ultimately the balance between what nature has given us and the way in which nurturing can improve or repress these genetic advantages. The best talents in the climbing world are not always the best athletes. Those climbers who have the motivation, the drive and the self-belief to succeed can overcome any handicap that they may have inherited. There is no magic formula; everyone, young or old, male or female can improve to the maximum of their potential if they have the desire and are willing to work hard to achieve their goal.

The path to reaching a student's maximum potential is not an easy one, but you can influence a student's climbing performance by:

● Improving their awareness of the hazards inherent in climbing and teaching them how to minimize the risks.
● Improving their ability to train effectively. It is said that those who enter climbing lacking in physical strength develop good technique straight away, whereas those who have the strength, tend to power through moves instead of learning good technique. Fitness does, however, have an important role to play in becoming a better climber because as we become pumped (muscles stop working due to a build up of lactic acid) the brain and muscles do not coordinate as easily, at which point, even the correct movements become inefficient.

Efficient climbers make the fewest movement errors. 'Blue Sky', VS 4b, 4a.

This chapter is concerned with what are possibly the most powerful ways in which you can influence climbing performance:

- By improving their movement skills. Learning the correct movement skills from the start of a climbing career can lay down a foundation that enables strenuous/powerful routes to be climbed more efficiently. Take movement skills out of climbing and all you have left is weightlifting.
- By changing their attitude towards climbing. Climbing is as much about confidence as it is in the body's ability to move, and your role is to give the students the opportunity and support to develop confidence. This important aspect can be achieved by helping them to become aware of the real dangers, more aware of how their body moves and to become fitter. Although learning movement is a powerful way of improving someone's climbing, for many students simply taking them onto steeper, longer and more exposed ground may also give them the experience and confidence to 'go it alone'.

> If you teach poor movement patterns and do little to improve a student's confidence, they will climb poorly whatever their genetic make-up and fitness level.

Movement should be taught before anything else on a rock-climbing course. However, successful teaching of movement will depend on how well the instructor can demonstrate things and how much they can inspire confidence in their students. On performance coaching courses it is possible that some students will climb extremes after a day or two. It is useful if the instructor can demonstrate movement and climbing techniques on real routes by leading them in a relaxed manner.

TEACHING MOVEMENT

Through a student-centred approach to the exercises described in this chapter you will be playing 'the inner game', expounded by Timothy Galloway's books *Inner Tennis* and *Inner Golf*. He identified that it is the subconscious side of our brain that coordinates the body, allowing us to make the intricate movements needed in sport, and it is our conscious side that tells us we are failures when we get something wrong. He wrote that 'The internal obstacles within our head are the biggest obstacles to performance.' Your skill is therefore to help the student learn by providing the environment for their subconscious side to do the learning. This is best done by self-discovery, because there is no right or wrong way to climb. Everyone has their own style, so be creative and develop what works for the students. Some will climb quickly, some slowly; keep it in perspective by remembering that creating flashy moves sometimes use more energy than simply powering through a difficult section.

> **The Benefits of Learning Good Movement**
>
> - Your foot and body movements will become more accurate.
> - Good/correct movements will become more consistent.
> - You will use less energy to execute the movements.
> - You will be better able to anticipate the movements ahead.
> - You will increase your confidence.
> - You will climb harder routes or existing routes with ease and in better style.

An occasional demoralizing aspect of teaching movement is that you can rarely change someone's climbing in a week or a weekend course although you may well witness some amazing transformations after just one day. Learning the infinite variety of movements in climbing, and making them automatic, takes practice and time. Some would say it is a life-long journey and the closer your students get to their genetic potential the harder any improvement becomes. Most instructors are not in a position to truly coach, with the exception of teachers, scout leaders etc, and they must lay down the tools that the student can use to progress themselves. The students practice must also be relevant. Months spent bouldering may develop great movement skills, but unless the skills are also practised on real climbs, where the movements compete with the brain's capacity to place gear, control fear and assess the route, they will not be of much use to your students.

For experienced climbers, the rock has a meaning and they have a language to describe climbing movement. Novices do not have this understanding or background experience and

IDEAS

A simple mnemonic that can be used to help you focus on teaching through demonstration and practice is IDEAS:

I   Introduce the technique, its purpose and give a brief description.
D   Demonstrate clearly.
E   Explain the key points demonstrated.
A   Activity and teaching 1:1.
S   Summary.

they must therefore learn the terminology in order to learn properly. Avoid terms like 'layback', and so on until they have developed an understanding of what it is and use general terms that mean something like 'keep your hips close in' or 'tiptoe like a ballerina'.

Each exercise in this chapter highlights one aspect of movement, but they can often be used to teach two or three things about footwork and body positioning.

THE WAY WE LEARN MOVEMENT

Effective instructing aims to provide the most appropriate conditions in which to bring about learning, so it is useful to have some under-

'The internal obstacles within are head are the biggest obstacles to performance' Regent street E2 5C Millstone edge.

standing of the way that your students learn motor skills. Students will have differing capacities to receive information through their visual, audial and proprioceptor (awareness of movement) channels. Some of them will need explanation of the underlying principles before they understand them, others will need to watch and some will have trouble feeling what their body is telling them. The aspect they will all benefit from is quality feedback.

An explanation of how we remember movements and can repeat them is that every time a climber performs a move or series of moves, the muscles, through their proprioceptors, send signals to the brain. The brain abstracts information about the movements, adds it to the information from our eyes and from what we hear and read, then synthesizes it into a set of rules – a 'motor programme'. We use a similar method when we learn a language. We do not learn every combination of words; instead, we learn the language by coming to understand a set of rules.

With practise and feedback, the brain's idea of what is required to make the movements becomes clearer, and the programme becomes more refined, consistent and eventually automatic. This programme is not a list of movements; it is a generalized plan that enables us to recreate the movements necessary to get up a climb. The more you add to the programme, the wider the variety of rock on which you climb on and the more frequently you climb, the more efficient the programme can become.

Learning the movements necessary for climbing is complicated by the fact that it is composed of mainly 'open skills' – the environment is constantly changing (the golf swing and tennis serve are examples of 'closed skills'). Rock climbing is not the same movement repeated over and over – it is more like free dance with an infinite variety of subtle movements When we start to climb there is a conscious involvement of the brain and the nervous system, but as we improve the involvement becomes more subconscious. Numerous messages about the climb, the position of all the parts of the body, the size of the holds, the distance apart of the holds, the angles and so on are sent to the brain and back again for interpretation. Using this information the brain filters out unnecessary messages and searches for the right set of rules to send back to the muscles which are going to make that particular move.

This constant conversation or feedback between your body and mind is called your 'kinaesthetic awareness'. If your motor programme is narrow and the feedback from your body is not clear, the corresponding movement will be inefficient. Novices therefore require much more effort to process a movement because their brain is less able to recognize the clues that their feedback link is giving them. An expert's brain is very good at identifying which clues are important and filtering out those which are not, thus allowing efficient movement. When the rules are organized and the feedback useful the movements can become subconscious or automatic.

When we are in control and confident we can choose our movements more consciously, but when the brain has to cope with stress such as the potential to fall off, concentration disappears and the feedback links are disrupted. At this point, only the most practised, deeply embedded and instinctive rules are available. Those climbers who have poor movements deeply embedded resort to poor movement patterns when they become anxious, gripping the rock tightly and becoming tired more easily than their experienced friends. This is because when good movement skills are automatic the brain is free to concentrate on other things such as style and preserving energy, and can use its spare capacity to sort out the problem.

This situation is further compounded by the fact that the rules our brain uses for creating movement are difficult, if not impossible, to change. Therefore if you learn to move poorly from the start, there is the danger that the most deeply embedded rules may be the wrong ones. Learning correct movement skills at the beginning of a climbing career is therefore vital, but, more importantly for the instructor, the students' ability to learn is influenced by what and how they are taught and the feedback they get from the instructor. Do not despair, the good news is that even if poor movements are already in place your students can practice good movement until it becomes the more automatic pattern even under stress.

Instructing climbing should concentrate on the aspects of climbing that characterize a succesful climber – someone with a broad and refined motor programme, good kinaesthetic awareness, an ability to read the rock, the fitness to stave off the pump, confidence in their abilities and an understanding of their limitations.

Do not make things look easy, make them look obvious. John Horscroft laybacking on Grit.

The motor programmes we develop for movement are general rules and it is therefore possible to transfer some of the existing movement rules/skills, developed from other sports, to a new technique or skill being learned. Therefore novices with appropriate movement skills and good kinaesthetic awareness developed in other activities are likely initially to develop faster than others. If they also have an inherited strong grip, the ability to focus and determination they may become one of the élite.

Stages of Learning

As students practise movement, they move from novice to their pinnacle (genetic potential). To do so, they pass through three stages of learning. The first stage of learning a skill is called the 'mental stage' (cognitive stage). This is where the student tries to understand what is required to climb efficiently. The instructor's role is to find a way of teaching the components of climbing and lay the foundations for good motor programmes. A video at the start showing some graceful climbers can often give the students an image of what is expected.

This is followed by the 'practice stage' where the student attempts to refine the skill. This is where the instructor can provide a positive environment, good feedback, knowledge and encouragement to allow the student to analyse their own performance.

The final stage of learning a skill is when it enters the 'automatic stage'. This is when the brain filters out unnecessary information and the student does not have to think about the skill and appears to flow through the moves on a climb. As a student moves into the automatic stage, an instructor's role changes from coaching the student to helping to maximize their performance. This poses a dilemma for you, because if a student has failed on a climb you must decide whether it is because they lack the skill, or whether they were anxious. With the latter, the instructor can coach anxiety control and try to provide an environment that encourages the student to succeed, that is, they coach to perform.

Teach, Play, Relax

Research has shown that after approximately 20 minutes, the learning process peaks, and additional practice may even undo the gains that have been made, so intersperse periods of learning with periods of play or rest or even go climbing.

USING DEMONSTRATION AND PRACTICE

Demonstration, explanation and practice are the primary ways to help students to acquire a mental plan for movement. Demonstration takes advantage of a very powerful learning principle, that of learning by imitation. A demonstration provides the shape to a movement, while the verbal description gives information about the amount of pressure or force and the speed you are using.

A potential problem with demonstrating perfect movement technique is that a novice may be unable to repeat it. This can lead to loss of confidence because the movement appears unachievable. Therefore, instead of demonstrating perfect technique for a student to recreate poorly or not at all, it is better to consider carefully what you are trying to achieve with the demonstration.

Do not strive for perfection straight away. Encourage students to allow their own development of the movement rather than limit their learning by trying to imitate you exactly. Ask whether what the student is doing will eventually lead to good technique – but remember that we do not easily unlearn old habits. In pursuing one idea of what constitutes perfect technique we also forget that we are all different shapes and sizes and most of us are stronger on one side than the other. Students watching you carry out a task have a different perspective than when they carry it out themselves, for example their left is your right. It may be beneficial sometimes to have them behind you. If it is knot tying, consider doing it ambidextrously.

If you cannot demonstrate things yourself, use someone else who the group perceives as an expert, or a member of the group. A video can also be used to identify a movement or slow it down or to view it from different angles. The video can either be of an expert or of students themselves. Students generally concentrate on one thing at a time, so do not talk while you are demonstrating – introduce it, do it and highlight any points to watch.

With more experienced students, demonstration is a tool that can be effectively used to give a visual model of the whole movement, providing the basic form or rough code of the movement and how the body moves. Once the student has the rough code and understands what is required, demonstration is redundant and improvement then requires repeated practice and verbal feedback from the instructor. Using demonstration with more advanced students can also convey details of a movement or even attitudes, for example, 'Look, you can take you hands off here if you use this technique'.

SPOTTING

Spotting is the ability to prevent injuries when practising movement on a climbing wall or on outside boulders. There is no reason why students, whatever their age, should not spot each other during a movement session. However, effective spotting by novices requires their full concentration and close supervision by the instructor.

Advice for Spotting

- Wear a helmet.
- Stop finger injuries – do not wear climbing harnesses.
- Remove all jewellery.
- Stand braced ready to support someone. A karate or boxing stance is a useful analogy.
- Keep your arms close to the climber, maybe even touching the body.
- Keep your fingers together so they are not bent back by the falling climber.
- Do not let a novice climber move above the height at which the spotter can grab their waist.

Protect the back and the head.

Spotters do not catch falling climbers, but slow them down, steer them to the best landing, and minimize the number of body parts hitting the ground. The size and skill of the spotter, the landing quality, plus the height above the ground all determine the seriousness of the fall. The advanced student is likely to climb higher, sometimes too high to be spotted effectively. Bouldering then turns into solo climbing and it may be up to the spotter to inform the climber when this becomes the case. Spotting more advanced students requires the climber and the spotter to have a greater understanding.

The falling climber should try to keep their limbs relaxed and adjust their torso so that they land on their feet. Crash pads are becoming popular and positioned correctly appear more forgiving, although they may tempt the student higher and into the realms of soloing.

It goes without saying that big people are the best spotters, but the hardest to spot. Consider using two spotters if the climber is large and continually examine the trajectory; is the climber coming feet first or back first? Watch their hips and back, not their fingers, and be aware it will all happen very quickly.

If the bouldering problem is steep, grab the sides of the climber's back just below the armpits and swing them back to a feet-first landing. This works best when the climber is not too high. On higher problems spot the student's hips and steer them to a feet-first landing. Be careful not to grab the student too low and push forward which would result in a headfirst topple backwards.

With younger climbers support them to complete the movements required.

If the student is having difficulty holding a position, then support them as you would with all movement techniques. Take as much weight as is necessary for them to do the move well. Then as they gather experience and strength reduce the amount of help.

Exercise: Spotting
Stand the students in a tight circle, each of them adopting the 'spotters' stance. Place one student in the middle and tell them to fall towards any of the other students. Take care that they do not become too boisterous. It can also be practised with one student walking between two parallel lines of students and falling randomly to either side.

WARMING UP, WARMING DOWN AND STRETCHING

A car started on a cold morning and screeched away may grunt and groan. It takes time for it to perform efficiently and the older the car the longer it takes to warm up. The human body is similar; take students straight onto a climb and they will probably not perform at their best and may even injure themselves. The tendons and ligaments of older people are more brittle, while the muscles, tendons and ligaments of young people are not only growing alarmingly quickly but also at varying rates, so they may have strong muscles before their tendons can cope with the strain. Even if young students do not noticeably injure themselves, they may be laying down the legacies of minor injuries that manifest themselves later in life.

The body should feel warm, but not tired at the end of a warm-up session. A short spell of five to ten minutes of running on the spot, skipping, circling arms, star jumps or any other

---

Why Warm Up?

'Warming up' increases the circulation of blood around the body, and opens the capillaries to feed the muscles and connective tissues with fuel and oxygen. It improves the efficiency of the chemical reactions, causing adenosine triphosphate (ATP – the energy molecule) to occur in the muscles, making them more eleastic and resistant to injury. Warming up also lubricates the joints, helps to prevent a permanent pump too early on and will allow recovery a lot sooner. Warming up prepares you mentally for the challanges to come. The way you warm up generally carries over – to how you climb later in the session. Warm up with smooth, precise movements and a positive attitude.

---

continuous but gentle movement warms the whole body and starts the blood flowing. When the approach to the crag is long, the warm-up need not be so extensive, but remember that the arms still need warming. Generally speaking the fitter or older the students are the longer the warm up needs to be. An excellent warm-up with youngsters is to form a circle, hands on knees, each pretending to be a jockey on a horse. Gallop without going anywhere, but lean to the left and right as if going round bends, speed up and go over jumps of different sizes, then sprint for the finish.

Warming up

There are four parts to warming up:

- Aerobic exercise.
- Moving joints through their full range.
- Stretching.
- Easy routes to warm up specific muscles and alert the body's awareness and coordination.

Teaching Movement

- Warm up and stretch.
- Do not be afraid to revisit seemingly basic concepts with students who climb harder routes.
- Use a video recorder.
- Intersperse rest periods with periods of activity.
- Do not teach too much or too quickly.
- Try to accommodate the different learning styles.

Once the warm-up has finished, take the joints through their full range of movements, starting from the toes and moving upwards, and ending with circling the arms and rotating the hands slowly and in control. If you are at a climbing wall move around for two or three minutes on very large holds as part of a warm-up. Next do some gentle stretching for five to ten minutes to help the body to acquire its full range of movement. Move slowly into each stretch and hold for fifteen seconds to allow the muscle to relax and extend beyond its initial length, then relax and repeat. Make sure that the back is as straight as possible and do not bounce on a stretch. This level of stretching does not increase the range of movements; if you want to become more flexible, you will have to dedicate more time to it and hold the stretch for longer periods of time (*see* Chapter Three, Improving Flexibility).

Three upper body, three lower body and two forearm stretches are usually enough (do not bend individual fingers back because there is nothing to stretch except the joint capsule). Do some twisting with two people linked by their arms back to back. Keep the bulk of stretching for the end of a climbing session when the body is turned in to the sort of movements required. Once the student has sat around for half an hour they are back to square one, so encourage them to keep warm and if possible repeat a warm up and stretch again before climbing.

If the first route is close to a student's maximum, their forearms will double in size and spend the rest of the day trying to deflate. To avoid this 'flash pump' do some very easy climbs first, even when on a climbing wall, and try to use the open palm grip (described later), working towards more crimp-type holds at the end of the warm-up. If you warm up carefully (use the pulse as an indicator of activity) through forearms may still become pumped they will recover more effectively. Most importantly, during these warm-up routes concentrate on movement technique.

Warming up with students before climbing has the added advantage that you can identify those who are less coordinated and those who carry an injury. Look at their accuracy of movement, their reliability (how many times does it take to master something), the speed they can move at, how fast they convert instructions. An awareness of their centre of gravity and how it affects their climbing is essential. How aware they are of their centre of gravity? Can they learn by watching you or are they better at listening to explanations. All these things may help you to tailor the day to each individual. Take notes if you need to. Enthusiasm is infectious, so smile, jump about and make them think that what they are doing is the 'best thing since sliced bread'.

At the end of a session it is just as important to warm down by repeating the process outlined for warming up. Warming down helps to remove toxins from the body that have built up during exercise and will help to reduce any aches and pains caused by stressing the muscles.

THE IDEAL VENUE FOR TEACHING MOVEMENT

Trying to learn movement while leading routes is a slow process because the mind is so busy with other things. The coaching of movement is therefore probably best done on a specific coaching course, although that does not mean you cannot introduce elements of movement while you are guiding a multi-pitch climb or teaching safety. Reinforce good movement techniques at every opportunity.

Points to consider when choosing a venue:

- A nice soft landing.
- A variety of easy problems.
- A variety of holds.
- Routes of various degrees of difficulty, angle and style.
- A variety of rock types.

Skilled route setting makes all the difference to a climbing wall. Undercover rock, Bristol.
Photo: Gavin Newman.

It is an impossible ideal to find, but indoor climbing walls are a good compromise, although they do cater mostly for those who use the wall as a form of fitness training. However, as more walls are used by climbers to learn techniques, the better they will become. Climbing walls most closely resemble steep limestone climbing but some innovative walls for example, are incorporating a lot more gritstone (undercover rock) features that require a more subtle approach.

Climbing indoors has distinct advantages:

- it is unaffected by the weather;
- it is relatively safe;
- many of the exercises are easier to do inside than out because the difficulties and holds are more easily selected and isolated;
- walls are a good place to look at more advanced body positions and other techniques.

There are, however, a number of drawbacks to using climbing walls that instructors should be aware of:

- If you just use climbing walls your students may only become good at movement on climbing walls. The 'climbing by numbers' style of climbing offered by flat panelled walls can be too specific for the demands of climbing outdoors and the holds are too predictable.
- Climbing wall routes often requires the climber to transfer as much weight over a hold as possible to complete the move, whereas on rock many moves, for example bridging, require opposition of the feet to stay in place.
- Modern walls have moved away from features found on real climbs, such as jam cracks, layback flakes and bridging, and very few walls incorporate routes that require slab climbing techniques. Starting on slabs is effective for teaching good technique for steep rock, but the opposite is not necessarily true.
- Reaching the top of many climbing wall routes depends partly on your 'ape index' (the relationship between arm span and body height), and levels of strength and endurance, and less on technique. Indoor routes would be more effective and realistic if they contained a lot of 'red herring' holds plus more smears and features for footholds.

Climbing walls can be better used for technique training by picking an easy route and climbing it without using the tops of the holds or by using features or panels. You may also find it useful (if the wall will allow it) to take your own box of holds along to the wall to create specific problems.

The above comments are supported by the observation that students making the transition from climbing walls to outside often have good stamina and strength, but find that they are limited by the more subtle movements required to climb on real rock. They are also usually lost when it comes to dealing with the time-consuming and energy-sapping characteristics of traditional climbing such as placing protection or the weather.

MOVEMENT EXERCISES

You cannot learn to climb well by simply reading about it. Gymnasts claim that they must practise a single move a thousand times before the brain has processed the rules and feedback that create it. The following eclectic exercises are not magic, they can only accelerate a student's learning if they are practised regularly and frequently. The skill of the instructor is to choose the exercises that suit the student and at the right time. They can be done whilst bouldering, low level traversing or on roped climbs but always within the comfort zone of the student.

You may find it useful to keep a record of the tasks you use with students. This will enable you to revisit a concept but use a different exercise to introduce it.

'The talented climber stands upright, in a naturally balanced position' – Dave Williams on Mousetrap E2 5b, 5a, 5a.

'A novice will lean into the cliff, their weight on both feet, their kees bent and their heels raised.'

THE RELATIONSHIP BETWEEN BODY POSITION AND FOOTWORK

On a less than vertical climb a talented climber stands upright, in a naturally balanced position, so that gravity forces the weight to the feet and allows the climber to see where to put their feet for the next move.

This may seem a simple concept to grasp, but it is more difficult to recreate on rock. A novice will often lean into the cliff, their weight distributed evenly on that both feet so neither foot is free to move, their knees bent and their heels raised (this causes tension and legshake). They will be stretching for handholds, pulling their body closer to the cliff, thereby making it difficult to remove their weight from either foot and

---

Centre of Gravity

To explain the concept of 'centre of gravity' to young students, try balancing a pole in the palm of your hand. The only way to keep the pole in position is to have the hand under the pole at mid span. The analogy is that the pole is the body and the hand the feet.

---

increasing their feeling of insecurity. Because their feet feel insecure, they then try to haul themselves up by their hands.

The main job of the arms and fingers is to hold the body in position while the feet place the centre of gravity so that the climber can push the body up the cliff. Pushing with the legs is more effective because it uses larger muscles than when pulling with the arms. There is also the less obvious method of pushing with the hands and this should be introduced early.

The exact position of a student's centre of gravity depends on their build. For most adult males it is about one inch above the navel; it is slightly lower in women. This difference in the position of the centre of gravity and lengths of the limbs means that everyone has a unique way of climbing and explains why it is difficult to teach someone to climb by forcing them to use particular holds that do not suit their body shape. Climbing is about allowing the rock to dictate the movements you make, not the other way round. There are no rules except this: do what works for you and conserves strength.

Exercise: Shifting the Centre of Gravity
Stand with feet shoulder-width apart; the centre of gravity then lies directly between the legs. Lift one leg without moving the centre of gravity away from the middle. It is impossible to stand with one leg off the ground. Now shift the centre

By pushing down with his right hand this climber has transferred his weight over his right leg, allowing his left to be raised.
Photo and climber Stefan Doerr.

Shifting his centre of gravity to the right this climber has freed his left foot to move easily. He will then place his left foot on a hold and move his weight over it and push upwards to reach the next hand hold.

of gravity over one leg before lifting the other. This shows the student how important it is to shift their body weight over one leg rather than holding their body weight in place with their hands and lifting the leg. The centre of gravity moves as the upper body moves around or as the lower body bends, twists and dips (i.e. the hips and knees) around the base created by the feet.

Exercise: Exploring Body Position
Walk up steps, move slowly and examine where the points of balance occur and how to transfer the centre of gravity from one foot to the other. Also compare how the body reacts when transferring weight with legs bent and legs straight.

Exercise: Moving Centre of Gravity
The student can hold the rock and move their feet and body as much as they can. The hands cannot move.

Advice about correct movement has historically consisted of 'use your feet', 'keep three points of contact' or 'don't cross your feet'. The first piece of advice means nothing to someone starting out and limits the configurations the body can adopt. It is akin to throwing someone in the deep end of a swimming pool and shouting 'use your arms'. The latter two pieces of advice are gross simplifications, creating the impression that climbers spend much of their time being static. In fact, research has shown that up to 70 per cent of the time on a route is spent moving and only 30 per cent being still. Of course, there may be pauses while we consider what to do or to place protection, but the aim is to move smoothly and fluidly, making a neat transition of balance from one point to another, even on overhanging rock. Moving with poise and grace can not only help to maintain a tranquil mind, but it also conserves precious energy, allowing an experienced climber to rest where a novice may struggle.

Exercise: Moving with Poise and Grace
Release the 'climber in everyone' by using some imagery tasks. The students can try climbing as though they are angry, or like one of the climbers on a climbing video, or as if they are on television, or as if their girl or boyfriend is watching them. The importance of precision, style and grace can be introduced by climbing like a ballerina. The opposite, climbing like a gorilla, shows how large, bounding movements can be counter-productive on rock.

Exercise: Climbing Smoothly
Try to climb without rushing. Concentrate on climbing slowly and gracefully without stopping. If your students are snatching for footholds or handholds, consider whether they have transferred their centre of gravity over the appropriate foot and found the most stable position for their body. (They may not understand how to use the holds.)

Exercise: Exploring Feedback
Exaggerate the movements. This may make your students more aware of how their body feels when it moves.

FOOTWORK

We all spend many years practising to use our hands precisely, but little effort is put into using our feet with the same accuracy. Precise and accurate placement of the feet is the secret to conserving upper body strength on steeper climbs.

Edging

Most climbers use the area around the big toe because this is the most sensitive part of the

Footwear

Students will be tempted to use old beaten-up rock shoes with the rationalization 'If I can do the moves in these old things it will be easy when I put my good shoes on'. However, they will get much more out of their coaching session if they practise in their best shoes.

Razor-sharp edges on rock shoes are not ideal for using on small rock edges because the rubber stretches when weighted and a slightly rounded edge is less likely to fold off the narrow edge.

foot, but a competent climber can edge with any part of it. Students may need to be shown how important it is to keep the sole of the foot flat and rigid and how to use the inside and outside edge of the front portion of the foot. To keep the pressure on the foothold when using the outside edge, try imagining that the toes are being curled over the foothold. The smaller the foothold the more important it is to keep the foot still and use the ankle as a hinge to prevent the upper body moving. Only place as much of the foot as necessary into large holes; putting your foot too far in may force the lower leg outward, thereby upsetting balance. It may be worth pointing out that we often put two feet on a hold, so do not obscure it with one foot.

Smearing

The goal with smearing is to get as much rubber as possible in contact with the rock. It is a technique that is impossible to practise wearing big boots. To maintain a smear on steeper rock

means that you have to bring the body out away from the rock to direct the force into the foot. It is possible to smear and edge, although you cannot edge a smear.

Exercise: Where to Smear
Students can examine the rock in detail with their hands and eyes, looking for every irregularity it has.

Exercise: Trusting the Weight to the Feet
Get the students to walk up, down and across progressively steeper sections of a slab until the limit of the grip of their footwear is found. The angle of rock they can tolerate depends not only on their footwear and the nature of the rock, but also on their ability to trust their weight to their feet. Try standing upright on a slab and lean forwards, lowering the body closer to the rock; as the body moves closer, the less the shoes will stick. Sometimes touching the rock with the palm of the hand before smearing can help the student to understand how to use the hold.

Footwork Exercises

Practise with different types of footholds (smears, edges, pockets and cracks) and on different angles of rock. Although the emphasis is on footwork do not focus exclusively on it – what may seem like poor footwork may actually be poor body positioning. A climber's aim is to find the best body position for gravity to force the foot to stay in place.

The smaller the foothold the more important it is to keep the foot still and use the ankle as a hinge to prevent the upper body moving.

For the foot to stay in place when smearing the force must be applied perpendicular to it. The more pressure the more likely it is to stay in place.

Look at the foothold until the foot is firmly planted on it. Dave Williams on the Rabbadda-Navarro route on El Fire Spain.

Exercise: Explore Precise Footwork and Balance

Scramble over small boulders, first using hands and then without, try a few twirls to build confidence. Place stones on the backs of the students' hands to take their minds off falling and to remove the temptation to use their hands. Climbing with clenched fists will achieve the same thing. Uncoordinated students can hold hands.

Exercise: Importance of 'Looking Down'

Novices often move their feet before they know where they are going to put them. Compare climbing without looking down to climbing without looking up.

Exercise: Introducing Accuracy and Precision

Inexperienced climbers dance their feet around on holds, rushing from place to place. Introduce accuracy and precision placement of the feet by climbing in slow motion or with no noise from the feet. This is especially effective on indoor climbing walls where the foot banging against the boards makes a lot of noise.

Exercise: Look at the Foothold

Many climbers look away at the last moment before their foot is on the hold. Practice looking at a foothold until the foot is actually on the hold by hovering the foot over the hold for a few seconds before placing it. This will help them study the possibilities the hold offers and make them make a firm choice of position.

Exercise: Encourage Efficient Footwork

Novices often focus on the biggest footholds, when in fact they should focus on their centre of gravity even if it means using smaller steps and smaller footholds. Climb using gigantic steps then little steps. Which uses less effort? To help the student to concentrate, get them to mark their progress themselves. Give the number ten to their largest step and the number one to their smallest step. Your students can shout out the number as they boulder. Smaller steps are particularly important on slabs.

Exercise: Reduce the Size of the Footholds

Using big handholds, reduce the size of the footholds each time. Consciously relax the grip on the holds to transfer more weight and hence force to the feet.

Exercise: Improving Confidence

To improve trust in your student's feet, place one foot on a poor hold and then stretch as high as possible to see how long the foot can stay there. Although this is something you would normally avoid when climbing it does help them to understand that. The higher they reach the more pressure is needed to keep the foot in place. To use footholds effectively push on them like you mean it. You can even hold the foot in place for the student to start with. By holding the feet in place on moves that are at a student's limit, you may enable them to work out how to bend their ankles and knees or shift their hips in ways needed to keep their foot solidly on the hold.

Exercise: Think Before You Move

To aid fluid movements the student should try to develop the habit of looking ahead for footholds while climbing and to assess the best place for the foot before moving, rather than halfway through a move. The student cannot reposition the foot once it has been placed on a hold.

Once the student moves on to steeper routes they may have to switch body position more often to reach handholds. This will then cause them to swop feet or swivel them on a hold.

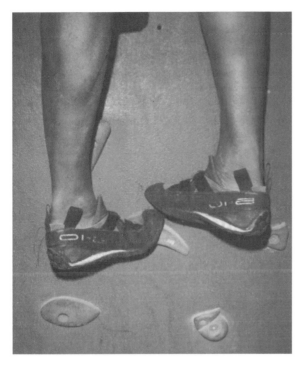

Swopping feet on a hold.

Exercise: Swivelling the Body
Try swivelling the body to change from outside edge to inside edge. This exercise is useful to introduce the link between the feet and the upper body because the students will have to move their centre of gravity around to maintain a stable position.

Exercise: Swopping Feet
Do the opposite to the previous exercise and look at swopping feet on the same hold. This is most easily done with the hips out from the wall. This exercise emphasizes swift, accurate changes and shows the student how important it is to realign their centre of gravity over the foot as soon as possible. To do this effectively they must make room for the foot being moved to land on the foothold. Rotate the ankle of the upper foot so that the toes point away from the foothold that the lower foot is on. Bring the heel of the upper foot towards the lower foot. Place the big toe of the upper foot a few millimetres above the big toe of the lower foot. Do not jump the foot; at the same time move the lower foot off the foothold and drop the upper foot onto the now vacant hold. The same principles apply when changing the outside of the foot; except

Switching outside and inside edges. Note the position of the knees in the second photo.

Commit yourself fully when making a high step/rockover. Note where the climber is looking.

that you now rotate the upper foot to bring the toes through first.

In general small steps are better than big ones, but there are times when a high step onto a new foothold may be necessary. This is called a 'rock over'. This can be stressful on knees so take care.

Exercise: Transferring Weight

When moving onto a foothold more than two feet up or to the side, you have to switch your weight deliberately (move your centre of gravity). Place the foot onto the best part of the hold, then smoothly move the hip over it, bending at the knee to keep the foot steady. The trailing leg may leave the rock completely; let it hang in whichever position maintains balance ready for the next move.

Making high steps emphasizes the importance of climbing smoothly and completing each move until the centre of gravity has been totally transferred over the new foot. If your students have trouble completing the move try exaggerating it further, similar to following through in tennis. Practise rock overs on slabs without using the

hands and then on steeper walls to show how foot positioning affects balance. Be careful of damaging knees on severe rock overs.

Using Feet Imaginatively

On steep and overhanging routes there are many tricks with the feet that can help to take the strain off the arms. Until now, we have only used the inside and outside edge of the front, but feet have two ends:

- The simplest way to use the feet imaginatively is to lock the toes in a horizontal crack, weight the heel and jam it in place. This can be used to help push the body towards the next hold.
- The same thing can be achieved by placing the foot sideways in a wider crack.
- Toes can also be hooked under a roof or in a horizontal break, to hold the body in place.
- Heel hooking is a way of attempting to use the foot as an extra hand above or to the side.

Students can practise with imaginative ways of using their feet on easy routes. The rest exercises used later are useful for practising imaginative footwork.

On steep routes look for the possibility of hooking the heel onto a hold as a third hand. The author on 'The Sentinel', E2 5C.

HOW TO USE HANDHOLDS

Rock offers a variety of holds that novices may never discover. To help your students to become aware of the variety and abundance of holds that may be available, describe edges, jugs, pockets, pinches, cracks, underclings and side pulls and send the students to find them before they even set foot on the rock.

Exercise: Looking for Holds
With young students (and not so young!), hide 'Smarties' over the bouldering area. This may encourage them to look for holds.

Exercise: Eyes-Closed Climbing
Eyes-closed bouldering (be careful if blind-folding young people) with or without a partner giving instructions increased concentration on other forms of information, for example, touch or where the centre of gravity is. The partner can describe the handholds and footholds and how to use them. The climber is blind, not stupid, so do not allow endless 'up a bit' type instructions. Eyes-closed climbing for intermediate climbers is looked at later in this chapter.

Exercise: Studying the Rock
Students can design their own boulder problems and mark them with a stick of chalk so that the rest of the students can try them.

Three Types of Handholds

No two holds are the same, but there are three broad ways of using them depending on their size, position and shape: open hand grip, crimp grip/ring grip and pinch grip. Like all movements, genetic factors such as joint length can affect which one a student prefers to use. However, because strength is position-specific, a climber who is skilled in all three methods can minimize the fatigue and stress among the different methods during a climb.

If a handhold is too small to accommodate all the fingers, try to give priority to the middle and ring finger because these are usually the strongest. On smaller finger holds keep the fingers together. If there is not room for all the fingers curl the others up to optimize the muscle/tendon system.

Taping Fingers to Prevent Injuries

Finger taping is best done using rings of 0.75cm or 0.5cm in tape on either side of the joints.

The 'X' method adds support over more of the finger. Take a turn around the base of the finger, then cross over the finger and take a turn around the middle of the finger. Cross back and take another turn. The tension will dictate the amount of bend in the finger.

The author on Sentinel E25c, Burbage North.

On a sloping hold the open palm grip is the least stressful on joints.

A crimp grip.

The Open Hand (Extended) Grip
In the open hand grip the fingers are not used to support each other. It is often used on rounded holds, layaways and undercut moves as it allows further reach. This grip is the least stressful on joints and tendons, but the most strenuous to use because the forearms must work hard to stop the fingers straightening out. On a rounded hold it is the quickest way to become pumped, so use the technique for endurance training.

A pinch grip.

The Crimp Grip
The crimp grip is a foreign configuration for the fingers and may need teaching to novices. A crimp uses the strongest digit, the thumb, to back up the next two fingers. It concentrates the forces to the tips making it useful on very tiny holds. Keep the thumb close to the rock to reduce leverage. However, it is the easiest way to damage fingers because they are contracted to their limit at the second joint.

The Pinch Grip
The pinch grip is a less than obvious way to use a hold. Try to use as much of the thumb as possible and keep the palm close to the rock to reduce leverage.

Contact Strength and Mechanical Advantage

A common reason for becoming pumped on a route is because the student is gripping the rock too hard. Contact strength is the amount of force applied to a hold. Exercises can be done to encourage understanding of this.

Exercise: Applying Force to Handholds
To demonstrate that the rock may be gripped too tightly, climb a route then repeat it by applying the minimum of pressure to the holds.

Exercise: Precision Use of Handholds
On hard routes the precision use of a handhold can be as important as precision footwork. Let students practise by keeping their feet on the ground and flowing across the wall from handhold to handhold.

Body position is important to direct the forces in the best direction but it can also affect the actual mechanical advantage that your hands have.

Exercise: Mechanical Advantage of Elbow Position
Unfortunately, moving the elbows out (chicken winging) creates a mechanical disadvantage for the big muscles, which makes it difficult to pull on a long move. Try the following: grip a hold in the crimp position with your elbow at 90 degrees to the wall. Test its holding power by pulling with the other wrist and then repeat it with the forearm pointing down parallel with the body. Which feels better?

Elbows in and elbows out, showing the transfer of forces to the hold.

THE IMPORTANCE OF OPPOSING PRESSURE

Body position affects how you can use certain holds – for example, a crack in a corner may be difficult to climb it facing straight on. It may be easier to twist the body sideways, use the edge of the crack for your hands and place your feet on the wall making up the corner (laybacking). On real rock many body positions require opposition of either the hands (the Gaston, *see* later), the feet (bridging) or both (laybacking). It is worth remembering that these body positions involve the whole body and not the feet or hands in isolation.

Laybacking

Subtle and not so subtle layback body positions can be found whenever you use a side pull, but classically they are found in cracks, corners and on arêtes. Laybacking relies on good technique mixed with a degree of strength and determination. Difficult laybacks require a keen awareness of centre of gravity to prevent the body swinging away from the rock. When laybacking on arêtes the heel can be hooked around the other side of the arête to keep the centre of gravity in the correct place.

Exercise: Laybacking
Find an arête or line of side pulls. The student can climb by leaning their body to one side. They should try to pull with the hands and push with their feet in opposition to each other. Keep the feet as low as possible. The steeper the rock the higher the feet must be kept to maintain the pressure, but the more strenuous it then becomes. Arms should be kept straight to lessen

Laybacking is one of the most exhilerating and committing forms of climbing. The author on Broadsword, E4 6a, Pembroke.

In its purest form bridging is where the legs are placed either side of a corner with the centre of gravity evenly distributed between the two. Steve Lewis on Profit of Doom, E4 6b.

Paul Donnithorne using opposing pressure between his back and feet at the top of a long sandstone pitch in Zion National Monument, Utah.

the strain on muscles and the inside hand is usually the highest. The hands and feet can be shuffled or leapfrogged up the rock but generally crossing over either hands or feet will put more weight onto the arms. If it is a crack, try jamming the ball of the foot into the crack.

Bridging (Stemming)

Bridging uses the feet in opposition to keep the body in place. It can make a strenuous position comfortable and it is therefore very important to practise the myriad of forms it can take. The only thing that may be keeping you in place is pressure through your feet, but do not forget the arms can also push. It is a very creative movement in climbing and is not only used in corners. It is worth experimenting with bridging on vertical and overhanging walls.

Bridging often requires a sophisticated use of the hands in order to free a foot for upward movement. Often you will use a push-pull combination with your hands. As the left foot is lifted the left hand must push against the rock low down and to the left side.

Exercise: Bridging
Try climbing corners of the wall using the feet only and no hands, or try climbing using just the walls for smears and no footholds. You can also use your hands by pushing against opposite

walls. Try changing feet by placing both against the same wall.

Chimneying

A chimney is defined as a crack big enough for the body to fit easily into. The method is to use opposing pressure between the back and feet (or knees if it is narrow). The hands are used to push the back away and up, but not too far or the feet can skid away. Chimneys are sometimes too wide for this, so they will then be bridged. If a chimney is wider than can be bridged, it becomes a problem because only lying across the gap will then allow progress.

Mantleshelf

This is the ability to gain a ledge, where there are no holds above it, with poise and grace rather than landing on top with a belly roll.

Exercise: Mantleshelf
Select the best part of a large hold or top of a boulder. Walk the feet up until your centre of gravity is as high as possible. Push hard on the top of the mantle to bring your body high. Step up and rock your foot over the mantle. Turn one

It may be easier to understand a mantelshelf if you compare it to getting out of a swimming pool. John Horscroft bouldering at Stanage.

Using an undercling. Note the use of the right/left rule or in this case the left/right rule. Climber: Trevor Massiah.

or both hands inwards to push and balance upwards. It is usually better to push down with the hand opposite the raised foot. Work towards narrower and narrower ledges.

Side Pulls and Underclings

Holds are not always horizontal and vertical holds (side pulls) or upside-down holds (underclings) they are often missed by climbers so it is worthwhile emphasizing them. Undercling holds allow the feet to be moved higher, enabling the student to reach a higher handhold. It is important that pressure is exerted through the feet to prevent them skidding away. The left/right rule described later is essential for performing side pull and undercling movements effectively, because you must sometimes use the outside edge of the foot opposite the handhold you are using. This allows the hip opposite the pulling hand to twist into the wall.

Exercise: Side pulls and Underclings
Introduce side pulls and underclings by getting the student to lean exclusively left or right as they climb or make very long reaches.

Gaston or Comici Technique

This technique is in the same genre as a side pull. It can be done with one or both hands. With both hands in a crack or on two holds, they pull in opposite directions to each other as if they are trying to open a lift door. Moving from this position usually requires leaning to the side. The opposite can also be done by pulling/ squeezing both sides of a large block.

Exercise: Gaston
Try climbing a route by using this technique on some or all of the holds. The student will have to move their centre of gravity around to find the least stressful position

THE IMPORTANCE OF BODY POSITION

Efficient climbing is a blend of creative footwork and use of the hands, but the way these are used depends as much on the body is positioned as

The left hand of this climber is pulling across his body in a 'Gaston'. Climber: Trevor Massiah.

on how well the feet are placed. The best body position is the one that directs gravity to force the foot to stay in place. Sometimes you should choose a hold not because it is easy to hold or push against, but because it is in the correct place.

Avoiding Overstretching

A temptation for all climbers is to stretch for the handhold because it is more reassuring to hold onto something large (this is a potential disaster on slabs because the feet lift off the rock as the heel rises). It becomes a problem when the climber focuses on the handhold so much that they become stretched out (try jumping when you have made your body as tall as possible) The reason a climber usually becomes stretched out is because their feet are not high enough (see the earlier photo of a novice) or because they are not supple enough.

Exercise: Preventing Overstretching
Ask the students to imagine that there is a box drawn in front of their head. Their hands must

not be taken above head height or beyond shoulder level. The student can then gain height only by using their feet.

Exercise: Staying Flexed
Suggest the students try moving their feet before they move their hands; the body will then stay flexed rather than extended. Try two foot movements before they move their hands. The student may end up in a 'frogged' position with their centre of gravity spread equally over their feet. Notice how moving the feet higher has enabled the student to reach further. The frogged position is a good time to look at how we sometimes have our heels away from the wall. In this position, the closer the heels are towards the rock, the more likely the student is to topple over backwards.

Linked with overstretching is when a climber leads with their arms and leaves the rest of their body behind, meaning that their centre of gravity moves further away from the ideal position above their feet. This will result in them becoming off-balance and may cause them to swing or barn-door off the climb.

A frogged position keeps the hips closer to the rock. When combined with straight arms it is a useful position when trying to rest.
Photo and climber: Stefan Doerr.

Compare the two photographs, where is the climbers centre of gravity (left) an off balance climber leading with his arms; (right) a climber in balance leading with his feet. Climber: Trevor Massiah.

Exercise: Moving Feet First
Ask the students to move their feet first and then their arms later and compare this with moving hands first and then the feet.

Positioning of the Hips

An important aspect of the hands body/feet link is the position of the hips. The steeper the rock, the more important this link becomes because it saves vital energy by keeping the weight over the feet but allows them to be seen during the moves.

Exercise: Importance of Hips
Traverse a wall, but bring the hips out to move the feet, then bring them back in to move the hands. This in/out movement does not apply on slabs.

Exercise: (i) Exploring Body Position
Traverse using any holds, but move the limbs in a specific order. Move hand–hand–foot, that is move both hands onto new handholds before you move either foot, then move hands again and so on. Then try foot – foot–hand. After a couple of sequences the body positions that the student has to adopt to stay on the climb become stranger and stranger. They will have to consider carefully how to position the limbs or the body core to maintain stability and balance.

The physics behind climbing is that the climber is trying to direct the forces through their feet. With the hips in close to the rock the weight is kept over the feet. Trevor Massiah on the Arrow, E1 5b.

Maintaining body-tension is important as the rock becomes steeper. Climber and photo: Stefan Doerr.

Exercise: Exploring Body Position
Find a wall with lots of holds and start from a resting position. There are five parts to the body – two arms, two legs and the torso. Try to move each part separately. It sounds simple, but in fact it is difficult to find the correct body position to move each part separately. The instructor can shout out right hand, right hand, left foot, left foot, body, for example. Try it while down-climbing or smearing on small footholds. This exercise is contrary to the idea that climbing is about flowing, so should only be used to highlight the importance of body position. It is also useful for introducing 'frogging' and 'Egyptians' (*see* 'Techniques as the Rock Becomes Steeper') below.

Exercise: Exploring Body Position
Find four footholds in a square configuration and use them to move around in a circle. This may also highlight those students who need to improve their flexibility.

TECHNIQUES AS THE ROCK BECOMES STEEPER

When climbing slabs, the body moves away from the rock to increase the pressure through the feet, but as the rock steepens it becomes more important to bring the body closer into the rock face and over the feet. Once the wall has become vertical the hips are best sucked in tight to the rock to keep the weight over the feet. When the wall is vertical or overhanging it is easier to reach and move by twisting the body sideways.

With gravity pulling the climber away from the rock on a steep route it is not enough for the points of contact to support a climber vertically; the hands and feet must hold the climber into the wall. This requires strength and body tension, a tautness that runs through the body, linking the hands and feet.

Exercise: Importance of Stomach and Shoulder Muscles
On a very steep route let the feet swing free then put them back on. If the student has difficulty doing this they may need to strengthen their stomach and shoulder muscles to maintain the link between the feet and the upper body.

The Left/Right Phenomenon

Watch how a lizard moves or Laura Croft in Tomb Raider 2 – arms and legs to the side, centre of gravity close to the wall, its head moving from side to side to keep its weight over its feet. The movements of a climber on an overhanging route are very similar. They mostly work in diagonals across the body by moving limbs left/right or right/left. On vertical and less than vertical walls, working in diagonals is often no more stable than working one side of the body or the other. On steeper walls gravity pulls the body away from the wall, making it easier for the body to pivot away from the rock like a barn door. On steeper rock working in diagonals has a distinct advantage especially when combined with twist locking.

Exercise: Left/Right Climbing
Find a steep route and climb by moving left arm and left leg, then right arm and right leg. Then try alternating the movements, for example, left foot, right arm, then right foot, left arm. Which works best? Think about elastic climbing – as one limb moves the opposite moves with it. You

Twisting sideways increases reach and uses the upper body more effectively. What would this climbers next move be?

Twist locks use the upper body muscles more efficiently on steep rock. Trevor Massiah on The Fascist and Me, E4 6a, 5c.

may find that these exercises introduce flagging – using the leg to counterbalance your body. Focus on the feet during this exercise because using left and right sides of the body require the use of both outside and inside edges and inside edges of the feet.

Twist Locks

The body is able to use some muscles more efficiently in certain positions – a good example of this is the twist lock. The body is strongest at locking off when it is turned towards the hold being locked because you can use stronger muscles. When you combine twisting with the left/right rule you create a very strong and stable position for the body. For example, if you twist into a left arm lock-off standing on the outside edge of the right foot, the body will then face left. The other foot may be inside edging, flagging or even just dangling in space. Twisting also allows the student to reach further; the longest reach is possible with the hand that is opposite the foot they are standing on. Letting the spare foot come off the rock can also extend the reach.

Exercise: Twist Locks
Pull up on free hanging rings as in gymnastics or use a rope ladder and lock on one hand. The end position will be the same as when twisting on rock – on rock the hands are fixed so the body has to twist, on rings the hands are free and can move. The upper arm is rotated to the torso; this has the effect that strong muscles such as the pectorals can work better. If the upper arm is rotated in the opposite direction, strong muscles become less effective.

Exercise: (i) Creative Twisting
To explain how twisting the body can make climbing easier find a steep route and try using the footholds differently each time. Be creative – rotate either hip into the wall and use the heel or outside edge of the foot. Twisting sideways and using the outside edge of the foot can be a disaster on slabs, but experimenting by climbing a slab sideways may teach the student a few things about balance.

Exercise: (ii) Creative Twisting
This exercise highlights a lot of things about twisting. Practise using undercling and side-pull

holds by taking a side-pull hold and pair with the appropriate edge of a foot. This can be used to explain the left/right rule above. Practise turning to both sides. (This may lead to natural flagging.)

Flagging, Back Stepping and Knee Dropping (Egyptians)

There are a number of techniques which are very effective on vertical and overhanging rock, such as 'back stepping', 'knee dropping' and 'flagging'. They may already have appeared naturally as the student learns to twist their body sideways and masters the left/right rule. With all of these techniques keep the hips in and the body as close to the rock as possible to direct the forces over the feet and add stability.

Exercise: Revisit Twisting
Adopt a bridging position then twist and put the outside edge of one foot on a hold. This trans-

An outside flag helps to maintain balance when you cannot change your feet to use the left right rule. Climber: Trevor Massiah.

Inside flagging combines a twist lock with a flag, using the stronger upper body muscles to reach. Climber Claire Carlisle.

fers more weight to the feet and increases the distance the student can reach.

To maintain balance on steep rock when only two points of the body are in contact the leg is sometimes used as a counter balance akin to the outrigger on boats, this is called 'flagging'. It can be done with the leg behind, in front or straight out the back and the foot does not have to be placed on a hold, but it is a good idea to keep it in contact with the rock whenever possible. The advantage of inside flagging is that it combines a twist lock with a flag and therefore uses the stronger upper body muscles to stay in place. Flagging behind helps to stabilize the body if it is in an out of balance position and trying to untwist (barn door). Inside flagging can also be used to avoid switching feet on an insecure foothold.

Exercise: Introduce Flagging
Stand the student in front of you and get them to lean forwards to reach for your hand. As you move further away, the student will automatically use a leg to counterbalance the body as it leans forwards.

The following exercises are most effective on overhanging rock.

Exercise: (i) Flagging
Using the exercise of four holds described earlier for switching the body weight around, stretch the right arm up for a hold and use the opposite leg as a counterbalance. Alternatively, reach the right arm up and leftwards so that the left leg is then flagged out behind the climber.

Exercise: (ii) Flagging
Find a single handhold on a very steep wall which is a layaway for the right hand and a single right foothold directly below this layaway. Reach leftwards; the upper body is on the left side of the foothold and therefore to maintain balance over the foot the left leg must be flagged out to the right to counter the weight of the body as it leans to the left.

Exercise: Preventing a Barn Door
On a steep route try to take both the left hand and foot off the rock – the only way to prevent the barn-door effect is to flag the foot (or change the configuration of the feet).

Exercise: Flagging/Rockovers
Climbing a line of small layaway holds in a straight line can highlight flagging, although it can also be used to introduce rock overs. Move up and down, adjusting the flagged eg to find the best spot for the counterbalance. It may be useful to refresh the idea that to stay in balance climbers often work in diagonals, such as left/right across the body.

Exercise: Introducing Back Stepping
Twisting can then be taken one step further by introducing back stepping (Egyptian), which is really a variation on bridging. Attain a bridged position between two holds on a wall, then twist the hips sideways and step one of your feet behind you and place the outside edge of the foot on a foothold. Keep your weight over the new hold and use the arm on the same side of the body as the back-stepped foot.

An 'Egyptian' or knee drop adds stability to a position. John Horscroft at Stanage Edge.

Exercise: Introduce Knee Drops
Knee drops are a more severe form of the back step and can also be introduced from a bridged position. After turning sideways and back stepping to place the outside edge on a hold, drop the knee and torso so that the knee bends downwards towards the ground. The aim is to keep your weight over the foot that has been back stepped by placing the dropped knee under your buttocks. This allows you to squat and keep your arms straight, thereby securing a rest position. If the back-stepped hold is high, place your foot onto it from a bridged position then pivot your feet to face away from it. A combination of twist lock and drop knee is a very stable position and transfers the forces to the legs. Knee drops can also be done with the forward facing knee and again produce a very stable position.

Exercise: Knee Drops

Traversing is a good way to introduce knee drops, flagging and twisting. Adopt a knee-drop position with the right hip into the wall, reach behind and rightwards for a handhold then step your feet around and sink into another knee drop with the left hip turned in. Reach forward and repeat in the other direction.

To protect your knees progress from back stepping to full knee drops. With practice, the back-stepping foot can be placed directly into a knee drop position. Eventually experiment with knee drops in lots of strange positions – for example, hook the toe on a ledge and twist the torso until the knee is in a dropped position. The knee drop can also be used by continuing a rock over until the knee drops beyond the foothold. It may even be possible to take a no-hands rest using this method.

LEARNING TO REST AND AVOID THE PUMP

In addition to learning efficient movement, learning to rest can have a profound affect on a climber's confidence and will therefore make a major contribution to success on routes that are more difficult. Much of the advice is common sense, such as the simplest way of resting is to down-climb to a rest spot then work out the moves rather than become pumped hanging on at the crux.

Being able to take adequate rest on a route depends on three factors:

1. **Body position:** maintaining the centre of gravity over the feet.
2. **Fitness:** the ability of the body to avoid the pump i.e. to clear lactic acid from the muscles.
3. **State of mind:** how many times have you been 'gripped' while placing a runner, only to find that you have relaxed as soon as it is in place?

Use the Whole Body

Remember to use the whole body when resting. As the rock becomes steeper keep your hips into the rock and your weight directly over your feet. If one arm is removed, shift your centre of gravity over the feet and to below the arm still hanging on. Use some of the positions discussed

A knee bar can take the weight from your arms. Photo and climber: Stefan Doerr.

earlier sections such as bridging and back stepping, Egyptians and knee drops to help you achieve this.

Do not forget the rest of the body for wedging and hooking – place the backside on a hold, hook the chin over an edge or use your foot as a third handhold, anything that can take the strain off your arms. The toe hook can help you maintain balance and your weight over your feet. Try the 'thumb catch' by laying or hooking the thumb over an edge and wriggling the fingers. Try laying the forearm across a hold. On small edges, alternate fingers and hands on the hold. 'Match' hands on the holds by making space between the fingers for the other hand. In a corner stem out and push the chest into the corner, or 'chicken wing' by putting arms or elbows against the walls. Try using knee bars by jamming a knee against a hold or roof and pushing with the foot to wedge it in place.

Using Your Arms Effectively

When climbing beyond the vertical, more of your weight comes onto the arms. Keep your arms low for as long as you can, using side pulls or under cuts to allow the blood to flow to the hands more easily. If you do have to hang on with your arms above head height try to keep your hand open as much as possible. When you can grip the rock with only enough force to keep you on the rock.

To rest effectively on steep rock keep the arms straight ('monkey hanging') by bridging or sinking into 'a squat', or by twisting and knee

Hanging on a straight arm puts the load on tendons and bone not muscle. Climber: Andy Cave on The Tippler E1 5b, Stanage Edge.

dropping,. You will then be hanging on bone and tendon rather than muscle.

Most people think of resting only while chalking up or placing equipment, but when the holds are large keep your arms straight while making moves. Straight arms have less leverage on them than bent ones and can compensate for

lack of upper body strength and they lower the centre of gravity.

Exercise: Straight Arm Climbing
Find a positive hold on a steep wall and assume a straight arm position. Then move the feet higher while keeping the arm straight and using it as a lever and the shoulder as a hinge. Now push with the legs – as the hips are rolled inwards towards the straight arm the body twists and increases the reach. Although you should strive to do this whenever possible, it is only really possible on climbing walls and steep limestone routes because they have a plethora of holds available.

Breathing/Shaking Out

Breathe slowly and deeply when resting and breathe out when you are making a strenuous move, just like weightlifters, even if the pump does not disappear it may help you to relax. If your arms are pumped hold them low to allow the blood to drain the lactic acid from the muscles. Shake them high (not violently) and let them drop. Stretch the forearms out by pushing your palm against a hold. Staying too long in one place may be counterproductive, so continue climbing as soon as your breathing has returned to normal.

Exercise: Resting
Shout 'stop' while the student is climbing; they then have to find a rest position and hold it for fifteen seconds. Limit the number of times 'stop' can be called. You can try to catch the student out.

DYNAMIC MOVEMENTS (DYNOS)

Climbing is about using style and grace, flowing from hold to hold, but there are times when you will need use the momentum of your body to 'snatch' for a higher hold. It is often used to overcome the need to hold a strenuous position statically. This can vary from a simple lunge of the hand to a full body leap or dyno. In either case the student should be trying to grasp the hold at the highest point of the movement when the body is motionless (the 'dead point'). Prior to lunging and leaping for holds be thoroughly warmed up, as serious damage can be caused to fingers and shoulders by incorrect technique.

Dynoing is a last resort. Stefan Doerr at Finale.

Bend the knees and sink down low. Try to propel the dyno with the legs, not the arms. Momentum is the key to success, so use the more powerful muscles in your legs; the arms should be used to pivot and direct, not launch. Breathe out as you push up, and on overhanging walls keep your arms straight. On less steep walls pull with your arms as you move upwards to keep your hips into the wall. Don't bounce beforehand. Crouch once and then do it.

Dynos need not be huge lunges – they may be a controlled dash for a hold. Before snatching for a hold, consider which hand is doing the holding and which hand the propelling. For example: the move is one where the right hand is on a good hold but needs to move to new hold, while your left hand is on a poor hold, only good enough to keep you in place. If you propel with the left hand you may fall off, but if you use the right hand to help you move and the left hand to stay in position and shoot your right hand out at the last moment you may grab the hold. It will move faster than you fall.

Exercises: Practising Dynos
Practise one-arm climbing, which forces you to latch onto holds quickly and accurately. Climb an easy route without pausing between moves and find boulder problems where the moves are not from two good holds. A variation is to traverse one-handed in both directions.

CRACK CLIMBING TECHNIQUE

Face climbing relies on exterior holds and more natural movements, whilst jamming in cracks is unnatural and can be painful when done poorly. To avoid bloody encounters when teaching jamming it may be a good idea to tape the students' hands and/or fingers. Also use a top/bottom rope, to avoid damage to fingers.

Sequence of Hands

The sequence of hand movements is the first thing to tackle:

- Jamming cracks in a face requires crossing one hand over the other.
- Jamming cracks in corners requires the hands to be shuffled because the body cannot be twisted side to side as easily. Which hand stays on top depends on which shoulder is against the rock.

Taping Hands for Jamming

Use 1.5in zinc oxide tape. Shave the hair from the hand and flex the hand as you tape.

Rip four 4in strips of tape, make a fist and overlap these strips across the bony part of the hand. Then take a strip from the littler finger across the back of the hand, between the index finger and thumb. Take the tape around the index finger, back across the hand and finish with two wraps around the wrist. Take another strip from the thumb side across the back of the hand to the outside of the little finger. Take the tape around the little finger, back across the hand and finish with two wraps around the wrist.

Remove the tape by cutting the wrist ties, it can then be revised.

Finger Jamming

- The best way to finger jam is to insert the fingers, thumb upwards or downwards (ideally above a narrowing in the crack) and wedge the knuckles in place.
- When using both hands, put the top hand in the thumb-down position; the lower hand can be thumb up or down. Placing the thumb downwards puts leverage and torque into the jam, which increases as the body moves higher. However, the thumb-upwards

method of jamming allows a further reach to be made for the next placement.

- When the fingers will fit into the crack but the hand is too big, try placing all the fingers in the crack and the thumb downwards against the wall (a thumb sprag).
- A harder but less tiring technique is to place the thumb in the crack and wedge the finger next to the thumb.

ABOVE A thumb sprag.

Hand Jams

Hand jams begin when the crack is wide enough for the hand to slide in as far as the wrist. The hand can be up or down depending on the crack. Push the fingers and the palm of the hand against one side of the crack and the knuckles against the other side and the hand will jam. As the crack widens place the thumb into the palm of the hand, giving it more bulk. When it gets too wide, form your hand into a fist shape and jam this in place. There are a number of methods of fist jamming, each depending on whether the thumb is placed outside the fingers like a boxer or inside the hand.

On pure crack climbs, the hands and feet may be twisted and contorted so they also jam in the crack. The hands keep you in place but the feet twisted sideways into the crack do the pushing. A few short movements with the feet are better than one long one.

Off-widths

Unless you happen to be a masochist the worst sort of crack is an off-width. Off-widths are more or less full body jams. The aim is to use the arms and legs to apply pressure to opposite sides of the crack. To do this, stick an arm in until it is a little past the shoulder then bend at the elbow pressing the palm against one side and the elbow, and shoulder against the other. This can be further adapted by lifting the elbow

Finger jamming.
Photo: Stefan Doerr.

A hand jam.

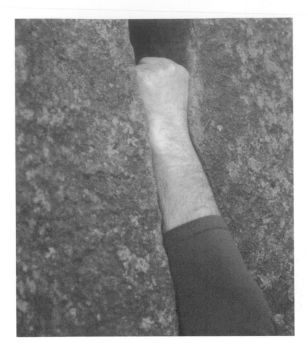

A fist jam.

Relief at the top of an off-width crack.

Paul Donnithorne jamming everything in a crack.
Zion National Park, Utah.

upwards until it becomes a good resting position. In all of these the outside arm pulls on the
outside edge of the crack at neck level.

To reduce the strain on your arms, do not let
your arms get too high above the head. The legs
are important and can be jammed by locking a
foot against one wall and the knee against the
other, or if it is small enough by jamming the
heel and toe in the crack. If the crack is just too
wide for heel/toe jamming try a T-stack. The
most important thing about off-widths is to
maintain a rhythm with your movement, using
the momentum gained from the push or pull to
initiate the next.

LEARNING TO READ MOVES

Technical ability has been correlated to how
well a climber can remember the moves and the
order in which they were made on a climb that
has just been completed.

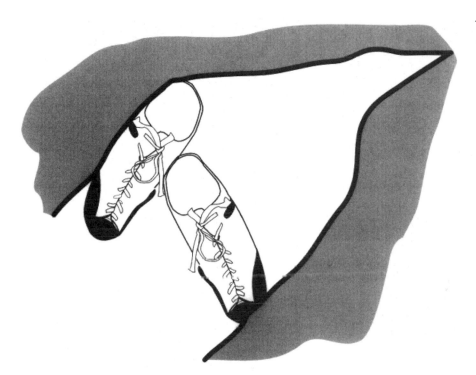

T-stack.

Exercise: Remembering Moves
Ask the students to spend time thinking about how they are going to climb the route. They should dentify the holds they are going to use and how they are going to use them. If the holds on the climb are small, ask the students to try to imagine that they are huge and climb as if they are. The student can try to remember what they did while they climbed; noting what felt efficient helps to accelerate the learning process. Use a video, to see if the students have done the move in the way they thought they would.

Exercise: Reading and Remembering
A fun exercise that helps students to read, remember and identify moves is for one student to use three handholds and step off; the next student uses those three and then adds three more, the next uses those six and then adds three more and so on.

Exercise: Stress-Proofing Movements
Speedy decision-making (stress-proofing) can be practised by pointing out the holds the students can use just before they move (an extendable ski pole is useful for this). You can use this exercise to train specifically feet or hands, pointing out which hand or foot to move.

Try to create moves that work on a student's weaknesses.

Exercise: Choosing Sequences Quickly
Speed climbing helps students to choose quickly which hold to use, and how to use it, and encourages them to select movements instinctively. It can help to stress-proof the moves so that the student selects them under moments of anxiety. However, speed climbing can also be counterproductive if it forces the student to climb in a poor fashion. The student should simply try to remove the pauses from their climbing. The opposite – slow-motion climbing – can also be useful by highlighting the subtle changes of centre of gravity.

Too many climbers have tunnel vision, only seeing the holds in a small area above them. If a student is having difficulty tell, them to look in a 360-degree circle around the body for any hold they may have missed.

IMPROVING BODY AWARENESS

The following exercises may help your students to be more aware of the internal information that their body constantly gives itself about balance, movement and the relationship of parts of the body to each other. The aim is to create an awareness of what the body is actually doing rather than what it appears to be doing.

Exercise One
Sometimes climbers focus too far ahead in their desire to climb and do not focus on the actual move they are doing. Your students can plan their strategy first and then climb, focusing on each movement.

Exercise Two
This can be done anytime. If it is done in a sitting position start from the head and move down and if lying start from the feet and move up. Close the eyes and relax, breathe smoothly. Work through each part of the body exploring how it feels. Can they isolate and feel each toe? Does their right and left arm feel different? How do their knees work? How much of their back can they sense? When the students have finished, ask them to open their eyes and return their attention to where they are.

Exercise Three
Practise movements with the eyes closed. Ask the students to try a movement with eyes open then attempt to recreate it with eyes closed. How did it feel? Try opening the eyes during the movements. Are the movements as the students imagined them to be? A video camera would be useful.

Exercise Four
Ask the students to close their eyes, relax and imagine themselves climbing a route or boulder problem. They should be watching themselves. Then imagine each part of the body is surrounded by a colour. This can help to isolate different parts of the body. The better the students become at imagery the more colours can be added.

Exercise Five
Breathing is important in increasing control over the functioning of the body. While the students are practising ask them to note their breathing. When they exhale and inhale? Do they hold their breath? How fast do they breathe? Ask them to vary their breathing and notice how it affects their performance, then return to their normal performance and see what affect this has had.

Exercise Six
Practise movement on both sides of the body and compare how it feels.

Exercise Seven
Exaggerate movements to highlight those parts of the movement that are under control and those that are not. It may help to release bodily tension.

TEACHING MOVEMENT ON ROUTES

Many of the movement principles looked at in this chapter can be transferred to the climbing session, but here are some games that can be used to liven up a flagging session and teach the students how to move:

- Place scarves, flags or sweets at the top of the climb and split the students into two teams so that they can have a relay race to retrieve them (the problem is that the belayers must take in quickly to prevent possible big falls).
- With very young climbers put 'Smarties' on ledges and in holes. This can take their mind off the exposure and make them look for handholds and footholds.
- Play 'Gladiators' – put a balloon, scarf or sticky label on somebody, and the chasing climber has to remove it. The students must not kick or pull the climber from the cliff – the thought of a finger being ripped from a crack doesn't bear thinking about.
- Place sticky labels on the holds or mark the ones that the students can use with a chalk stick. Any climber succeeding on the climb is able to remove one label or chalk mark. Do not remove three in a row otherwise the climb may become impossible.
- Speed climb, either on parallel routes or the same route. An easy route ensures that good movements are maintained.
- Down climb the route.
- Find a harder route and spend some time with the students looking for rests and ways of doing the moves. Ask them to try to link the sections and moves together mentally.
- Video the students. There is often an amazing transformation in climbing style once a student knows that their attempt is being recorded.
- Try one-arm climbing, one-foot climbing or two people holding hands.

HELPING STUDENTS TO CONTROL THEIR FEAR

If you do not feel alive when you climb, you not only feel dead in your heart but also physically heavy.
Marius Morstad, University of Oslo.

Samurai warriors believe you cannot be an effective warrior until you are not afraid to die. Although a respect for danger is healthy, a student may not reach their pinnacle if they are preoccupied with falling off in safe situations. It does not matter how fit they are or how well they move – if they let fear or phobia get in the way and become tense and nervous they will climb that way. Being frightened is not the problem – it is how you cope with it that matters.

We cannot all develop the mental control that top climbers have, but like technique and strength training students have frontiers to expand. Although other sports accept that mental control can be acquired by training, climbers are slow to realize this potential. Mental training takes time and effort to produce results.

The first thing to realize is that many conditions affect performance:

● Some crags are intimidating. If so, try bouldering first or do some easy climbs before trying the harder route.
● Are the student's thoughts positive or negative? (*See* 'Self-Belief', page 69.)
● Are the students climbing with someone they trust? Build confidence and use a good belayer.
● Have they had a row? (*See* 'Relaxation', page 68.)
● Are they tired or hungover?

Non-Specific Advice

● Be at your best, don't venture on your hardest lead when you are not happy.
● Fool yourself and climb as if the holds are big.
● Expect success.
● Know your partners.
● Plan ahead.
● Rehearse the moves.
● Strive for elegance.
● Become calm at rests.
● Double your runners up.
● Down-climb if in trouble.
● Listen to your inner voice.
● Breathe in a controlled manner.

● Are they worrying about failure? (*See* 'Imagery', page 69.)
● Do they really want to climb the route? (*See* 'Concentration', page 68.)

An important start to developing self-belief and giving your students the incentive to improve is to help them to create realistic goals. Choose routes that test them but do not intimidate them. Success breeds success. Motivation is personal but is affected by outside factors, so an instructor can help a student by encouraging them, (confidence takes a long time to enhance but only seconds to destroy), and creating an atmosphere where they want to and are able to succeed. If you can convince them that 'practice makes perfect', improvement is more likely to occur.

You will often be involved in breaking down barriers and preconceptions about climbing harder routes. Some students assume that top climbers employ the same tactics as they do to get up a route. Remember, there are no rules in climbing – it is okay to top rope a route or abseil down to place runners prior to leading as long as this does not interfere with other climbers.

Anxiety

There are two sorts of anxiety – the positive, for example adrenalin before a route, and the negative, which destroys the chances of success. Anxiety is an important part of arousal, but when it becomes too much it can affect performance. The Catastrophe Cup model is a theory that describes how once our anxiety has gone over the crest of a hill it is unrecoverable i.e. once performance has been affected it cannot be regained straight away. At the point of peak arousal we become frozen in a state where half of us wants to stay and half of us wants to go home. Instructors are often tempted to push the students too hard; but once they have gone over the crest of the wave (peak performance), there is only a short distance before the student will crash off the crest of the wave.

While there is no cure for anxiety, there are things we can do to lessen its affect on our climbing. If the tension can be released by focusing, self-belief, relaxation and so on, the 'flight or fight' syndrome can be channelled into climbing. Self-awareness may help with understanding what the point of peak arousal feels like.

The way an instructor talks and describes a route can have a calming influence on the student. There are a number of ways an instructor can minimize stress levels and induce calm. Imagery and relaxation techniques are all useful. Saying 'pull yourself together' and 'take a deep breath' are not enough. First of all, the student needs to recognize the anxiety and its source. If a student is recovering from a fall or an injury you can get them alternately to relax and then create positive images of what may happen if they fall off.

Relaxation and Concentration (Focus)

Relaxation is a temporary and deliberate withdrawal from climbing which allows you to recharge your physical, mental and emotional energy. Concentration is a withdrawal of atten-

Focus on the move, not the camera. Climber: Lucy Archer on the Isle of Skye.

tion from factors that are not relevant (also sometimes called focusing). With practice, these techniques can be improved even during a climb. The problem that you may have with relaxation is that you may be waiting for something to happen, the metaphorical light to illuminate the mind, but this is the exact opposite of what relaxation is meant to do – you are trying to enter the 'no-mind' zone.

There are two levels of relaxation – total and momentary – that depend on how much time you spend relaxing. It is best to do total relaxation after, rather than before, a climb, otherwise you may feel too relaxed. Momentary relaxation is best done prior to a warm-up, when you are anxious or when learning a new skill and prior to imagery.

Watching a film may seem like relaxation, but if the film is exciting it actually increases emotional arousal. Many of the relaxation methods used in the West come from Eastern yoga and meditation techniques (see 10-minute yoga by Dowald Butler). Most techniques of meditative relaxation slow down the metabolism and calm you by occupying the mind with something simple. Here are two methods described briefly:

- Go to a quiet room. You can reach a deeper state of relaxation by lying down, but this may remove some of the alertness you need to climb and should not be done until after climbing. Take each muscle group in sequence and tense then release it. Keep aware of the difference in tension.
- You can also try imagining that you are filled up with liquid. Let it flow out of your toes very slowly until empty.

When we are under stress, one of the body's natural safety mechanisms is to narrow attention to what is perceived as essential for survival. In climbing, this can have unfortunate consequences. We tend to become obsessed with handholds and style consequently deteriorates, we narrow our focus to holds immediately in front of us and fail to see crucial holds on the periphery, we search for gear instead of making the moves. Concentration or focusing may help you to distance yourself from worries that are beyond your control. It is a case of learning to put aside distractions and stay with the present. There are many methods for practising concentration.

One is to sit in a chair and place a photograph of climbing in front of you. Relax and spend five minutes without moving, noticing as many qualities of the photograph as you can. Another is to find a quiet spot and sit comfortably upright and close your eyes. Begin slow, deep, quiet breathing, paying attention to the deatils of each breath. How fast? How deep? When you feel relaxed, count each of the exhalations. When you reach ten, start again. If your mind wanders from the counting, also start again. With practice, doing this for ten minutes becomes easy.

Exercise
Focusing practice on easy climbs by focusing on one aspect of movement such as hand placements, using the minimum of grip. If your attention wanders, just refocus. Try to take thirty seconds over each movement. In time, you will be able to transfer your focus between different tasks, which can make concentrating easier when you get into difficulties on a climb.

Imagery

In the 1930s Dr Edmund Jacobson showed that imagining tensing and relaxing a muscle actually influenced the muscle. The brain is not always capable of distinguishing between something that has actually happened and something that was imagined. Movement imagery is closely linked to where the rules for movement are stored. When you imagine a movement, electrical impulses travel to the muscle the movement would require therefore providing kinaesthetic feedback. The term 'imagery' is better than 'visualization' because you are not simply seeing yourself but also feeling yourself climbing. The more accurately you teach students to imagine themselves climbing well the better climbers they can become.

Imagery is not daydreaming about the great climbs you want to do – it is an acquired skill that requires the same effort and discipline as working out in a gym. It is, however, a short cut to better technique, so next time you are daydreaming about a climb try to direct it so that you climb with style. Always start a practice session with relaxation to remove any clutter. Look at a problem and imagine yourself doing it. This can be done either by looking through your eyes and seeing yourself, or by imagining someone else doing it. Where will your hands

---

Imagery Strategies

- Relax first.
- Concentrate.
- Use all your senses not just sight.
- Try to imagine scenes in explicit detail e.g. krabs clinking). It doesn't have to be climbing.
- Use photographs or video to improve the mental picture you have of yourself climbing.
- Mentally practice a difficult section of a climb as well as physically practice it (movement rehearsal).
- Eliminate images of failure.
- Use the present tense to describe things.
- Create positive but realistic images of yourself dealing with problems on a climb.
- Work daily to change negative images to positive ones.
- Set specific goals.
- Lots of 5 or 10 minute sessions are best.
- Enjoy it. If you are bored, stop.

---

go? Which way will your body shift? Feel yourself doing the moves: how your weight shifts, how the sideways move will shift your fingers on that knob. Smell the rock. Climb the entire problem in your head before you grab the first holds. It takes time to become good at imagery so do not be dismayed if you lose concentration after one move. Some studies have shown that the critical moment just before you nod off to sleep is a good time to practise imagery. Be realistic – it is no good imagining you are the best climber in the world, imagine yourself climbing at your best. Above all, be positive, do not let the slightest negative thoughts enter your head. The use of mental training and in particular imagery is the single most important characteristic that sporting champions have over their less successful competitors' so practise it.

Self-Belief

Self-belief is believing that you can do what you set out to do. When we think about insecurity, worry about who is watching or what might happen if we fall off we go to pieces.

Be aware of your thoughts while climbing because it is possible to train your mental thoughts to be more positive, causing you to move more efficiently and with better precision. Positive thoughts allow you to focus and relax. Negative thoughts increase muscle tension.

Instead of fighting fear it may help to go through everything that can go wrong and develop an answer for each of them but this can be counter-productive with novices.

Under stress we lose access to all but our most ingrained movement patterns and if they are poor ones the climb can go pear shaped very quickly. With practice, you can stress-proof your movements by increasing the stress and fatigue gradually. This can be duplicated by the instructor distracting the students as they climb. As the students revert to poor technique decrease the difficulty of the climbs.

Psych up by imagining how it feels to stand at the top of the route, relax your muscles. Talk to yourself inwardly or outwardly; this is something used by a lot of climbers without them realizing it. Positive self-talk or affirmations can reinforce positive image, for example. 'I can get up this route'; 'The crux is hard but its well protected'; 'I've climbed much harder on a top rope'. Negative self-talk can have a negative effect on self-image and climbing ability, for example 'It's too hard'; 'The crux is steep and I may not get protection in'; 'I found an easier route than this desperate a few months ago'; 'I won't make it'. The instructor can help by saying things like 'You can climb it', rather than 'Give it a go' or 'Try and climb it', which both give an opt out. It may help to climb an easy route first.

It is possible to talk yourself 'off' a route by consciously trying to control what should come naturally. You may hear students talking to themselves, 'Come on you can do it, twist your body, reach up, pull hard, place your feet on the two small holds and reach for the jug, keep going ... too late you've blown it'.' The instructor can help students to trust their skills while climbing and not to think too hard about the detail. If they are becoming anxious, try to distract them by focusing on something general like using the feet with precision. Focus on regular rhythmic breathing. Look ahead and concentrate on the next move, rathre than on falling or failing.

Climbing a problem the student can flow up is a good start to any route that is going to push them. Get them to concentrate on the positive feelings that success evokes. It may be beneficial to talk through the consequences of something going wrong, but only if the consequences are not too serious, such as they will only fall off.

Centring

When fear becomes too much, try a technique stolen from martial arts called 'centring'. Close your eyes and relax for a few moments, take a deep breath and focus on the middle of your forehead. Breathe out slowly, feeling this focus travel down the body to just below your navel. This is the centre of gravity of the body. You should feel relaxed and in balance. Hold this sensation for as long as possible. If you add a positive statement to this and smile it may help see you through the moment of panic. It can be done before or during a climb.

Break the route down into sections, providing places where the students can retreat, or choose a short boulder problem. Direct the students' thoughts inside before they leave the ground. Tell them to shut off any distractions and get them to affirm their belief in their ability, and visualize the sequence of moves, the texture of the rock, body positions and how excited they are. If negative thoughts arise, centre and think positively.

Simply concentrating on the here and now can be a great help rather than thinking 'what will my mates feel if I fall off this?' Some athletes use a 'box strategy' where they imagine a desk with a box on top. They imagine themselves writing down a word or phrase that sums up what is worrying them and then fold the paper and place it in the box. The worry has been set aside, but can be returned to later by imagining taking the paper out of the box and dealing with the problem.

Try to practise the following things away from the pressures of a climb!

Before Climbing

- Imagine yourself to be somewhere else even if it is for a few seconds, or read a book.
- Relax and create a positive image of yourself climbing the route.
- Say some positive things to reassure yourself that all is well.
- Climb an easy route first to calm yourself.
- Imagine the worst thing that can go wrong and get rid of it into a box.
- Break the route into sections or islands of retreat.
- Accept using aid and rests on routes that are too hard for you. This can break the mental barrier of the next grade.

During a Climb

Most of the above can also be used during a climb, but here are a few additional things that can help:

- Breathing – The simplest advice for staying calm is to remind students to breathe, and keep breathing evenly through moves. If you hold your breath you will be tense and your muscles will not be getting the oxygen they need. As with weight training, exhale while making the moves. If you can control your breathing you can control your heart rate, which can then control the higher-level functions of the brain. When in doubt breath out. Erratic breathing can induce panic.
- Concentrating on something other than the fear may help your climbing. Have a statement that you use, for example silent climbing, which focuses the mind on using your feet, or 'grip less', which helps you to calm down and grip the rock less.
- Relax, close your eyes, breathe and transport yourself to a desert island or somewhere quiet.
- Talk to yourself positively.

THE ART OF FALLING

Fifty years ago the adage was that the leader should not fall, but new and more reliable equipment means that climbers fall off all the time and live to tell the tale. Falling incorrectly can result in injuries and maybe learning to lead courses should cover the art of falling off either through a practical session or at least a discussion. This does not mean that you teach falling as an acceptable part of climbing, but if a student is going to fall off they may as well learn to do it properly. It is debatable whether practising falling will remove your fear of it, but if you are going to attempt a route that is making you nervous it may be a good idea to fall off straight away to remove any nervousness.

Intentionally falling off can be done by having a safety rope set up so that if the runner comes out the student does not hit the ground, or by making sure the gear they are going to fall onto is bomber. Practise with the full rope out at the top of a climb, when there is more rope to absorb the forces and less damage is likely to occur to the rope. Falling correctly needs practice and can help improve a student's confidence.

Anne May and Guy Wilson discussing the moves at Stanage edge.

Trevor Massiah, preparing for landing.

To take falls correctly takes confidence and practice. Students must accept the risks associated with practising falling. Teach the student to avoid falling by climbing down to a rest point, if at all possible, before they tackle a strenuous part of the climb. Explain that it is always preferable to convert the energy used by hanging on to complete the route.

Before teaching falling, take stock of the consequences. Is the student going to hit anything? Are they going to pull gear out? Is the belayer awake? When a fall is inevitable, warn the belayer and fall gracefully, not to look good but to avoid injury. A calm, supple body is less susceptible to injury. A falling climber should fall in control, facing the rock and avoiding tumbling. If you fall on a slab slide down on the feet, pushing away with the hands. Keep your legs bent and apart so they can act as shock absorbers. Do not freeze up or go limp. Keep the rope running cleanly or it may become wrapped around a leg which can tip you upside-down so. Be careful about grabbing the rope as you fly past, as this can result in rope burns, but once you are comfortable with falling off hold the rope in front of you to stabilize the landing. Only grab the runner as a last resort (they do come out) and do not put your finger through a bolt hanger – subsequent removal to clip into the bolt is difficult.

TEACHING COMMUNICATION (CLIMBING CALLS)

Understanding climbing calls is important, but knowing when to use them is vital. It seems a touch ridiculous for the instructor to shout 'Climb when ready!' and for the climber to reply 'Climbing!' when they are standing next to each other. What else is the climber going to do? It is, however, important to have a clearly thought-out sequence of calls so that when the instructor is out of sight or the weather and the wind are stealing the words the student does not stop belaying before the instructor is safe and will not dismantle the belays until they are safe. Climbing calls are designed to be kept to a minimum so that when words float away in the breeze, but the rope has been making characteristic movements, an educated guess can be made about what has been shouted.

If the crag is crowded, it is useful to add the person's name to the call. Instructors when working with young people may have fun making up their own calls such as 'To infinity and beyond!' instead of 'Climbing!'.

The sequence of climbing calls is:

- Once the lead climber has reached the top of the climb and attached to the belay anchors, they can shout down **'Safe'**. This informs the second that they do not have to belay the leader anymore.
- The second removes the rope from the belay device and shouts **'Take in'**. This tells the leader that they can pull up the spare rope without battling with the second trying to get the rope out of the belay device.
- When the rope comes tight, the second shouts **'That's me'**. This tells the leader that it is the second on the end of the rope and the rope has not become jammed somewhere.
- The leader puts the rope into the belay device and when he is ready to take responsibility for the second, shouts **'Climb when ready'**.
- The second starts to dismantle the anchors if on a multi-pitch climb (and not before) and shouts **'Climbing'**.
- The leader acknowledges that they have heard the call by replying **'Okay'**.

There are a number of other calls that may be needed, such as 'Watch me' to ensure the belayer is still awake. If there is too much slack in the rope shout 'Take in'. Shout 'Slack' or rope when some rope is required but avoid shouting 'take in slack' because it can be misheard and confused, often with frightening results.

When sport climbing, shout 'Lower me' to inform the belayer that they can pay out the rope to lower from the belay chain.

Avoid shouting 'watch out below I have knocked a rock off' as the rock may have hit the ground by the time the sentence has been finished. Instead shout 'Below'. There are also a number of calls to avoid such as 'Belay on' and 'Belay off' as they are unnecessary and confusing.

Finally, if communication with a student is likely to be difficult, brief them what to do if they cannot see or hear you. Rope tugs are confusing – simply tell the student to climb when the rope comes tight. Learn to whistle very loudly. One whistle means that you are safe.

CHAPTER 3

PHYSICAL TRAINING

If you do not understand how to perform an exercise correctly, talk to a qualified fitness instructor. If any of your students has any health problem or is taking medication for high blood pressure or some other health problem that might affect a fitness programme they should see their doctor.

Some top climbers claim they do not train; what they actually mean is they do not train systematically. All athletes can be coached and trained to reach their individual pinnacles of excellence and even though climbing is more complex than other sports, climbers are no exception.

Physique, muscle fibre characteristics, heart and lung size and other factors affecting performance are inherited. A depressing fact is that only about 1:1,000 of us will ever develop the grip strength to emulate the élite. However, factors such as diet, training and the type of sports your students undertake when young may affect the expression of their inherited characteristics. Some students have a cool head or the ability to learn new skills quickly, others may be naturally strong. The élite few have them all.

Age is No Barrier

Anyone who maintains a good level of fitness can perform at a high standard until they are old. Strength declines as we get older, especially above fifty years of age, because fast twitch muscle (important for fast explosive movements) turns to slow twitch muscle (important for endurance) and there is evidence that older climbers lose strength quicker than younger ones when they stop exercising. Older climbers should therefore train on a regular basis to limit the regression of their muscles. Do not, however, expect the same gains from fitness training as youngsters whose metabolism and growth-hormone-saturated bodies are primed to pack on muscle.

The tendons, ligaments and cartilage of older students are also more easily damaged, plus the rate of healing slows. Older climbers should

therefore be obsessive about warming up and down. Older students can place the emphasis on footwork, balance, flexibility, body position and the development of cunning to get up routes. Be aware that the motor programme we learn does not disappear with age, although the ability to recreate movements may be diminished by decreasing strength and stamina. However, the saying 'You cannot teach an old dog new tricks, is nonsense – it just takes longer.

Do Men Have an Advantage?

Men are on average 7 per cent taller, have longer arms, broader shoulders, narrower hips and

---

Training Fallacies

- **'No pain, no gain'** – training should not hurt. If it does it is a sign of a problem that should not be ignored. Discomfort is different; it is a natural consequence of muscle fatigue. Learn to recognize the difference.
- **'You need to tear muscle to build strength'** – weight lifters may traumatize muscles with excess weight, but it is not necessary to develop strength. It can take four to six weeks for the muscle to recover from significant tearing of the fibres.
- **'Go for the burn'** – this is associated with the lactic acid build-up in the muscles and although not dangerous, it is not necessary for effective training.
- **'Lactic acid causes soreness'** – lactic acid is cleared one hour after exercise; after that, soreness is due to swelling and muscle trauma. Jogging slowly or squeezing a soft ball after training will help to reduce the trauma.
- **'Muscle turns to fat'** – both are specialized cells and while a reduction in training will cause muscle cells to decrease they will not change into fat cells; only overeating creates fat cells.
- **'You must push your body to the point of failure to improve'** – it may be beneficial a few times and for power training but the body cannot recover if every session is to your limit.

Louise Thomas and Glenda Huxter on 'The Onion Eaters', E2 5C, Pembroke.

Males are better physically equipped than women for strenuous routes, but this should not be viewed as an advantage at the start of a climbing career, because women get around strenuous sequences by developing technique at an earlier stage. Remember that as muscle size doubles, strength only increases by 60 per cent.

THE BASICS OF TRAINING

Training does not simply build more muscle, it improves the performance of existing muscles, respiration and heart function. It also builds tougher bones, ligaments, tendons and connective tissue by creating changes in the muscle, its blood supply, the level of enzymes and other chemicals necessary for its efficient functioning. Training improvements are likely to be most dramatic when the initial fitness of a student is low. As fitness improves more effort is needed to make gains. In other words, the better you become the harder you have to work to improve. Common training terms are:

Overload
This distinguishes training from exercise. If you overload a muscle by pulling harder or for longer than previously or lift a weight heavier than last time the body can adapt to allow you to lift the weight or climb the route more easily. The rate of improvement depends on the following factors: frequency, resting, intensity and time (duration).

much less body fat. Women are more flexible and possess better balance because of their slightly lower centre of gravity. Despite these physiological differences, there is no evidence to suggest that women should use different training methods from men for rock climbing.

Training Tips

- Increase the amount of exercise gradually, then progressively overload the system with more intense training.
- Make training enjoyable and specific for rock climbing.
- The amount of time spent exercising is more important than the amount of effort. It is better to run one mile in fifteen minutes than half a mile in four minutes.
- Breathe evenly and learn to work through fatigue, but also learn to back off before exhaustion hits.
- Be consistent. One day of practice is like one day of clean living – it doesn't do any good in the long term. There are no short cuts.
- Do not sit down or stand around when resting between bouts of exercise, keep moving to keep the blood circulating and get the waste products removed from the muscles.
- Do as little as is necessary and rest.
- If you are tired or 'not feeling 100 per cent', adjust the training to suit.
- Try varying the rest days to find out what is best for the individual.
- Experiment with light, medium and hard training days for variety.
- To assess whether the body has recovered create a set warm-up regime where it is possible to assess how the body is feeling.
- Generally stamina training requires less rest than strength and power training.
- A regular training partner will make it more difficult to back out and allows for more feedback.

Frequency and Resting

It is during rest that the body is recovering and the muscles adapting to the stresses imposed during overloading, allowing them to cope better with the stress next time. This resting and growth is called 'super compensating'.

There is only a fine line between a routine that improves performance and one that ruins it. Muscles learn by growing and improving their links with the nerves as well as improving the efficiency of their energy systems. If you climb before the muscle has gone through this process of rest and growth the recovery of the muscle is cut short. If you climb at the exact point that the muscle has recovered, but at the same level as last time you will neither improve nor regress. If you avoid rest days altogether it can lead to regression. However, if training becomes infrequent or not intensive enough its effects will be diminished. Fitness is lost twice as fast as it is gained.

For an average student training two or three times each week is enough, but for more advanced climbers it can be increased to four. Since the best training for climbing *is* climbing, gym training is only required when insufficient climbing is being done. It is not a substitute for the genuine article. For maximum gains, allow the body to recover for twenty-four to seventy-two hours after a session. The actual time spent training depends on the severity of the workout and individual genetics. Do not spend more than six weeks on the same programme. Vary it before reaching a point where no progress is being made (plateauing). Beginners can vary their training on a daily basis, for example, train strength and power on Monday, anaerobic endurance on Wednesday and stamina on Saturday. A medium-level student should mix and match the different methods, but with increased fitness should concentrate periods on one whilst maintaining the others.

Duration and Intensity

This describes how hard you push the student. The volume of training is related to the duration (distance or time taken for each repetition of an exercise or session) and the intensity of that exercise. Climbing involves periods of both low- and high-intensity activity, so ensure that this is built into a training programme. The training you do may also depend on the type of climbing you specialize in. Are you a one-pitch sport climber, a bouldering specialist, a gritstone fan or a mountaineer?

It is probably better to vary the intensity of training – for example, one, an easy session, and four, a hard session. Start at one and work up to a four, then take a rest day.

Goal Setting

There is no doubt that a structured training schedule is more effective than a haphazard approach. Even for those students who do not have a definite goal, a planned programme of training is still useful as it can focus attention on improvement and may help them to feel they are not wasting their time. Goal setting takes into consideration the student's lifestyle and should be designed to develop and maintain technique, flexibility, endurance, strength and power in that order, but above all it should be designed so that the student wants to do it. It should also be designed to reduce the chances of injury, prevent strained tendons and ligaments and allow a faster recovery between climbs. Variety is important because keeping to one training regime – for example, stamina training on the same gently overhanging wall with small holds – does not improve your ability to climb big roofs on big holds. Even on fingerboards the students should vary their routine and the angles they hold.

Targets can be set for a student's training in the long term (this summer), medium term (one month) or short term (one day). The majority of students will probably wish to peak during the summer or for a specific trip, but have short-, medium- and long-term goals, regardless of whether the programme is two months long or over four years like Olympic-standard athletes.

The instructor's role is to help the student identify the weaknesses that are limiting their performance. A slight change in a weak area can have a greater effect on performance than any improvement in an already strong area.

Do Not Train to Total Fatigue

If you are bouldering or training one-arm pull-ups the main training effect is better coordination of the muscle fibres and of all the muscles working together. Therefore do not ruin the learning effect by doing too many repetitions, ruining quality and becoming too fatigued.

Therefore, allocate more time to improving weaknesses and less to tweaking strengths. *The student's* most difficult task is to ensure that the goals they decide upon are achievable and that the means to achieving them are enjoyable.

A useful mnemonic to help a student focus on what their goal is and how to achieve it is **SMARTER**:

- **Specific:** How much harder and by when? It is not specific enough to say 'I want to climb harder'.
- **Measurable:** Has the goal been achieved? Specify the number of routes at a particular grade.
- **Agreed:** Do you really want to achieve this?
- **Realistic:** Is this goal feasible? Setting goals too high results in failure. Don't be afraid to change the goals to make them achievable.
- **Timed:** Have time limits been set for achievement?. Don't forget rest days and even rest weeks.
- **Exciting:** Does the student enjoy the training? If not, make changes.
- **Recorded and reviewed:** Keep a written record so that the success of a training schedule can be seen and measured.

ELEMENTS OF FITNESS TRAINING

Training can be divided into a number of elements: warming up, warming down, flexibility, strength, power and endurance.

- **Warming up, warming down:** sore muscles are inevitable when you start training because the muscle fibres are not used to being stretched. Warming up, warming down and stretching are very important to reduce the trauma. For example, running shortens the muscles at the back of the legs which can be counterproductive to climbing, so stretch hamstrings after running. Warming up and down is covered in more detail in Chapter 2.
- **Flexibility:** this is covered later in this chapter. Stretching the muscles around a joint on a regular basis will improve flexibility, or at least maintain the current level of flexibility depending on how long each stretch is held. The type of climbing to be undertaken may dictate how flexible you need to be, for example gritstone and slate require a greater degree of flexibility than steep limestone because they involve wider bridging moves and obscure body contortions.
- **Isometric and isotonic strength:** strength, along with technique, of course, is required to perform short, hard crux moves. This requires the muscles in the fingers, forearms, upper arms, shoulders, upper back and stomach to be strong for climbing. The degree of strength required for other muscle groups is quite specific to the type of climbing undertaken. For example, as long as your legs are strong enough to get you to the crag that is sufficient for pure rock climbing. However, if you are into alpine climbing more time should be spent on strengthening the legs. Strength can be subdivided into isotonic for example, pulling up, and isometric, which is the ability to hold a static position, for example, locking off.
- **Power:** this is defined as strength against time and is the ability to perform dynamic moves.
- **Endurance (stamina):** this is the ability to perform a move over and over again. The muscle relies on adenosine triphosphate (ATP) for its energy. However, there is only enough of this in the muscle for three–five seconds of activity and so the body relies on the production of ATP through the breakdown of glycogen. The breakdown of glycogen is done aerobically (with oxygen) or anaerobically (without oxygen). Whether you use oxygen or not depends on the pace (intensity) of the activity you are doing. **Aerobic endurance** is defined in climbing terms by a long climb of a relatively low standard where oxygen is in plentiful supply and the waste product of muscle contraction (lactic acid) clears away naturally and other factors such as glycogen reserves limit climbing. **Anaerobic endurance** is defined by the dreaded pump. It typically occurs on routes with few rests. The anaerobic pathway also produces lactic acid which cannot be cleared away and limits the anaerobic system, because only a certain amount of lactate can be stored in the muscles. It will eventually stop muscle contraction (the pump).

Muscles can use both systems, but when climbing the arms gain their energy largely anaerobically, because when the muscles contract isometrically they squeeze shut the capillaries supplying them with blood and oxygen. It is therefore important to relax when climbing, to grip the rock with minimal exertion and to take advantage of rests whenever possible. The aerobic pathway uses energy efficiently, while the anaerobic pathway is almost 95 per cent less efficient.

Endurance training can also be subdivided into power or strength endurance by working different groups of muscles one after another. This will make the heart work harder while training individual muscles for strength or power.

A GOOD START

Rock climbing, with its deliberate stop–start motion, is not particularly stressful on the aerobic system, but aerobic fitness is essential for long mountain routes. It is also a good base from which to start any more advanced training. When it is done consistently aerobic training will lower both resting and exercise heart rates, increase the ability of muscles to use oxygen, increase blood volume and cardiac output, lower the chances of injury and illness and reduce body fat. Aerobic fitness, however, is not developed overnight and can only be achieved over a period of years.

Walking, running, biking, skipping, stair climbing, ski machines, rowing machines and so on are all useful for improving aerobic fitness. Running is especially effective because it is weight-bearing and strengthens bones, but if you have problems with your hips, knees or ankles, you may want to avoid running. Biking is as effective as running, but you will have to do it for longer to have the same effect. It also changes the stresses from legs to the lower back. Swimming is the least stressful, but it does not train body weight and unless you have good technique it is difficult to keep your heart rate sufficiently high.

The actual time spent doing aerobic training depends on an individual's goals and their starting fitness level. Students with low fitness may benefit from twenty minutes twice a week, very fit students may do sixty minutes up to four times a week, but should not to exceed five times per week. The effectiveness of aerobic training can be gauged by measuring resting heart rate as soon as you get out of bed (the carotid artery is the easiest and is in the neck just to the left of the windpipe). Within four to six weeks it may have dropped a few beats per minute. It is also a good measure if you are feeling a bit 'under the weather'.

If you get bored working at the same pace for twenty minutes, vary the pace ('fartlek' or interval training) by raising the heart rate to 80–90 per cent maximum for short bursts. Fartlek training is particularly useful for alpine climbing as it mimics the type of exercise in the mountains.

Burning Fat Through Aerobic Training

The real key to climbing well is to improve your strength to weight ratio. When exercising at a moderate rate (70 per cent of the maximum heart rate) the body copes by burning a mixture of carbohydrate and fat, but when exercising strenuously (85 per cent of maximum heart rate) only carbohydrates can produce energy fast enough. The body finds it difficult to convert fat into carbohydrate and therefore uses its carbohydrate reserves instead.

> To work out your approximate maximum heart rate take your age away from 220, for example, if you are forty your maximum heart rate is 180.

The best way to burn fat is therefore to exercise at 60–75 per cent of your maximum heart rate. It is surprising how easy it is to attain 60–75 per cent of your maximum heart rate. An exercise pulsometer can be useful to keep you in the correct range. More calories are used by sixty minutes of moderate exercise than twenty minutes of exercise that leaves you exhausted.

PHYSICAL TRAINING NOT INVOLVING CLIMBING

Aerobic exercise will give you an essential base, but it will do little to promote the forearm and finger strength needed by climbers. If your chest has slipped to your stomach and you are pear-shaped all aerobic training will do is to make you a smaller pear. If you also want a good shape you must tone the muscles through resistance training, such as training against a weight which could be your body or a weights room.

Weight Training for Climbing

Climbing uses muscles in specific ways that are rarely found in a standard weight-training programme, therefore select exercises which imitate climbing movements. Physical training of the upper body and fingers (all other strengths are wasted if you cannot hang on) provides the best results, but do not underestimate the importance of stomach muscles to maintain the link between feet and hands. It is better to train strength first followed by endurance, but do not train for power until you have made steady gains in strength. In order to make gains safely, it is important to keep the muscles balanced so always train the muscles that work in opposition to avoid injuries.

Weight-Training Tips

- Work with a partner.
- Warm up, stretch and warm down with a lower weight.
- Maintain a steady rhythm and control the descent of the weight.
- Start with the weaker side, but do the same amount of reps and weight on each side.
- Use a full range of movement.
- Use loose weights as they do not have a single plane of movement.
- When using machines do not let the weight touch the stack.
- Use a mirror to check you are doing the exercises correctly. Quality is more important than quantity.
- Keep control on the downward phase.

Strength Training

In simple terms, lifting large loads for a small number of repetitions improves strength. First of all, find how much can be just lifted for ten repetitions (reps). Then work at 80 per cent and repeat three times, increasing the weights until three sets of the one set max can be done. Then find your new max and start again. This is called 'cyclical progression' and can be applied to all strength training to prevent reaching a plateau. Do not be tempted to emulate body builders and push huge weights. Increasing muscle size by a 100 per cent only increases strength by 60 per cent.

A 'pyramid' approach can be effective for strength and endurance training. Start with

---

Weight-Training Exercises to Improve Overall Strength and/or Endurance

- Put one session of pushing muscles for every two or three pulling sessions.
- Dips – don't go really deep, as it stresses the shoulders (chest and front of shoulders).
- Back extensions.
- Crunches are better than sit-ups.
- Lat pull-downs (lats and upper back).
- Lat push-downs.
- Rowing with an overhand grip (middle and upper back plus forearm).
- Flyes.
- Bench press.
- Wrist curls and reverse curls.
- Bicep curls for under cuts.
- Squats and calf raises can help one's ability to stand motionless on a hold but leave running and general aerobic exercise to improve leg endurance.

---

minimum reps on maximum weight, and then gradually reduce the weight and increase the reps. This method means that you work strength when you are fresh and endurance when you are more tired.

Remember each workout should increase slightly in intensity – the same workout over several months will not have the desired effect. Endurance training does little to improve contact strength, but training contact strength will have some effect on forearm endurance.

Endurance Training

Endurance training improves the ability to keep going – for many students this is the most limiting factor in their climbing.

When weight training for anaerobic endurance, decrease the weights or reduce the intensity of the exercise to 70 per cent, but do three sets of fifteen to twenty repetitions or until just short of failure (this can be recognized as the point where breathing becomes difficult and further effort is doubtful). Repeat four to six times. The length of rest is crucial and should be no longer than twice the exercise time.

Power Training

Training for power is similar to strength training, but the movements are as explosive as possible. There is no such thing as finger power because fingers do not move explosively. For

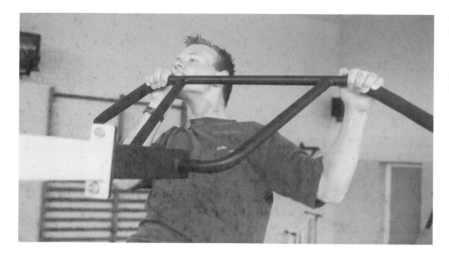

Typewriters. Being able to do hundreds of pull-ups will not necessarily enhance a student's climbing ability.

longer routes training for power should be matched by endurance training.

Some climbers use a training method called plyometrics (super recruitment training). Used in conjunction with strength training it can develop explosive power, for example, for dynos or jumping. The theory is that the body has a safety mechanism which causes the muscles to stop contracting at a certain point so as to avoid injury. Plyometrics can cause the muscle to override this safety mechanism because the force is generated very quickly. Over time the safety margin is expanded and the muscles pull harder. It is, however, a very fine line between success and injury and unless someone is already particularly strong, this method of training is best avoided. Power does not develop rapidly in young people and can be hard on young joints.

FITNESS TRAINING THAT MIMICS CLIMBING

The best exercises for climbing are undoubtedly those that mimic real climbing.

Pull-Ups

Surprisingly, standard pull-ups are not as useful as one would expect. However, variations of them can enhance the more important ability to lock-off (the ability to keep one arm bent while reaching for a hold with the other) and the ability to pull on small holds. Pull-ups can be used for strength or endurance exercises, depending on whether the weight attached to the student is increased by attaching weights to their harness or decreased by clipping a bungee

cord to it or placing it under the feet. Resting the feet on something higher can also achieve the same thing and mimics the angles of overhanging rock.

A good way to do a standard pull-up is slowly, palms facing away. Take 30 seconds to 1 minute to do a pull-up and the same to lower down. A variation of this is to do four pull-ups in a minute, then rest for a minute, then four more in a minute and continue until it is no longer possible to achieve four. When 20 minutes has been achieved increase the sets to five.

To avoid injury, the next series of exercises should not be attempted without assistance from a bungee cord until at least fifteen pull-ups have been achieved.

A good method of training for lock-off strength (isometric) is 'typewriters'. This exercise involves pulling up until the chin can be touched against each hand, repeating it until no more can be done. The wider the hands, the harder it is. As soon as these feel easier, try 'Frenchies'. This involves pulling up and holding in a two-arm lock-off for 7 seconds, then lowering down slowly. Pull up again; lower halfway and lock off again at 90 degrees; repeat, but lower to 120 degrees; repeat.

Locking off with one arm can be practised by pulling up and locking off using one arm while holding onto a towel wrapped around the bar with the other. The lower the towel is held the harder it becomes. Move slowly downwards; do not suddenly drop. Once it can be done with the towel, it should be tried without. If the student cannot do a pull-up, then start at the top and lower slowly down in control and without stopping.

Finger Training

Finger training is vital – if a student cannot hold on it is irrelevant how strong their shoulders are. To minimize the chance of injury, train fingers gradually and tape the base of them, but remove the tape after exercise to allow the blood to flow again. Use only the 'open grip' not the 'crimp grip' (see Chapter 2) as this strains the joints. Grip exercisers are good for warming up the fingers, but they are not effective for training because we do not use our fingers dynamically when climbing.

A good introductory finger exercise is to put two loops of broad tape over a pull-up bar and hang by two fingers of each hand for 15 seconds. Once this is easy, decrease to one finger.

It is important to give fingers a minimum of three days' rest each week and to train the antagonistic muscles on the back of the hand by reverse wrist curls.

Fingerboards

These are one of the best ways of gaining finger strength, but students who are new to training should avoid them. Warm up thoroughly by flexing the fingers, stretching the forearms and massaging to reduce the 'claw' effect of short-

Pinch a book and raise and lower it up to one hundred times. This is an effective and safe way of improving finger strength. Do it with the hand facing up and facing down.

ening tendons. However, do not bend each individual finger back because this will damage the joint. Joints dry out when they are not moving, so vary the training and allow fingers 2–5 minutes between sets and increase the rest period between training sessions. Vary the angles of holds so that the strength gained is not too specific and have the students' feet supported on something or by attaching bungee cords to a harness or under the feet. Alternatively, the fingerboard can be mounted out from a wall with some footholds placed on the wall. Weight can also be added to the harness or a bum bag.

Start any training session by warming up on larger holds, then move to smaller ones or add weight. The most common way of using a fingerboard is to 'dead hang' in an open palm grip for repeated 15-second stints, resting for a minimum of 2 minutes between hangs. Improvement is possible without using desperately small holds. Work for twenty-five to fifty hangs. When the student can hang for longer than 15 seconds, use a smaller hold or add weight.

The pyramid structure discussed under weight training works well for dead hangs. After

For the majority of climbers gaining finger strength is the priority.

warming up, start with the smallest holds, gradually moving to bigger holds but hanging on for longer.

Because there is no foot contact, fingerboards involve using muscles in ways rarely found in climbing. Finger training can mimic the rhythms of rock climbing by using the 'grip–relax–grip' sequence. This involves moving the hands around the fingerboard. Develop ten to twenty movements on small holds then shake out on a large hold and repeat – aim to achieve about ten rotations. This exercise is based on the fact that blood flow stops to the forearms every time a hold is gripped and only resumes once the forearms have relaxed.

Campus Board Training

Campus boards start at approximately head height and consist of an overhanging board with ten wooden rungs. Wolfgang Gullich first used the campus board in 1988 to train for 'Action Directe' in the Frankenjura, Germany. These

Campus board training is a recipe for disaster unless someone is already very strong. Climber: Trevor Massiah.

boards have a reputation for being the most advanced, intensive and potentially damaging form of training that has been developed.

The theory is that while bouldering is very good for developing strength and power, the more often a boulder problem is done the easier it becomes, and at this point the problem has little use for power training. Campus boards require little technique, meaning that any improvement comes from an increase in power and is therefore measurable. They can also be used for an endurance workout.

Before using a campus board warm up for 45 minutes. Build up any session slowly and try to use only the open-palmed grip. The most basic way of using the board is to simply climb the board using whatever rung spacing strength allows. Either match hands on each rung or walk the hands up alternately. Large moves on large rungs train the arms more, whereas smaller moves on smaller rungs train the fingers more.

The campus board can be used for plyometrics or static moves. Plyometrics can easily damage shoulders, elbows and fingers; it should be avoided by anyone who does not already have immense strength and can do no more to improve their technique. Plyometrics is best exemplified by dropping down or jumping up between small holds, ideally on a campus board and without feet on holds. Power throws involve trying to take one hand up one or more rungs.

Static recruitment training involves hanging for short periods of 2–3 seconds, with enormous weights attached to a harness. Static moves such as locking off involve climbing the board without leaping.

PHYSICAL TRAINING USING CLIMBING

The best way to improve for climbing is undoubtedly to go climbing frequently, but not all of your students will have unlimited time available. Bouldering indoors or outdoors can be a very effective method for improving strength, endurance, power and technique. Remember to train movement skills before physical training.

Bouldering

Before bouldering, warm up and increase the intensity gradually – do not jump on the hardest problems immediately. Wooden holds are the best for strength training because they are kinder to skin and their inherent lack of friction increases the need to hang on more. Real rock is the best for developing a combination of strength, power and technique together.

Novices can benefit from a random hit-or-miss approach to improving strength, so long as a variety of problems and holds are used. Some of the exercises used earlier for practising movement can be adapted to train students, such as the stick pointing out holds – one student does three moves, the next does his three, three more are added and so on.

The principles of training for strength, endurance and power training that were discussed earlier apply to bouldering, for example, stamina training involves lots of climbing of easy, low tendon-stress routes, whereas strength and power training involves short sequences of hard moves. However, there are a few extra things to consider. If the boulders or problems are so steep that the students can only use big holds they will train arm strength rather than finger strength, so for improving finger strength try to use holds that are to the first finger joint. Try to make up a five- to eight-move problem using different angles and types of holds. Progress by keeping the same angle but decrease the size of the holds or visa versa. This will prioritize finger or arm strength.

The aerobic pathway is best trained by slow, easy distance training – that is, climbing lots. For training anaerobic endurance, low-intensity, high-duration training works best. Do circuits of predetermined moves up and down, diagonally and horizontally. To improve power and coordination try quick moves between small holds on a variety of angles and holds. For more controlled static strength try problems that force you to lock off to reach the next hold.

For those students who lack the body tension to climb overhanging rock, walk them along an overhanging section of the wall, taking their feet further and further under until they are traversing with their feet on the wall. If they are finding the movements on the wall difficult, support their body. Traversing indoors or outdoors involves a small range of movements, and moving across is not the same as moving upwards. However, traversing is a great way of building finger and forearm stamina.

Resting is important. Rest for one minute per move and for twenty minutes for every forty

Climbing walls are great places to teach. Trevor Massiah enjoying himself at Undercover Rock, Bristol. Photo: Gavin Newman.

minutes of hard bouldering. Aim for maximum quality and forget about burning out on easier problems at the end.

Using Climbing Walls

Climbing walls can vary from a full-blown leading wall to a small wall in a cellar. Many climbers visit climbing walls with the aim of getting pumped as quickly as possible – this is a mistake. A better idea is to try something which will inevitably result in becoming pumped while doing your utmost to resist the onset of fatigue. Learning to rest and recover is a most desirable skill. Becoming pumped on climbing walls usually means the end is in sight, but on rock cunning will provide rests with knee locks, shoulder jams and even chin rests (see Chapter 2 for using a climbing wall for technique training).

It is preferable, therefore, to train your body to rest quickly in-between pumps and to avoid the pump in the first place. Do a route or a circuit on a small wall, but instead of resting off the climb find a rest place that allows the students to repeat the route again. When it can be done three to five times, find something harder and do the same. This mimics real climbing, where routes can take much longer to climb than they do indoors.

To train anaerobic endurance, work the muscles at 80 per cent of their capacity until close to failure. Create circuits on climbs, familiar to your students, of a set grade. The climb should feel easy to start with and then become harder until the students can no longer climb. This is called interval training. Start on a route that they can do eight to sixteen times with short rests, building up over time by reducing the number of routes but making them last longer with longer rests. The rest between circuits should be just enough to allow the student to complete another one.

Aerobic endurance is best done by constant rhythmic climbing for ten minutes on easy routes, without getting pumped. This may seem like a long time, but outside a route may take an hour or more. Endurance training can be done on routes with big holds to limit finger damage and where the students can also concentrate on climbing with technique. If the students are fit enough so that they do not become pumped on a vertical wall, do not just move to smaller holds, but consider using a steeper wall where gravity has a greater effect. Vary the routes attempted because training stamina on a gently overhanging wall does not help the students to gain power on big roofs.

Lock-off strength can be developed on a climbing wall by reaching for a hold but not touching it for 5 seconds, then repeat. Initiate traditional climbing by stopping in the middle of a crux and pretend to place a piece of gear and clip the rope in. Endurance and dead-point technique (hitting a hold and keeping hold of it) can be developed by using one arm while traversing.

System Training

This is a method of training developed by Rudi Klausner, the former German national coach. System training is more complex as it involves the whole body and a wider variety of holds. It is therefore less stressful on tendons and is suitable for climbers of all abilities.

Most climbers who have a bouldering wall tend to arrange the holds randomly, which is the total opposite to other forms of physical training. System training mixes the two disciplines. A typical workout performs a number of exercises on a wall that has identical holds mirrored for left and right hands and feet. Through repetition and isolation of basic movements, positions and grips, these exercises systematically exhaust the muscle.

Typical exercises involve hanging for 10 seconds, moving to the next hold and repeating six to ten times. Movement exercises that mimic climbing movements or reach exercises where the climber pulls to their maximum reach and returns to the bottom hold in control can be developed. Any movement can be mimicked, such as frogging, laybacking and so on.

This method of training has the advantage that the same movements are performed on both sides of the body and any weakness can be spotted and worked on. The major benefit is isolation: a certain hold can be exhausted, then a new hold can be used. The whole body is worked because muscle tension must be maintained throughout the body.

Use proper foot placement, body position and body tension. Technique is lost as soon as body tension disappears. Make complete movements so that the whole technique is mastered. You can help the student by pushing at the hips when the body sags. System training is not about doing problems, so do not compete with anyone – train your own weaknesses.

TRAINING JUNIOR CLIMBERS

Young people mature at different rates and we should not set blanket ages for different practices and training methods. The National Coaching Foundation states that 'Specific strength or weight training must not be given to children before bone development is complete, usually about age 17.' The muscle forces in strength training are very similar to those required during climbing, therefore when training young people it is important that movements producing high muscle and joint forces are not used.

A high incidence of injuries, burnout and post-viral fatigue syndrome in junior athletes in new sports where guidelines have not been set has been reported, for example, in mountain biking. It is important that sufficient rest follows sessions. There should be a sufficient intake of energy to replenish muscle glycogen so that the usual growth can take place. The muscles of

---

Tips for a Safe Junior Programme

- Do not use movements that create high muscle and joint forces.
- Allow sufficient rest.
- Slow, low-intensity exercise is best.
- Do not make movements repetitive.
- Be aware that children overheat easily.
- Children should drink plenty of water.
- Climb on a variety of rock types and steepnesses.
- Training should not be too intense, vigorous or specific.

---

children favour aerobic rather than anaerobic work because they utilize glycogen slowly. Children are therefore better at steady, low-intensity exercises.

Routes should not be too long but should have hard sections followed by rests and easier sections.

Full bone growth may not occur until twenty to twenty-five years in some cases. Between ten to fourteen years children are particularly vulnerable to growth plate injury as a result of chronic repetitive damage, which can have serious consequences. Injuries to the growing tissues of children and adolescents make them especially vulnerable to a variety of problems, such as biomechanical abnormalities, which may result in further injuries later in life. Try to consult parents to decide whether full growth has taken place (for example, are they still buying larger clothes or shoes?), and until then avoid movements that are repetitive. Children are also more prone to overheating because their sweat glands are less effective and because children breathe faster they lose more water, so make sure that they have plenty to drink.

It is vital that juniors concentrate on climbing on a wide variety of rock types and steepnesses and become aware of the risks and how to cope with them. Try not to sidetrack them into less relevant training such as weights, fingerboards and the like. Direct their training to improvement of the neuro-muscular coordination, combined with a slight increase of aerobic power. Training should not be too intense, vigorous or specific. More stamina-based training is better than anaerobic endurance or strength, and avoid overloading the muscles.

TRAINING NOVICE TO INTERMEDIATE CLIMBERS

Ben Moon, the world's strongest climber in the 1990s, said, 'Young people worry too much about training … The time to start training is when you stop improving.' Novices should climb and boulder a lot, create gains from getting out climbing … end of story. The only reason for spending extensive periods in a gym is if the weather is bad or there is not a crag close by. If there is not a nearby crag or climbing wall, build one. Novices need to watch other climbers and continually practise technique.

Novices can get all the gains in strength and endurance that they need from climbing and bouldering. If visiting a crag or wall is not possible, then low-intensity, high-volume work-outs for endurance are better and safer. Climbing lots of routes rather than burning out on one very hard route is preferable.

Advice for Novice to Intermediate Climbers

- Practise technique above all else.
- Train or preferably climb regularly.
- Practise mental control techniques.
- Use low-intensity, high-volume training.
- Work antagonistic muscles.
- Mimic climbing movements with any exercises.
- Forget stressful exercises like fingerboards.
- Vary the exercises.
- Maintain cardiovascular fitness.
- Keep a good power to weight ratio.
- Warm up and stretch before and after climbing.
- Work flexibility weekly.
- Be patient.

TRAINING INTERMEDIATE TO ADVANCED CLIMBERS

If the student climbs less than extreme, keep to the previous schedule and even then ask some fundamental questions before launching into a hard training programme. If their power to weight ratio is poor, then get them to lose weight and do more general training before embarking on a specialized training programme. If they do not already practise technique they can improve rapidly by concentrating on it first.

When training more advanced climbers it becomes difficult to identify weaknesses and it is too easy for them to train what they are good at. The secret for advanced climbers is to identify

---

Advice for Advanced Climbers

- Identify whether strength, endurance, power or technique is lacking.
- Work lock-offs.
- Work technique first train later.
- Work hard and rest well.
- Finger train gradually.

---

whether technique, strength, endurance or power is lacking. The likelihood is that it will be all of them! Stories of climbers spending more time in their cellars than climbing are common, so they must decide whether they want to be strong or a good climber.

NUTRITION FOR CLIMBERS

(J. Worsley, Sports Science Lecturer, Pembrokeshire College)

Strength to weight ratio is on every climber's mind, but climbers come in all shapes and sizes. Their diet should provide a balance of nutrients, whether their food preferences are the staple jam and peanut butter sandwiches or black pudding and chips.

What Are a Climber's Energy Requirements?

A climber's energy requirements consist of basic energy requirements plus specific extra energy requirements needed for climbing:

- A fit 35-year-old male requires approximately 1.3 kcals/hour/kg.
- A climber weighing 70kg (11 stone) therefore requires 2,184 kcals just to stay the same. A two-hour climbing session requires approximately 8.5 kcals/kg/hour, that is 1,190 kcals.
- The total calorific intake required is therefore 2,184 + 1,190 = 3,374 kcals.

Active climbers may find that an intake of energy above this level is necessary to sustain performance. This is a guideline only and will obviously depend on height and the size of the skeletal frame. Women generally have a lower metabolic rate and are smaller, which means fewer calories are needed to maintain the desired weight or fat percentage. Women also normally have a higher fat percentage than men.

A good power to weight ratio is important when routes move to the vertical and beyond.
Photo: Gavin Newman.

Below is the recommended daily intake of energy (Government guidelines are currently under review).

Table 1: Recommended daily intake of energy

Age Range	Occupational Category	Kcals/Day
Boys		
9–11		2,280
12–14		2,640
15–17		2,880
Girls		
9–11		2,050
12–14		2,150
15–17		2,150
Men		
18–34	Sedentary	2,510
	Moderately Active	2,900
	Very Active	3,350
35–64	Sedentary	2,400
	Moderately Active	2,750
	Very Active	3,350
Women		
18–54	Most Occupations	2,150
55–74	Very Active	2,500
	Most Occupations	1,900

A Question of Balance

A climber's energy requirement is provided by a mixture of carbohydrates, fats and proteins. A balanced diet ideally contains energy-providing carbohydrates as a major part of the diet (57 per cent), the body-building proteins (13 per cent) and the protective fats (30 per cent).

The energy yield is as follows: carbohydrate four kcals/g, fats nine kcals/g, and protein four kcals per gram. Therefore, the 35-year-old male climber in the example on page 85 requires:

- 57 per cent of 3,374 = 1,923 kcals i.e. 1,923/4 = 480g of carbohydrate
- 30 per cent of 3,374 = 1,012 kcals i.e. 1,012/9 = 112g of fats
- 13per cent of 3,374 = 439 kcals i.e. 439/4 = 110g of protein

Vitamins and minerals are necessary in small daily amounts and occur naturally in most foods. Finally, the importance of proper rehydration is often overlooked. Insufficient rehydration will certainly limit performance and if continued can cause injuries to joints and tendons.

Carbohydrate

Carbohydrate occurs in three types of food:

- Starchy foods, such as rice, pulses, cereals and pasta (these also contain vitamins and minerals as well as protein).
- Simple sugars, including confectionery and glucose drinks.
- Fibre, the indigestible carbohydrate found in cereals, fruits and vegetables.

Carbohydrate should make up 57 per cent of an adult's total energy intake because it provides the fuel for muscle contraction (glucose) as well as all the other processes continually taking place in the body. The requirement is about 480g when actively exercising and should consist mainly of the starchy variety of foods. Carbohydrate is broken down into glucose, a form of sugar carried in the blood to the cells. It is glucose that allows all active processes to take place. Any unused glucose is converted into glycogen stored in limited amounts in the liver and muscle tissue. Unfortunately, the human body does not store vast amounts of glycogen so a regular intake of starchy foods is required.

Energy replacement, after a particularly strenuous climb for example, should be considered a priority as glycogen levels will be largely depleted and the capacity of muscles to refuel is greatest within the first hour after strenuous exercise.

Sweet foods may give an immediate boost to perceived energy levels, as well as tasting good, but this is short-lived and does not satisfy the appetite, leading to a tendency to over indulge, with the excess kilocalories being turned into fatty tissue. These foods also bring the risk of dental disease and because very few contain vitamins and minerals, filling up on them can cause a shortfall in the daily requirement. At the crag itself flapjacks, bananas, apples and whole-grain bread with cheese or ham will begin the restocking process, offering an immediate glucose boost, and replacing some of the minerals lost in sweat, thereby satisfying the appetite without the need to resort to chocolate bars.

Fibre provides the push needed to expel waste products from the digestive tract by keeping those muscles involved healthy and fit in a similar way to the external muscles. This prevents disease such as cancer of the colon and disorders such as constipation, and allows rapid removal of waste products from the body. Roughly 30g of fibre are needed on a daily basis, a figure that has declined with the over refinement of modern foods in the Western diet. Try to include fresh, raw or lightly cooked vegetables and two pieces of fruit in the daily diet and use whole-grain bread, pasta and rice, as these are excellent sources of fibre.

A common expression used in connection with carbohydrate is 'glycogen loading', which is the active process of increasing glycogen stores to maximum levels prior to strenuous exercise. A simple method of achieving this is to consume your normal high-carbohydrate foods the day before if you know that you are attempting a particularly challenging route, but to refrain from exercising. This will ensure that muscle energy reserves are at optimal levels for that peak performance.

Protein

This is the part of the diet that supplies the building materials for growth and normal body development and the repair of tissue after injury, whether accidental or through exercise and training. Proteins such as hair, skin and muscle are made up from about twenty smaller units called amino acids. Some of these amino acids are 'essential' in the diet as they cannot be manufactured in the body. The easiest source of protein is from animal origin as this provides a wide range of amino acids. Chicken, fish, eggs, cheese and milk are good examples. Vegetarians need to make sure that their protein comes from various sources such as soya, pulses, cereals and nuts in order to ensure that the full range of amino acids are being taken in. Increasing protein intake will not increase muscle mass; that will only happen with an increase in resistance training. After injury or a particularly hard climbing session it is advisable to increase protein intake from 13 per cent to 20 per cent to promote tissue repair.

Active climbers have an interest in maintaining low fat percentages in the body as this is wasted material to them and extra weight to haul up the crag. Try not to use red meats and processed meat products as a source of amino acids because these are full of saturated fat which causes weight problems and impairs cardiovascular functioning. For the same reason, eggs and cheese should be limited in quantity, although cheese in particular contains an extensive range of essential amino acids. Skimmed or semi-skimmed milk has a low fat content whilst maintaining a high protein level. The amount of fat in the diet can be closely monitored by scrutinizing food labels.

Protein also brings with it the substance that is essential for replacing short-term energy supplies, creatine. However, supplements of creatine, used by rugby players and track athletes, have no proven benefit to climbers. As long as the diet contains adequate amounts of amino acids there is no need to resort to tablets. The long-term effects of creatine supplementation have not been investigated and may possibly have a toxic action on the liver.

Fats or Lipids

This section includes solid fats such as lard and butter as well as fatty fluids such as oil and cream. Fat is excellent if you wish to gain weight or like Sir Ranolph Fiennes, you need a huge energy intake for crossing the Antarctic from coast to coast. The average climber, however, should avoid excess fats and limit intake to those fats already in foods such as bread, meat, fish, cheese and eggs. This will provide the essential fatty acids required for cell manufacture after exercise or during growth and will also provide the fat-soluble vitamins, A, D, E and K, which are required for a healthy body. A certain amount of fatty tissue in the body is necessary for the protection of internal organs and insulation against cold temperatures and for the production of hormones that regulate the mechanisms of homeostasis (maintenance of the internal body environment). This includes systems involved in metabolic rate, fighting infection, waterproofing the skin and glucose levels in the blood. About 25 to 30 per cent of the total energy intake should be lipid in origin, consisting mainly of unsaturated fats such as olive oil, mackerel, tuna, nuts and lean white meat. Saturated fat and cholesterol have been highlighted as being detrimental to health and should be limited, though not totally eliminated, from the diet. Omega 3 fatty acids that have been acclaimed in recent research as being beneficial to healthy cardiovascular function are to be found in herring, mackerel, pilchards and other oily fish, as well as in the olive oil that has kept Mediterranean peoples healthy for centuries. Margarine was developed due to wartime scarcity of butter and is designed to provide a nutrient-rich substitute. However, like many foods in the modern diet it has been chemically processed, and these artificial foods should be avoided, along with white flour, sugar and processed meat and vegetables. Beware of hidden fat in food – read the labels carefully.

Climbers are often prone to joint stiffness and to alleviate the condition cod liver oil capsules have been shown to be effective in some instances.

Vitamins

These micronutrients fall into two categories:

- The water-soluble vitamins B and C that need to be absorbed on a daily basis as they are not stored in the body.
- The fat-soluble A, D, E and K vitamins that are stored in the body.

There are published Recommended Daily Allowances (RDAs) for most of these vitamins and the RDAs will be covered easily in a balanced diet without resorting to tablets. Supplements are only necessary if, for some reason, the overall energy intake is markedly reduced, as during illness for example. The B vitamins should be taken together rather than singly as they work better in this way.

The water-soluble vitamins are sensitive to excess intake of alcohol, pain killers and anti-inflammatory drugs, as well as smoking – these all impair absorption so please bear this in mind when analysing your diet.

Minerals

The human body uses a vast array of these, but they will all occur in sufficient quantities when a balanced diet is eaten and when the nutrients are not cooked completely out of the food, as with over-boiled vegetables. Vegetables should be either steamed or eaten raw whenever possible, and should always be fresh as both vitamins and minerals are lost in storage. Tinned vegetables are so over-processed that manufacturers add nutrients to them, as well as flavourings such as salt and sugar. Read the label to make sure you know exactly what you are getting. Frozen foods in theory should be full of nutrients, but the consumer has no way of assessing the state of the food prior to freezing and nutrient content will mainly depend on this. It also depends to a lesser extent on the efficiency of the freezer and the method of preparation prior to eating.

The important minerals for climbers are iron, calcium, phosphorus, sodium and potassium.

Iron

Iron is essential for the transport of oxygen and as such is important to all those who exercise, about 18mg per day being required. It is found in meat products, nuts, seeds and green leafy vegetables. A small increase may be required by females who need to compensate for iron lost during menstruation. Those on restricted intakes of energy need to be aware that their iron intake may suffer, resulting in anaemia.

Calcium

Calcium is necessary for healthy bones and there is a constant turnover of this mineral with exercise. Foods providing good quantities are milk, cheese, nuts, green vegetables and bread; the daily requirement is about 1.200mg.

Phosphorus

Phosphorus is present in grains, cereals, meat, milk and green vegetables and is essential for energy production, as well as healthy bones and teeth. It is required in similar quantities to calcium and works closely with vitamin D.

Sodium

Sodium is present in most foods, especially refined products, and supplements will not be necessary. Good sources are cheese, bacon, fish and meats. It assists in nerve impulse transmission, fluid balance and acid/base regulation and is lost in sweat, but not in sufficient quantity during normal climbing sessions to warrant replacement with tablets. In the case of endurance or prolonged climbing sessions in warm conditions extra salt should be taken in food prior to the exercise, so as to compensate for the anticipated increase in loss. A good tip is to taste the sweat on your face to see how salty it is and assess losses in that way.

Potassium

Potassium is found in meat, milk, vegetables, bananas, cereals and nuts and does a similar job to sodium. This mineral, though lost in sweat, is not lost in as large a quantity as sodium. A banana after the climb should balance this out.

Hydration

Hydration is possibly the most important part of the diet, especially when training. Lack of fluid will result in decreased performance, manifesting itself as muscle cramp, disorientation, headaches and nausea. Students should sip 500ml to 1l regularly before, during and after exercise. Thirst is not a good guideline for evaluating the state of hydration because this reflex is extremely slow and by the time this occurs you are already dehydrated. Factors such as humidity, wind and temperature will also affect fluid loss. A good measure of full hydration is that urine is clear and copious.

Before climbing, ensure full hydration and post-exercise begin replenishing fluid at once. Drinks containing alcohol and caffeine dehydrate the body and should be avoided the night before. Water is fine for moderate exercise, but if the students are working hard and sweating a lot some glucose and salt can help the absorption of fluid.

Sports drinks are expensive and most are energy replacement drinks that contain high levels of easily absorbed sugars. This is not a good idea during exercise because the high sugar content triggers the release of insulin, which causes the body to store energy. The words to look for on sports drinks are 'isotonic' – meaning of a similar concentration to body fluids, 'hypotonic' – meaning a lower concentration and 'hypertonic' – meaning a higher concentration. Hypertonic drinks do not aid rehydration and are designed to replace muscle glycogen. Isotonic and hypotonic are the best bet for rehydrating.

Commercial drinks are expensive and it is easy to make your own. For a hypotonic drink mix 750ml water with 250ml fruit juice and add a pinch of sea salt. For an isotonic drink mix 500ml fruit juice/500ml water and add a pinch of sea salt. If the priority is fuel replacement just add a pinch of sea salt to 1l of fruit juice.

Surprisingly, cold drinks are absorbed faster so keep the drinks in the fridge.

Dieting

Power to weight ratio is important in climbing and we all feel the need to lose weight at some time. This should be done carefully and sensibly to ensure that you have enough nutrients to perform well. Although there is some evidence that the propensity to put on weight is inherited it is ultimately through overeating and too little exercise that the genes express themselves.

Throw all your diet magazines and dietary products in the bin. If the $35 million Americans spent on dietary goods worked, 55 per cent of them would not be overweight. Good dieting is a balance between reducing your normal food intake and increasing aerobic exercise to raise the body's metabolic rate and burn calories. Neither is efficient as a dieting tool on its own. If you go on a starvation diet and do no exercise you may not lose any weight because the body's metabolism (rate of burning food) slows down to reduce its energy requirements. This is what helps us to survive famines! It also explains why, when you start eating normally again, you put on more weight because it takes time for the body to adjust its metabolic rate.

Do not become fixated on weighing yourself because as you exercise you reduce fat and develop muscle, which is heavier. Body fat is a better way to judge progress. Most good fitness gyms or colleges with a sports science department may be able to do this for you.

You should look out for signs which indicate that your food, mineral and vitamin intake has become inadequate, for example brittle and dull hair, flaking skin, cuts and bruises taking longer to heal and lethargy. It is a mistake to lose weight rapidly because it just piles back on when you stop dieting.

The body uses a large proportion of energy actually digesting food, therefore it is best to eat small amounts often. If you believe that you do not eat very much but you keep putting on weight, keep a list of everything you eat – everything, even a chip from someone else's plate. Most importantly, keep active and maintain a high metabolic rate.

IMPROVING FLEXIBILITY

(J. Worsley)

'Racehorse don't stretch so why should humans?'
Gordon Pine, 1950

Sport performance has benefited from scientific research since Gordon Pine's day and in the

Mike Rose at 'Undercover Rock', Bristol showing the advantages of a flexibility programme.

realm of flexibility each climber can now choose where they would prefer to be along the continuum from immobility to joint dislocation. Although improving flexibility has many benefits for climbers, it is by no means synonymous with the ability to climb. There are, however, benefits of flexibility training that make it essential for all climbers. Flexibility is defined as the capacity of a joint to move through its full range of movement or motion.

Benefits of Improving Flexibility

The relaxation of stress and tension in muscles has been shown to:

- increase sensory awareness;
- decrease post-climbing muscle soreness;
- increase blood flow (therefore oxygen) to and from the working muscle prior to exercise;
- maintain the full range of movement (ROM) around the joint when strength training;
- reduces injuries caused by overextension of joints;
- increase the ROM;
- increase the sense of health and well-being.

Some climbers have a natural genetic advantage in flexibility, but others can make up for this with the correct stretching regime. Flexibility programmes are best designed to progressively increase the usable ROM of joints over time. It is beneficial to include all joints, whilst emphasizing the important ones for climbers. Like all training, vary the programme regularly. A selection of stretches is included later on. As with all exercise, it is important to warm up thoroughly before any stretching session and to stay warm during it.

Limitations of Joint Flexibility

The Type of Joint.
Joints are simply a meeting of bone and bone, or bone and cartilage called articulation and are structured for strength (hip) or flexibility (shoulder), which explains why the shoulder is more prone to dislocation.

The Skeletal Muscle Tissue
When muscles contract they become thicker and shorter. They are also able to stretch and return to their normal shape and size. Muscles that remain in shortened positions for a long period of time, for example when weight training, experience a reduction in flexibility, which causes a reduction in joint flexibility. Muscles also work in pairs (agonist and antagonist). In order to maintain maximum flexibility both muscles can be trained equally. Muscle contributes about 41 per cent of the restriction to movement around a joint, but are most easily worked when seeking improvement.

The Ligament and Joint Capsule
Ligaments attach to the bone and are responsible for joint stability. These make up about 47 per cent of the resistance to movement of a joint, but the danger in stretching these is that the joint may become destabilized and so should be done by trained professionals only.

The Tendons
These transmit tension from the muscle to the bone and so produce movement. Very fine finger movements in climbing require inextensible tendons that transmit the smallest of muscle contractions and any overstretching can cause injury and deformation. Many climbers stretch their fingers by bending them back as far as is possible, but as they are controlled by tendons this is in fact bad practice. Tendons only limit joint ROM by 10 per cent, so are not as significant a factor as muscle, ligament and joint tissue.

The Skin
Skin is not completely elastic and only limits ROM by 2 per cent. By application of vitamin E cream the skin can be encouraged to maintain maximum elasticity.

Miscellaneous Factors
- Females tend to be more flexible due to differing hormone levels.
- As aging takes place, flexibility decreases. Older climbers should therefore stretch more frequently.
- Muscle temperature increases ROM, therefore warm up before climbing.
- Excess fat around a joint can limit its ROM.
- Scarring from injury can limit ROM.

Developing Flexibility

With all stretches consider whether the joint is designed to travel in the direction you are stressing it.

Exercise: Ballistic Stretching
This involves some form of rapid movement or bounce once the stretch position has been reached. This is dangerous for individuals unused to this form of exercise and often leads to injury.

Exercise: Static (Passive) Stretching
This involves easing into the stretch position and holding it for increasing lengths of time, normally 5 to 120 seconds. As the sensation of stretch diminishes, the stretch can be extended. This method is effective and safe.

Exercise: Proprioceptive Neuromuscular Facilitation (PNF) Stretching
This involves the use of a towel or partner to provide a force against which the limb may push in an isometric contraction (muscle remains the same but the tension increases). This is held for roughly ten seconds, then the normal stretch resumed. This assisted stretching is very effective, especially on the hip joint, but requires care by those creating the resistance.

Designing a Programme

Follow the guidelines below to produce a schedule that targets a student's individual goals:

- Warm up (see movement Chapter 2).
- Ensure that the stretch stimulates the desired muscle group. Target areas important in climbing, such as hip flexors, which are essential in getting the foot up high.
- The stretches must be anatomically safe.
- The joint and muscle must be placed in a position that has not been previously achieved.
- There should be a feeling of tension in the muscle but not pain.
- The stretch should be maintained for a minimum of ten seconds, gradually increasing to two minutes.
- Do not hold your breath.
- Build flexibility gradually and regularly.
- Stretching can be done anywhere, including at the kitchen sink.

The Stretches

Here are some example stretches that are useful for climbers, although the list is by no means comprehensive. Most of these stretches are easily adapted for use with a partner who can increase the stress placed on a particular muscle group. Music can often aid concentration during these sessions. Balance the training of muscles in pairs and do not allow great differences in strength or size of the muscles to build up as this will eventually lead to misalignment of the joints.

Exercise: Neck and Shoulders
Sit or stand with straight back, shoulders down away from the ears. Lower the chin to the chest, feeling a stretch at the back of the neck. Increase the intensity by easing the head down further by applying light pressure to the top of the head with both hands. Repeat diagonally left and right.

Exercise: Upper Back
Stand erect with good posture, feet hip distance apart, stomach pulled in and loose knees. Tilt the pelvis under the body trunk. Extend both arms out at chest level and interlock the fingers. Look downwards. Feel the stretch between the shoulder blades.

Exercise: Chest
Stand erect with good posture, feet hip distance apart. Let the knees go loose and tilt the pelvis beneath the trunk of the body. Clasp the hands in the small of the back. Gently ease the elbows

Upper back.

Exercise: Shoulder/Lower Back
- Stand with the feet hip distance apart, knees relaxed. Extend both arms above the head and link fingers. Push upwards. Extend this to the lower back by leaning slightly backwards and pushing the arms further behind the ears.
- Stand or sit. Bring one arm across the body at shoulder height. Hold the raised elbow with the opposite hand and gently apply pressure. Feel the stretch in the lateral shoulder. Repeat on the other side.
- Take the arm behind the body and grasp the elbow with the opposite hand. Apply pressure feeling the stretch.
- Stand upright. Place the hands on a wall behind the body as close to shoulder height as possible, with fingers pointing outwards. Flex the legs to lower the shoulders and ease into the stretch, feeling tension in the anterior shoulder.

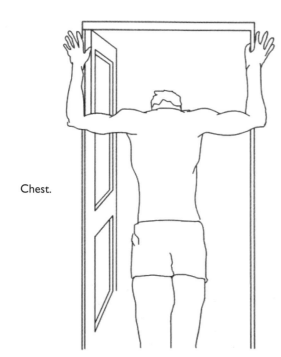

Chest.

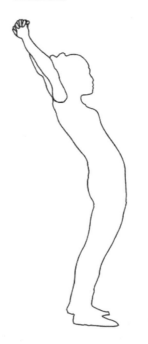

Shoulder/lower back.

towards each other without arching the spine. Feel the stretch in the front of the chest. An alternative is to face a doorway or corner and place the flat forearms and palms either side. Elbows should be at shoulder height. Lean slightly forward to feel the stretch in the pectorals of the chest.

Exercise: Side Stretch
Sit, maintaining an erect posture, feet flat on the floor, and hands on hips. Lean sideways, not forwards or back. Intensify the stretch by lifting one arm then leaning over using it as a weight. Release the back by sitting upright in a chair, feet on the floor, and gently curve forward, chest between the thighs. Feel the stretch along the back.

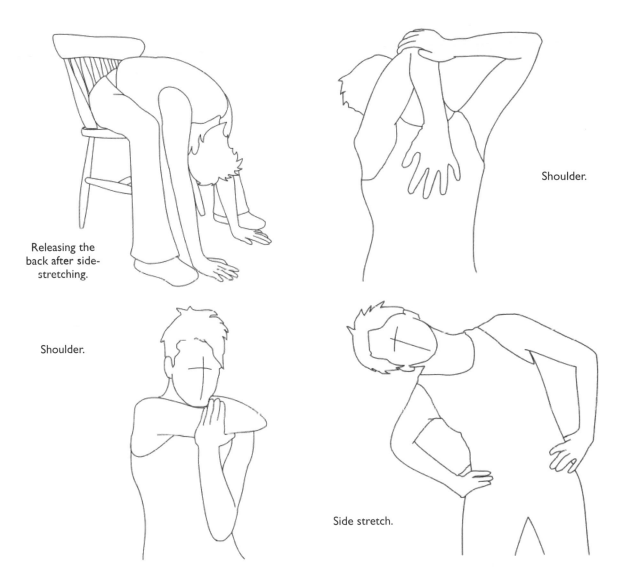

Releasing the back after side-stretching.

Shoulder.

Shoulder.

Side stretch.

Exercise: Front of Leg (Quadriceps)
Stand upright with one hand used for balance on a chair or wall. Flex one knee forward towards the buttock while slightly bending the support leg. Grasp the foot and further bring it towards the buttock without overstretching the knee joint. Feel a stretch in the front of the leg. Repeat on the other side.

Exercise: Abdomen and Hip
Lie face down with the body extended, palms by the hips, fingers pointing forwards. Using the arms in this position raise the head and the trunk whilst keeping the hips on the floor, feeling a stretch in the abdomen and upper thigh areas.

Exercise: Hamstring
Lie flat on the back in front of a doorway so that the raised leg is extended through the doorway flat on the floor. Increase the stretch by sliding the buttocks closer to the door frame. To increase further, wrap a towel around the raised foot and pull the leg away from the frame towards the chest.

Exercise: Back of the Knee
Sit upright on the floor, legs straight out in front. Bend one leg inwards so the heel touches the inner thigh of the opposite leg. Flex the foot of the straight leg and reach for the toes, pulling them back towards the trunk. If you cannot reach use a towel.

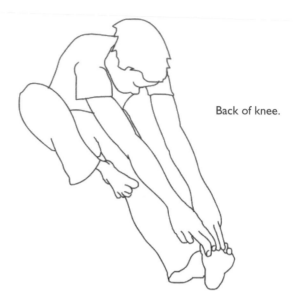

Front of leg.

Back of knee.

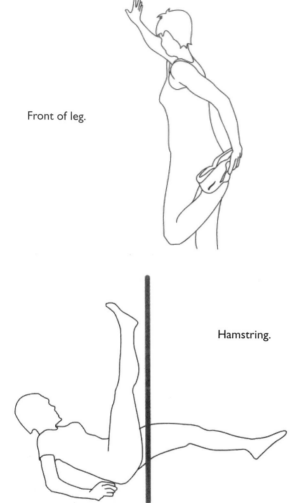

Hamstring.

keeping the other leg straight and lean against the wall with a straight spine and pelvis. Keep the heel of the back foot flat on the floor throughout and the toes of both feet pointing forward. Bend the arms and move the weight forward, hold the stretch in the lower leg. Also stretch the lower leg by flexing the knee of the back leg and hold.

Other Beneficial Exercises Are:
- Hanging from a bar or doorframe with straight arms and slightly flexed body to stretch the back and spine.

Exercise: Hip Flexors
- Sit upright on the floor and bend the legs outwards so that the soles of the feet touch. Hold the ankles and lean forward with a straight back, pulling the feet towards the groin. Feel the stretch in the groin area.
- Sit upright on the floor with the legs extended. Flex one leg and place the foot on the floor outside the straight leg, just by the knee. Twist the trunk away from the flexed leg and place one hand on the floor for support and the opposite elbow in front of the flexed knee apply pressure. Feel the stretch in the hips and buttocks.

Exercise: Lower Leg
Stand upright slightly more than arms' length away from the wall. Bend one leg forward,

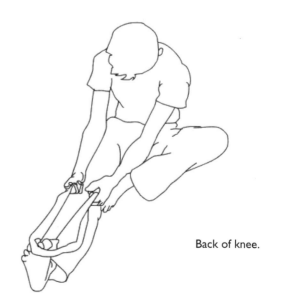

Back of knee.

Hip flexor.

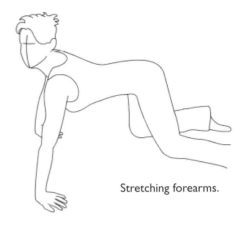

Stretching forearms.

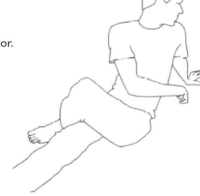

Hip flexor.

- Kneel on all fours with the fingers pointing towards the body. Lean back gently to stretch the forearms.
- Calf muscles can be stretched by rising onto the toes and holding, first with feet together and then with toes pointing in and heel out and then the reverse.

Controversial Stretching Techniques

There are certain practices that have been shown to be potentially damaging to joints.

The Hurdlers Stretch
In this technique one leg is bent backwards while in a sitting position and the other straight out in front. It was traditionally used to stretch the hamstring but it places undue strain on the knee ligaments and stresses the knee cap.

Lower leg.

Controversial techniques (i).

Inverted Single or Double Hurdlers Stretch
One or both legs are bent back and the body leans backwards. This overstretches some tissues and crushes others, jams joints and can pinch nerves.

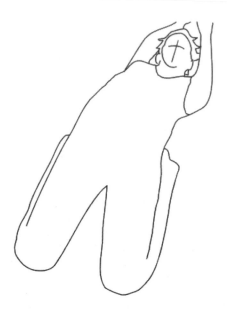

Standing Straight Leg Toe Touch
An old favourite. This stresses the discs, ligaments and sciatic nerves of the lower back.

Shoulder Stand and Plough Stretch
This causes abnormal stretching of the upper
spine that throws the head forward in a poor
posture. The heart and lungs become compressed and there is a risk of tearing the ligaments of the spinal column.

Controversial techniques (ii) and (iii).

CHAPTER 4

THE CLIMBING ENVIRONMENT

Instructors in the UK have the privilege of working in some of the world's most diverse and beautiful landscapes, but this privilege carries with it a heavy responsibility. There is a hugely increased pressure on our cliffs and crags from climbers and instructors and there is an equal environmental pressure to reduce that burden. Always try fit your safety and teaching requirements within the all-encompassing framework of environmental sensitivity.

If instructing practices are not adapted to demonstrate a concern for the environment there is every possibility that our activities will be curtailed by an outside, non-sympathetic body as demonstrated by the recent closure of whole areas to climbers in Germany and the USA. This is a salutary lesson to us all.

Adrian Wilson on Crack Basher, E2 5C, Abbey Buttress, South Wales.

USING OUTDOOR CRAGS

(Dave Turnbull, BMC Access and Conservation Officer)

With increasing recreational pressures on the countryside the environment has never been a bigger issue in climbing than it is today. In a country as small and densely populated as the UK the relationships between recreation, nature conservation, agriculture and land ownership are in a constant state of flux and sometimes conflict. This section focuses on how conflicts can be avoided and environmental impacts kept to a minimum by adopting good practice and developing a sound appreciation of access and conservation issues.

Responsible Use of the Outdoors

British cliffs may be small by overseas standards, but arguably they offer some of the most concentrated and geologically diverse climbing to be found anywhere in the world. Many of our cliffs and mountain regions are also highly valued for their natural landscape features and the wildlife they support and are protected from damage and disturbance under both UK and EC legislation. Around the country today there are literally hundreds of crags and upland areas with fragile access arrangements, seasonal climbing restrictions and controls over group use, parking, approach routes, dogs and many other issues. Responsibilities for managing countryside recreation and nature conservation are spread amongst many different organizations including National Park Authorities, nature conservation bodies and major landowners such as the National Trust, the Forestry Commission and the water companies.

It is the responsibility of all climbers and instructors to help protect our cliffs and mountain regions for the future and also to safeguard access to them. 'Sustainable development', a concept which has come to the fore since the Earth Summit in Rio 1992, applies equally to climbing and mountaineering activities as it does to mineral extraction, infrastructure development or heavy manufacturing industry. To the climber, sustainability means balancing our personal and commercial aspirations with the carrying capacity and sensitivity of the areas we visit and use. It means acknowledging and accepting our environmental responsibilities, adopting and promoting good practice and appreciating the needs of other people who visit, work and live in such areas.

Rights of Access

Many of the cliffs we climb on are on private land with no formal right of access. In the UK, mountaineering governing bodies including the British Mountaineering Council (BMC) and Mountaineering Council of Scotland (MCofS) have always had a policy of working closely with farmers, conservation bodies and landowners to agree access arrangements that satisfy conservation and land-management concerns whilst permitting access for climbers and walkers. On the whole this approach has been successful, but it relies on goodwill from both parties and can be fragile as user pressures on the countryside increase. In the late 1990s the Government strengthened its commitment to granting a statutory right of access to 'open country', that is mountain, moorland, heath and downland

Entering MOD land in Pembrokeshire.

(and sea cliffs in England), and this is anticipated to become law in 2002. The Countryside Bill, as it is known, may help to clarify climbers' and walkers' access rights on open country and an associated mapping exercise will help to define open access land and areas subject to closures. The Bill will differ slightly in England and Wales whilst in Scotland a totally different approach is being adopted that will probably give more access than in England and Wales, but with more weight given to landowners' concerns when they are relevant.

Cliffs and Mountains – Management and Protection

Cliffs can be important for many different reasons including climbing, nature conservation and geological interest. Some of the crags and mountains we climb on are very important for their wildlife and geological interest and have statutory protection against damage and disturbance under the Wildlife and Countryside Act 1981. Cliffs provide nest sites for colonies of seabirds as well as threatened species such as peregrine and chough; some cliffs lie in botanically sensitive areas such as semi-ancient woodlands, while others support important plant communities, lichens, mosses and liverworts in rock crevices and on open faces. The most important sites are identified as Sites of Special Scientific Interest (SSSI) and National Nature Reserves and are also under European legislation (see Table 2).

Conservation and countryside management in Britain are complex issues that involve many organizations and individuals with different responsibilities as summarized in Table 3. Over the last thirty years or so climbers in Britain have worked closely with conservation bodies and landowners to develop voluntary access arrangements that protect important animals and plants from damage and disturbance. In England and Wales alone, climbers support well over 150 seasonal climbing restrictions to protect important species of nesting birds as well as some permanent restrictions to protect endangered cliff plants.

Seasonal Access Restrictions and Land Closures

Many cliff faces and areas of mountain and moorland are subject to seasonal access restrictions or temporary closures owing to cliff and

Table 2: Nature conservation and landscape protection in England and Wales

Designation	Legislation	Description
Sites of Special Scientific Interest (SSSI)	Wildlife and Countryside Act 1981	Areas of ecological or geological conservation value designated by English Nature, The Countryside Council for Wales (CCW) and Scottish Natural Heritage.
Special Protection Area (SPA)	EC 'Birds' Directive 1979 (79/409/EEC)	Areas of international importance for birds where steps must be taken to avoid pollution incidents, habitat deterioration or disturbance (e.g. Southern Pembrokeshire is designated as a SPA because of its chough population).
Special Area of Conservation (SAC)	EC 'Habitats' Directive	The Habitats Directive requires EC member states to maintain or restore certain important natural habitats and wild species of flora and fauna.
Local Nature Reserve (LNR)	National Parks and Access to the Countryside Act 1949	Areas of local nature conservation importance established by local authorities.
National Nature Reserve (NNR)	Wildlife and Countryside Act 1981	There are 197 NNRs covering 79,526 hectares in England alone, e.g. Cressbrook Dale, Peak.
Area of Outstanding Natural Beauty (AONB)	England and Wales	AONBs contain the finest countryside in England and Wales outside the National Parks. They are designated by the Countryside Agency and CCW whose role it is to advise farmers, conservation bodies and local authorities on management policies within these areas. AONBs include the North Pennines, Gower, the Wye Valley and the Forest of Bowland.
Heritage Coast (HC)	England and Wales	Coastal areas of high landscape and conservation value. Over a third of the coastline of England and Wales is designated as Heritage Coast and a third of this is owned by the National Trust. Heritage Coasts are defined by local authorities and have special protection against development.
Environmentally Sensitive Area (ESA)	England	ESAs are designated to help control environmental damage caused by agriculture. Grants are available to farmers who agree to adopt farming practices that safeguard the landscape, wildlife or archaeological features. Large parts of the Peak District, Dartmoor and the Lakes have been designated as ESAs.

ground nesting birds, game shooting activities, fire risk or possible disturbance to livestock (for example, during the lambing period). Information about restrictions and land closures is available from the BMC and other governing bodies and by far the most common restrictions encountered by climbers are those which protect cliff nesting birds. The UK is internationally important for many wintering, migratory and nesting birds, notably seabirds and waterfowl. All wild birds, their eggs and nests, are legally protected under the Wildlife and Countryside Act 1981. Rare or endangered birds such as peregrine and chough are classified as Schedule 1 species under the Act and are protected by special penalties. Some birds are listed as Red Data Book species if their populations are internationally significant; if they are scarce or

Table 3: Organizations involved with conservation management in the UK

Organization	Function
English Nature	English Nature is the Government's statutory nature conservation agency in England. It is responsible for designating and administering (SSSIs) and for establishing NNRs. It has power under the Wildlife Protection Act to prohibit activities (including recreational pursuits) that may damage SSSIs. The Head Office is in Peterborough and there are twenty-one regional offices.
Countryside Agency	The Countryside Agency works to sustain and enhance the natural and cultural resources of the English countryside. It designates AONBs, encourages opportunities for public access and advises the Government on new access legislation.
CCW and Scottish Natural Heritage (SNH)	CCW and SNH are the Government's nature conservation agencies in Wales and Scotland. Unlike English Nature, they have a combined responsibility for nature conservation, landscape protection and the encouragement of public access. CCW is responsible for designating AONBs in Wales.
National Park Authorities	National Parks were established under the National Parks and Access to the Countryside Act 1949 (amended by the Environment Act 1995) with two main purposes: to conserve and enhance natural beauty, wildlife and cultural heritage, and to promote opportunities for understanding and enjoyment of the special qualities (of the Parks) by the public. If these objectives conflict, the National Parks Authorities are obliged to attach greater weight to conservation than recreation under the 'Sandford Principle'. National Parks also act as local planning authorities and are responsible for managing rights of way.
National Trust	The National Trust is a charity set up in 1895 to protect and manage places of historic interest and natural beauty in England, Wales and Northern Ireland. The National Trust is Britain's biggest private landowner. It owns large parts of Snowdonia, the Lake District as well as extensive sea cliff areas in South Wales (Gower and Pembroke), West Penwith, North Devon, Swanage and Anglesey. The Trust takes a positive approach towards public access.
Royal Society for the Protection of Birds (RSPB)	The RSPB is a charity with over one million members and 700 members of staff. It owns and manages wildlife reserves throughout Great Britain (e.g. at South Stack, Gogarth) and actively campaigns for bird protection at a national and international level.
Country Wildlife Trusts	The Wildlife Trusts are voluntary conservation bodies that aim to protect and enhance wildlife habitats and to promote understanding of wildlife. There are 47 individual Wildlife Trusts (usually based on counties in England and Wales) and they manage well over 2,000 sites including climbing areas such as Eridge Rocks and Chee Dale.
Water Companies	Statutory water companies such as Severn Trent and North-West Water own large areas of land, some of which are managed for nature conservation and recreation. Climbing areas owned or managed by water companies include Calvers Rocks, Pex Hill and Castle Rock.

declining breeders in Britain; or restricted in distribution or particularly culnerable. Table 4 shows some of the main species that climbers are likely to come across on the crag.

Most seasonal access restrictions for nesting birds operate between 1 February to 15 August, depending on the location and species present. The BMC encourages conservation organizations to review restrictions on an annual basis and to remove them once birds have finished nesting. This process relies heavily upon local climbers working closely with ornithologists

Table 4: Some bird species regularly found in climbing areas

Species	Significance to Climbers
Peregrine	The peregrine is a Red Data Book species (i.e. rare or endangered) protected under Schedule 1 of the Wildlife and Countryside Act 1981. The peregrine nests on coastal, mountain and moorland cliffs throughout Britain. It normally lays three–four eggs between mid-March to May and the chicks fledge the nest from late May onwards. Persecuted by gamekeepers and egg-collectors in Victorian times and by pigeon fanciers during World War II its population hit its lowest level in 1963 due to the effects of pesticides. Populations have now returned to pre-war levels in most regions.
Raven	Raven numbers declined substantially last century when it was eradicated from most of England. The raven is a large black crow commonly seen in the mountains of Snowdonia and the Lake District. It is also making a comeback in the Peak District and nests on a number of sea cliffs. The raven nests early in the year (four–six eggs between late January to February) and the chicks fly the nest within ten weeks.
Ring ouzel	A moorland nesting bird occasionally seen in Peak District and Snowdonia. it resembles a blackbird with a white throat and successfully nested on Stanage Edge during the 1990s.
Owls	Owls are distributed throughout the British Isles and occasionally nest on cliffs (e.g. Brimham Rocks in 1999). The barn owl has suffered long-term decline in Britain and is protected as a Schedule listed species.
Chough	The chough is a Red Data Book species which is protected under Schedule 1 of the Wildlife and Countryside Act 1981 and the EC Birds Directive. There are around 300 breeding pairs in Britain. It nests on sea cliffs in Wales, (e.g. Pembroke, Gogarth and Craig yr Aderyn) and Western Scotland. The chough is a member of the crow family, laying three–five eggs between April and June. The chicks fledge the nest by mid-July. Habitat loss, land-use change and persecution are the main threats to species survival.
Auks (Razorbills, Guillemots)	Guillemot and razorbill are Red Data Book species which inhabit coastal and offshore water and nest in large sea cliff colonies. Around 145,000 razorbills breed in Britain (20 per cent of the world population) and over a million guillemots. The main threats to survival are oil pollution and food shortage. Both species nest in Pembrokeshire, West Penwith, Swanage and Anglesey.
Kittiwake	One of the commonest breeding seabirds in Britain, the kittiwake nests in colonies on sea cliffs and islands. Numbers in Britain and Ireland have increased since 1900 and there are now over 500,000 breeding pairs.
Cormorant and Shag	Cormorant and shag nest in most sea cliff climbing areas in Britain (e.g. Little Orme, Pembrokeshire, Devon and Cornwall). The shag is slightly smaller than the cormorant and can be distinguished by the tuft of black feathers on its head.

to identify precisely where birds are nesting and when they have finished nesting. Information about seasonal access arrangements is widely available in guidebooks, the climbing press and the BMC website. In Pembrokeshire, Swanage, Gower, the Lake District and many other areas signs, marker posts and information boards on cliff tops or approach paths are used to identify restricted and non-restricted areas.

Getting Involved with Conservation Projects
Climbers have a long history of working with ornithologists and botanists on conservation projects requiring difficult access to cliff faces. In Pembrokeshire, the Lake District and Lancashire, for example, climbers have regularly assisted with bird ringing and monitoring work, whilst in Morocco, climbers have had long-term involvement with a project to create new nesting ledges for the endangered Bald Headed Ibis on a

Ringing choughs.

stretch of crumbling sea cliffs. Elsewhere, climbers have carried out rhododendron clearance work on cliff slopes (Lundy, 1998) and ecological surveys of cliff vegetation (Avon Gorge and the Lizard).

Good Group Practice

One thing is certain with regard to managing groups, there is always someone only too happy to tell you what you are doing wrong and how it could be improved. There is also little doubt that intensive use of crags by groups can have detrimental effects on the crag environment in terms of rock damage and footpath erosion and so on. The BMC, the Mountain Leader Training Board (MLTB), outdoor centres, instructors and guides have gone to considerable efforts over the years to develop guidelines and regional good practice publications to help address sensitive group management issues. Specialist advice is now available for groups operating in the Peak District, Lake District, Dartmoor, Pembrokeshire, southern sandstone and Snowdonia. Careful management and planning of group activities can help to reduce impacts on the crag environment and conflicts with other users. Some of the key issues that

group leaders can take into account are shown in the chart opposite.

One of the surest ways of keeping your impact to a minimum is to stay in touch with changing access arrangements and sensitive issues at specific crags. Access information is available from many different sources including guidebooks, climbing walls, shops and websites. The BMC website (www.thebmc.co.uk) includes a Regional Access Database recording all crags in England and Wales with reported access issues – including those with special requirements for group use.

USING CLIMBING WALLS

(Steve Richardson, Undercover Rock)

The proliferation of modern indoor climbing facilities is partly responsible for the recent increase in the popularity of rock climbing. Gone are the days spent serving an apprenticeship in the hills, building gradually on previous experience with caution and a real awareness of the risks involved. Climbing can now be experienced by a quick trip down the local gym in

A group of young people under instruction at Newton Head, Pembroke.

Group Management and Planning

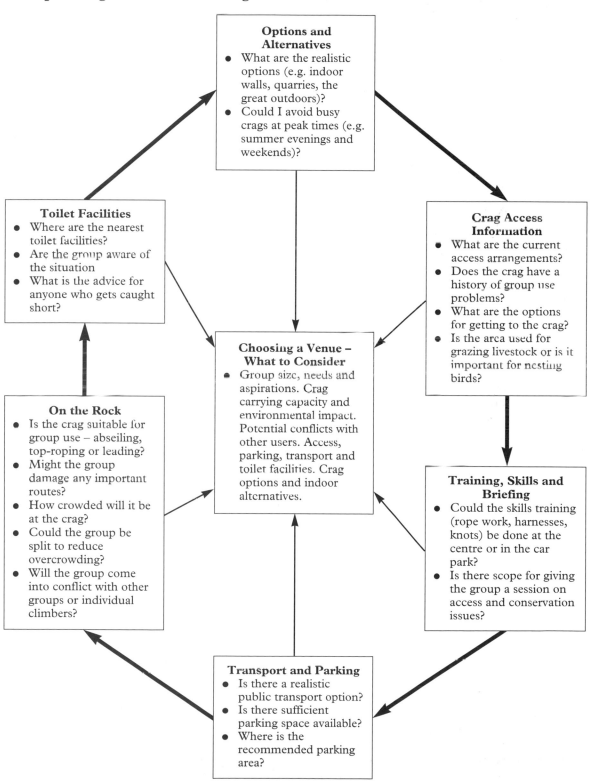

Options and Alternatives
- What are the realistic options (e.g. indoor walls, quarries, the great outdoors)?
- Could I avoid busy crags at peak times (e.g. summer evenings and weekends)?

Toilet Facilities
- Where are the nearest toilet facilities?
- Are the group aware of the situation
- What is the advice for anyone who gets caught short?

Crag Access Information
- What are the current access arrangements?
- Does the crag have a history of group use problems?
- What are the options for getting to the crag?
- Is the area used for grazing livestock or is it important for nesting birds?

Choosing a Venue – What to Consider
- Group size, needs and aspirations. Crag carrying capacity and environmental impact. Potential conflicts with other users. Access, parking, transport and toilet facilities. Crag options and indoor alternatives.

On the Rock
- Is the crag suitable for group use – abseiling, top-roping or leading?
- Might the group damage any important routes?
- How crowded will it be at the crag?
- Could the group be split to reduce overcrowding?
- Will the group come into conflict with other groups or individual climbers?

Training, Skills and Briefing
- Could the skills training (rope work, harnesses, knots) be done at the centre or in the car park?
- Is there scope for giving the group a session on access and conservation issues?

Transport and Parking
- Is there a realistic public transport option?
- Is there sufficient parking space available?
- Where is the recommended parking area?

Ian Vickers at Undercover Rock, Bristol.
Photo: Gavin Newman.

what, for many, is perceived as being a safe environment. Like it or not, climbing walls are an established part of the climbing culture and will continue to attract new people to the sport.

With increasing numbers of people coming into the sport, climbing walls are regularly used by instructors to introduce people to the sport. The Mountain Leader Training Board (MLTB) has recognized this and includes the use of climbing walls as an important element in the Single Pitch Award (SPA). It would, however, be naïve for any instructor introducing people to climbing via an indoor climbing centre to be concerned only with the running of a safe and enjoyable session for their students indoors. Instructors must also consider their responsibilities in terms of educating people about the wider climbing issues and the environment in which we work and play.

Climbing Wall Development

Early climbing walls were usually part of a university, school or local sports centre such as Mile End and Sheffield's Hallam University. They consisted of brick edges and inset moulded features on existing internal brick walls and were generally vertical in nature with the addition of small roofs. They were primarily suited to bottom-roping and bouldering type

activities and the facilities available for lead climbing were limited or non-existent.

In 1992, however, two dedicated indoor climbing centres were opened, Undercover Rock in Bristol and The Foundry in Sheffield. This represented a major change in the provision of indoor climbing facilities in Britain, offering extensive climbing surfaces which feature bottom-roping, leading walls, bouldering facilities and specialist training equipment, such as Bachar ladders and campus boards. Over the next few years other entrepreneurs realised the potential business opportunities climbing walls offered and several more major centres opened across the country. Some of these walls have been developed with private investment and some using extensive grant funding from lottery applications and the Sports Council.

The Association of British Climbing Walls

The increasing number of facilities and numbers of people using them has resulted in concerns about Health and Safety issues and the threat of litigation. This, together with the need for greater professionalism in the industry, has encouraged climbing wall managers to combine resources and form the Association of British Climbing Walls (ABC).

The ABC was set up in 1994 as the representative body of climbing centre and wall managers and owners, with members from both private and local authority managed facilities. It is a trade organization whose main objective is 'to develop good management practice and operation of artificial structures and to foster good relations within the industry'. One of the main aims of the ABC is the development and benchmarking of safe practice and quality management processes for operating climbing centres and walls, thus ensuring a high standard of safety and customer care, compliance with current Health and Safety legislation and so far as reasonably practicable, to discharge their duty of care to all customers.

Any existing or new climbing centre or wall development may apply for membership of the ABC, but in order to be accepted as a full member they must comply with the ABC 'Guidelines for the Management and Use of Artificial Climbing Wall Structures'. This set of guidelines, prepared by a Technical Committee of the Association, recognized by the British Mountaineering Council and endorsed by the Entertainment National Interest Group of the Health and Safety Executive, is designed to ensure that the wall is operated and maintained in a safe and professional manner.

Further information on the ABC can be obtained from: The Association of British Climbing Walls, c/o Bristol Climbing Centre, St. Werburgh's Church, Mina Road, Bristol, BS2 9YH or from their website www.abcclimbingwalls.com.

Climbing Wall Instruction

It is generally perceived that climbing wall instruction is an easy day out in a well controlled environment free from objective hazards, and in some cases this may be true. However, busy climbing walls require excellent group management skills and place additional, somewhat different, demands on instructors to those experienced in the outdoor environment.

Entry Requirements
The majority of modern climbing walls have specific entry requirements for individual climbers and for instructors working with groups, but these may vary from wall to wall. It is advisable to check prior to any visit with a group to avoid disappointment. This section outlines the basic requirements for climbing walls operating to current best practice guidelines.

- Most indoor climbing walls allow a registered member of the facility to sign in and take responsibility for up to two guests. Anyone wishing to take responsibility for a larger number of people, whether adults or minors, will need to have some form of qualification. The MLTB SPA is the minimum level of qualification required. However, some centres also have a site-specific qualification.
- To become a registered instructor you must already be an individual member of the climbing centre. This is normally a simple matter of completing a registration form, which asks you to confirm your basic level of competence and binds you to agree with the centres terms and conditions of use. Make sure you take the time to read these because they will indicate what is acceptable practice in the centre (this may vary between different centres).

- You will be required to produce evidence of your instructing qualification, the validity of your first-aid certificate and in some cases proof of public liability and instructor indemnity insurance. Some centres may take extra steps to check your qualification with the MLTB. You must ensure anyone for whom you are responsible is aware of and abides by any relevant conditions of use.

Site-Specific Qualifications
Due to an increase in the use of climbing walls by school and youth groups, led by teachers or youth workers with no specific interest in teaching rock climbing in the outdoor environment, some climbing centres offer a site-specific qualification. Prospective group leaders undergo training, a period of consolidation and an assessment which will allow them to bring groups into the climbing centre. Such awards are generally not transferable to other centres. The MLTB publishes a set of guidelines for climbing centres wishing to run such awards, with the aim of defining a common syllabus and setting standards in terms of those people able to provide such courses. Course providers should be Mountain Instructor Award or Mountain Instructor Certificate award holders and ideally they should also be SPA course providers with specific knowledge of climbing wall operating procedures and practices.

Running a Climbing Wall Session

If you are unfamiliar with a climbing centre a prior knowledge of their entry policy for groups and the facilities available is invaluable. The following questions will assist you in planning a constructive and worthwhile climbing session. The list of questions is clearly not exhaustive and specific climbing walls will present their own problems.

- What is the best time of day to take a group – when is it not too busy?
- Do you need to book your group in advance?
- Is there a maximum group size per instructor?
- What is the cost of hiring additional instructors if required?
- Do you require your own third-party liability and indemnity insurance?
- What is the centre's pricing policy and are you entitled to any discounts?

- How many top-ropes are available and what is the type and angle of climbing surface?
- Are there any suitable bouldering facilities?
- Are there any changing and warm-up areas?
- Is there any provision for people with disabilities?
- Is hire gear available and at what price?

Group Management and Responsibility

In recent years there has been considerable press regarding the impact on and use of outdoor venues by groups under instruction and SPA instructors have been particularly targeted for criticism. The SPA syllabus does identify and address these issues and it is down to the instructor to act responsibly and sensitively. However, it is easy to forget that the same issues arise when working in climbing centres. It must be remembered that, with the exception of a few walls which have dedicated areas for group use, you are working in a close environment with other climbers who have as much right to be there as yourselves.

Climbers and instructors operating in the outdoor environment accept and understand that climbing is a risk activity and most will be constantly aware of their surroundings and adjust their behaviour accordingly. Unfortunately, this same level of awareness is often absent in the 'safe' environment of a climbing wall and the resulting complacency can lead to accidents. Instructors should be aware of the impact other users may have on their group. For example, there is always the risk of someone lowering or falling onto another climber or member of your group. The intense nature of indoor climbing can also cause muscle or tendon injuries, particularly in young climbers and where an inadequate warm-up has occurred.

You can help to minimize your impact with a bit of forward planning:

- Plan your session but be prepared to be flexible.
- Where possible try to avoid busy times, particularly evenings and weekends.
- Do not monopolize one area of the wall for long periods of time.
- Keep control of your group.
- Brief your group on relevant conditions of use and safety issues.

- Avoid kitting up in the main climbing area.

Some practices that are acceptable and commonplace in climbing centres are potentially dangerous in an outdoor environment and it is important that you educate your students about the folowing:

- Belayers standing away from the base of the wall. This is common practice on steep overhanging walls, but could compromise runner placements on traditional routes.
- Complacency and lack of attention particularly whilst belaying. In climbing walls even the most experienced climbers are not immune from this particular affliction.
- Gri Gris are widely used in climbing walls and are often the first belay device used by novice climbers. These are not suitable for traditional climbing (see Chapters 5 and 6 for further information).
- It is common practice in climbing walls for belayers to use the harness abseil loop for belaying rather than tying into rope and using the rope loop. The number of accidents that have occurred on sport routes of more than 25m illustrates that this is not always a good idea.
- Novices often attach themselves to top-ropes using a screwgate krab. Having established in their minds that this is normal practice they then go on to attempt lead climbing attached to the rope in the same way.
- Overestimating one's ability. Indoor walls are excellent training facilities and novice climbers can reach a respectable standard very quickly. However, the ability to regularly flash F6b+ in a climbing wall does not necessarily equip you with the skills to climb E3 5c outdoors.

The Future

Despite their problems, climbing walls are an excellent resource. They provide the perfect place to introduce people to the sport and have the benefit of always being dry. Most modern walls provide excellent facilities for teaching technique and performance coaching. Hopefully in the future we will see more walls providing separate resources for instructors, thus ensuring that there is no reason whatsoever to go out to a crag.

CHAPTER 5

EQUIPMENT

Choosing equipment twenty-five years ago was simple because there was a limited range available. Since then, many weird and wonderful climbing inventions have reached the market place with the result that there is a bewildering variety of equipment, which can make it difficult for instructors and climbers to choose the best tool for the job.

Having a good knowledge of equipment helps you to give informed and interesting answers to questions from your students and to provide accurate advice as a technical expert. That said, the most important elements for safety are familiarity with rock climbing, good judgement based on previous experience and an understanding of how to use the equipment – why it does what it does is less important.

FORCES AND FALLING

To understand why climbing equipment is so strong we need to examine how forces are generated and absorbed during a fall.

The rope is your life line. Adrian Wilson in-flight from the Butcher, E3 5C.

Units

The breaking strains for climbing equipment are described in Newtons (N) rather than kilograms (kg). A Newton defines the force required to break climbing equipment and it is usually very large. Force rating is far more informative than mass rating, because the same force can be generated in two ways: a small mass under huge acceleration or a huge mass under small acceleration. In other words, hanging a car from a krab may generate the same amount of force as a climber taking a long fall.

The definition of force is any action or influence that accelerates or changes the velocity of an object. An object experiences force when it is pulled or pushed by another object. The unit of force is the Newton, which is the force necessary to accelerate a mass of 1kg to 1m/sec2; this force is approximately equal to the weight of a 100g object at sea level. A kilo Newton (KN) is the force required to accelerate 1,000kg to 1m/sec2.

How are the Forces Generated in a Fall Absorbed?

As a climber ascends, they gain potential energy (the energy of position); when they fall this is converted into kinetic energy (the energy of momentum). The amount of kinetic energy is dependent on the climber's weight and the length of the fall.

When the rope stretches, catching the falling climber, some of the energy is converted into heat by friction of the rope fibres. The remaining energy is dissipated and absorbed by the friction of the rope sliding over krabs, the movement of the belayer, knots tightening, rope sliding through the belay device, krabs flexing and even runners popping out. Any energy left over is transmitted to the climber, the belayer (or belay anchors) and the protection. The energy, which is held by the belayer, is transmitted to the other side of the krab and to the climber, but reduced by a third by friction. However, the same physics that allows pulleys to help raise a weight acts against us when we fall

UIAA/CEN/PPE/3 Sigma Rating

These abbreviations relate to outdoor equipment and appear on manufactuers' brochures.

The **Union International des Associations des Alpinism (UIAA)** is a European Union formed in 1928 to ensure that climbing equipment was safe. In 1964 they set the first safety standards for climbing ropes. Today, alpine clubs from more than eighty countries participate in the UIAA, which provides standards for gear ranging from karabiners to ice axes.

In the early 1990s the EEC decreed that climbing gear must be standardized and approved within their already **Comité Européen de Normalisation (CEN)** industrial safety system. The UIAA is now an advisory body to the CEN. The CEN sets standards for all climbing products sold in Europe.

The European Directive 89/686/EEC states that **personal protective equipment (PPE)** is 'any device or appliance designed to be worn or held by an individual for protection against one or more health hazards'. This also includes items of equipment used within a system or safety chain (e.g. rock anchors). It has been illegal since July 1995 for a manufacturer to sell equipment without the CE mark within the European Economic Area. The CE marking comprises five numbers and a letter. The first two are the year of manufacturer, the following three numbers the day entered into stock and the letter identifies the person responsible for final control.

This may give you confidence in your equipment, but in recent years the UIAA and CEN tests have become antiquated and some of the information relatively useless. For example, putting a camming device into a vice and pulling to failure may tell you how strong the unit's axle and stem are, but it doesn't provide much information on how well the cams hold in rock. The UIAA is currently improving its tests to reflect more accurately the use equipment is put to.

and the two forces are added together to act on the protection.

The energy created by a fall and the force the belayer applies to stop the climber reaches a maximum when the rope has stretched fully. This is called the impact force (IF). A strange fact is that the IF does not depend on the length of the fall, it depends on the fall factor, which is the distance fallen divided by the amount of rope paid out and describes the severity of a fall. It ranges from 0 to 2. Zero is where there is no

Interesting Fact

A climber will fall 40ft (12m) in 1.6 sec. In the following 1.6 sec they can reach 170ft (52m) and be travelling at 70mph (112 km/h). It is not very reassuring to know that they will not exceed 155mph (250km/h).

force on the rope and 2 where the leader falls, with no protection in place, therefore all the forces are transmitted to the belayer and the rest of the safety chain.

A leader fall of 5ft (1.5m) therefore transmits the same force to the protection, the climber and the belayer as a leader fall of 50ft (15m). Although the longer fall generates more force, this force is absorbed by the longer rope. This is of course a simplistic view because the energy created in the longer fall acts over a longer period of time and is therefore more stressful on equipment.

Let us take the example of a climber weighing 82kg (13 stones). He generates 7.46KN in a fall factor 1 and 10.18KN in a fall factor 2 (these figures are generated from a low-stretch system without the dynamic elements described earlier, such as knots tightening). The protection receives almost double this, 20.36KN. The fall factor 2 is a worst-case scenario and provides the baseline for how strong climbing equipment

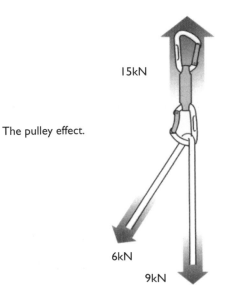

15kN

The pulley effect.

6kN

9kN

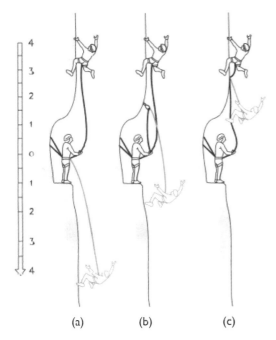

Fall factors.
(a) Fall factor 2
(b) Fall factor 1
(c) Fall factor 0.5

needs to be, for example the minimum gate closed strength for a krab is 22KN.

On a final note it is possible to generate a fall factor above 2 by taking the rope in as the climber falls through the air. This does reduce the final length of the fall but also reduces the amount of rope available to absorb the fall and therefore increases the fall factor above 2. The opposite is also possible and paying the rope out can reduce the fall factor.

Dynamic Belay

The figures above were generated from a low-stretch system. In reality, it is difficult to create the circumstances where a true low-stretch belay occurs. Normally in a fall ropes stretch, knots tighten, the belayer is pulled upwards and some of the rope slips through the belay device. However, some belay devices are more dynamic than others. The Petzl Gri Gri is an example of a predominately 'low-stretch' belay device where the rope is stopped immediately. If the Gri Gri was clipped directly to the belay anchors then all the forces would be transmitted to the climber, his protection and the belay anchors. The

important concept to grasp here is that a low-stretch belay transfers all the forces to the belayer, climber and the belay, whereas a dynamic belay that allows some of the rope to slip can absorb some of the forces. The majority of belay plates and tubes allow some slippage.

Vectors
When two protection placements are connected or a sling is placed around a boulder, the measure of the angle formed at the junction between the two pieces or the sides of the boulder determines how the load is distributed. The greater the angle, the worse the distribution. At angles greater than 120 degrees, loads begin to multiply rather than being distributed.

The mathematics describing these forces is trigonometry. Take the example of a rope strung between two trees. If a climber weighing 80kg (12½ stones) (UIAA test weight) is hung from the middle he would exert a force of approximately 80N. This application of forces is called a vector.

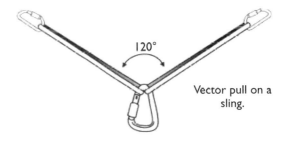

Vector pull on a sling.

To calculate the force on one anchor we need to make the following calculation:

$F = F1/\text{Cosine } X$ where
F = force on one anchor
$F1$ = half the force from the climber, i.e. 400N
X = half the angle created by the climber hanging in the middle of the rope.

This creates the following forces:

- when the angle is zero, i.e. the rope is hanging down vertically, the force is 400N
- when the angle is 30 degrees the force is 449.43N
- when the angle is 45 degrees the force is 526.3N
- when the angle is 80 degrees the force is 1,290N

- when the angle is 99 degrees the force is 25,470N
- when the angle is greater than 100 degrees the force is theoretically infinite.

Combining the 99-degree example, where the load on the anchor is 25,470N, with the other half of the system creates an angle of 198 degrees with a total load of 50,940N. This means that the total system must be able to hold 50,940N or 50.94KN, that is sixty-four times the climber's weight. A static rope has a typical tensile breaking strain of 30KN. This is the reason why the rope on a tyrolean traverse should not be tensioned to a point where there is no give in the system (this is in fact virtually impossible to do).

ROPES

A rope must be able to withstand severe forces without causing injury to the climber, must last a long time and be pleasant to handle. A tall order for a twisted piece of man-made fibre!

Approximate Rope Strengths	
11mm dynamic	21KN
9mm dynamic	15KN
11mm static	30KN
5.5mm cord	0.65KN

Ropes are divided into two types, dynamic and low-stretch (sometimes called static ropes). Dynamic ropes absorb the impact forces generated in a fall and must be used in all climbing situations, whereas low-stretch ropes are designed for abseiling, tyroleans and caving and must not be used for climbing. The difference can be compared to that between a spring and a wire cable. If a climber falls on a wire cable more of the force is transmitted to them, resulting in a broken back.

Rope Construction

Ropes were not commonly used until the mid-nineteenth century and even then many climbers still regarded it as unbecoming and something to be ashamed of. In the days of W P Haskett-Smith, the leader did not fall for fear of the rope breaking, but visit a climbing wall or

Kernmantle rope construction.

sports crag nowadays and you will see climbers falling off with impunity. It is even a common sight on adventure climbs. This change in attitude has been due, in no small part, to advances in rope construction.

Until the early twentieth century, climbing ropes were acquired from the marine industry and were hawser-laid manila or hemp of about 12mm thickness. They were stiff, heavy and unwieldy and did not stretch very much. The greatest development came with the onset of the World War II, when the resultant shortage of man-made fibres led Du Pont to create ropes made from nylon. The 'Hawser-laid' construction continued to be used, but they were lighter, stronger and more pleasant to handle. After World War II, Edelrid introduced a new construction of rope called the kernmantle and this is the method by which all modern ropes are made. Kernmantle ropes consist of a multi-stranded core (kern) surrounded by a tightly braided sheath (mantle). Both are made of individual strands of twisted nylon.

The core is the major load-bearing element and is made by braiding or twisting the fibres. The sheath protects the core and is largely responsible for the way the rope handles and its durability. Its strength and physical characteristics depend on how well the core and sheath function together. A tightly woven sheath tightens the rope, making it stiffer but keeping the dirt and water out, while a loosely woven sheath is more supple. Individually, the two components are weaker. Dynamic and low-stretch ropes are made by the same method.

The dynamic element is introduced into the rope by steaming the core.

Although they are not CE approved, Hawser-laid ropes are still used by some groups, especially on sandstone crags because it is easier to clean the sand from the rope strands. However, the irregular surface of the rope makes it unsuitable for use with mechanical belay devices and it is less pleasant to handle.

Characteristics of Dynamic Ropes

For a rope to be certified it must pass a series of stringent tests by an independent CE-approved laboratory. The current rope test was invented in the late 1950s by Professor Dodero in France and has been updated several times since. In the test, 40m of rope is dried for at least twenty-four hours in an atmosphere of less than 10 per cent relative humidity and then conditioned in an atmosphere of 20 +/–2°C and 65 +/–2 per cent relative humidity for at least seventy-two hours. The drop tests are carried out at room temperature within ten minutes of removal from the conditioning atmosphere.

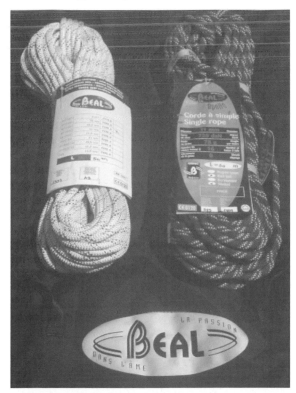

The rope tag contains a wealth of useful information, but do you know what it means?

The label contains most of the information useful to climbers: fall rating, impact force, diameter, length, weight, coating, elasticity, sheath slippage, knotability. However, there are some things not contained on all labels such as handling, kinking and advice on colour.

Fall Rating

The European Standard specifies that a climbing rope must survive a minimum of five consecutive drop tests (falls), with a five-minute rest in-between. The test for a single rope involves dropping an 80kg weight 4.8m on 2.8m of rope, with the rope running through a simulated anchor which is about 30cm from the fixed anchor. For double ropes the weight is reduced to 55kg. Since both ends are statically anchored, there is no dynamic element to the test, so it is an extremely severe one (see the section on forces above), unlikely to occur in normal climbing falls. Fall rating is used as a big selling point, but since neither a ten-fall nor a five-fall rope can break under normal conditions, the increased safety is largely irrelevant; it may, however, indicate improved durability in extreme uses.

Because the Dodero Test does not actually reflect real climbing falls, the following properties are more important.

Impact Force (Dynamic Properties)

The Impact Force (IF) is the load transmitted, via the rope, to the falling weight during the first test drop and it is a measure of the rope's ability to absorb the energy of a fall (its dynamic properties – see the section on forces above). The IF of different brands can vary by as much as 25 per cent. The UIAA sets a limit for this force, called the maximum impact force (MIF), at 12KN for single ropes and 8KN for double ropes.

When the test is repeated with five-minute intervals, the measured IF increases by 28 to 59 per cent due to the gradual loss of the rope's dynamic properties, but most stay below the UIAA maximum for the five falls. The ability of a rope to absorb the forces created in a fall decreases with age – that is, the IF transmitted to the safety chain increases with age and use.

The IF is an important factor when deciding which rope to purchase for leading traditional climbs, because as a climber falls he is generating a force that is subsequently transferred to the climber, the rope, the protection, the belay and the belayer. Falling onto a lower IF rope is more comfortable, transfers less force to the protection and decreases the chances of it pulling out. However, low IF ropes are often associated with high rope stretch, which increases the chance of hitting a ledge or the ground. A rope with low IF will not last as long, therefore those who do not require a low IF rope, such as when bottom-roping, may like to look for a higher IF rope.

Price

A higher price does not necessarily mean a better rope. However, be sceptical of rope 'specials' or bargain models, because the easiest way to make a cheaper rope is to drop a strand from the core or thin the sheath to cut nylon costs. While these ropes still pass the UIAA tests, they suffer in durability.

Diameter

The UIAA classifies dynamic ropes as single (1), half (½) or twin ropes (∞). Single ropes vary from 9.4mm to 11mm. Half-ropes are used in pairs and clipped alternately through runners; they vary from 8.1mm to 9mm. Twin ropes are generally less than 8.5mm and differ from half-ropes in that both strands must be clipped through all the protection points. Twin ropes are not commercially available in Europe any more because half-ropes have become so thin.

Single versus Half-Ropes

There are many questions an instructor will need to ask, but if the students are keen traditional climbers persuade them to buy two half-ropes.

- Will the students be lead climbing?
- Keen traditional climbers will soon 'out climb' a single rope, although a single will suffice for wall/sport climbers.
- Two half-ropes are more expensive. Can students share the cost?
- Have they experience with double ropes?
- Will they be multi-pitch climbing?
- Double-rope technique combines lower IF with the security or two ropes if one is cut.

The diameter given on the label of a rope is not in fact the actual diameter of the rope. A rope's diameter is measured by hanging a weight on 1m of rope. Weight (gm/m) is a better method for comparing ropes. The more gm/m the thicker the rope.

The advantage of large diameter ropes is that they last longer, are easier to handle, make abseiling more comfortable and tangle less. Small diameter ropes have the advantage of being easier to clip into protection, produce less drag and make abseiling down long routes easier.

Typical Weights gm/m of Beal Ropes		
● Apollo	11mm	78g.
● Top Gun	10.5mm	69g.
● Booster	9.7mm	61g.
● Stinger	9.4mm	57g.
● Verdon	9mm	49g.
● Iceliine	8.1mm	42g.

Length

For over one hundred years the standard rope length was 120ft (36.5m), but in the 1960s and 1970s 45m ropes became standard. Nowadays, 50m, 60m and even 70m ropes are normal. Longer ropes decrease the number of belay stances needed on long routes, but have the drawback that they are heavier. Longer ropes also have the advantage that because falling usually wears the first 10m, the end can be cut off and still leave a usable length of rope. Some half-ropes are sold in 100m lengths, which means that two ropes do not need to be tied together for abseiling and avoids the chance of the knot becoming jammed on abseils. These ropes are very heavy for one person to carry.

New ropes shrink after braiding, so what you actually purchase may not be exactly 50m, for example. Some manufacturers allow for this by cutting the ropes longer than stated, but the ropes can also be a few metres shorter. With use, a rope can lose up to 5 per cent of its length.

Marking the middle of the rope is important, but avoid using marker tape because it tends to get caught in belay and abseil devices; instead use one of the manufacturer's marker inks. Avoid marker pens because the solvents may affect the nylon.

Weight

Smaller diameter ropes suggest that they will be lighter, although this is not always the case. Making them denser (packing more strands inside the sheath), can make ropes smaller, but may not change the weight. Furthermore, weight is only really important to rock climbers on long, desperate pitches or when carrying them in the mountains in winter.

Dry Coating

A wet rope is more difficult to belay with and abseil on. It also abrades more easily, stretches more and may freeze solid. It can be very difficult to tie knots in frozen ropes and they are up to 40 per cent weaker at −40°C than a dry rope. A rope can absorb more than 50 per cent of its weight in water and the 'Holy Grail' for rope manufacturers is to create a rope that does not absorb any water.

Paraffin wax was used for many years to add a dry coating, but this attracts dirt. Silicone and Teflon are the most common modern dry coatings, although Beal have recently started coating each fibre with fluoride and heat-polymerizing it. There is no accepted standard for comparing dry treatments; some companies treat the individual fibres and claim their method is superior, whilst those that soak the rope say it seals the pores and is longer-lasting. However, no rope is fully waterproof.

Newly coated ropes are slicker, creating a lower drag through krabs, and they are therefore more abrasion-resistant. Manufacturers claim their treatments increase the life of a rope by up to a 150 per cent. This may be true when the rope is new, but abseiling and belaying remove surface coatings rapidly. Dry treatments also increase the price by approximately 15 per cent. To add to the confusion, an untreated, tightly constructed rope with a closely woven sheath is likely to be more water-repellent than a loosely woven, coated rope. Furthermore, the coating on a rope may be temporarily improved by spraying with Edelrid Dry Rope or washing the rope in Nikwax's TX10.

Elasticity/Stretch

Manufacturers could conceivably produce a rope with a very small IF by using rubber, but it would be useless for climbing, jumaring and abseiling for obvious reasons. The UIAA therefore sets a limit on elongation under load for dynamic ropes of 8 per cent for single and 10 per cent for double ropes. This is not the elongation that a fall would create, but the stretch created by hanging an 80kg weight on the rope. Manufacturers do not produce figures for the stretch created by the forces generated in a fall as it is very difficult to measure, but one series of tests showed that with a 66ft (20m), factor 1 fall, an 11mm rope stretches over 26ft (8m), that is 40 per cent. This figure would be expected to be greater with a half-rope.

Sheath Slippage

Excessive slippage of the sheath over the core makes a rope wear more quickly, but has the advantage that it decreases the likelihood of it cutting over a sharp edge and makes for softer handling. Some dynamic ropes come with zero sheath slippage, especially those with a braided core construction and these last longer.

Knotability

To test the knotability of a rope a simple overhand knot is loaded with 10kg for one minute, then the weight is reduced to 1kg and the interior of the knot is measured. The ratio of rope diameter to the interior knot diameter is given on the rope label. The UIAA norm is 1.10. The lower the ratio, the more knotable the rope is and subsequently the more supple it is.

A more supple rope knots more easily and because the individual fibres tend to bend rather than break, they are more abrasion-resistant. Stiff ropes are more durable, easier to untie after loading and are less prone to tangling.

Colour

Colour is irrelevant when buying a single rope, but when buying two half-ropes make sure they are different colours and easily differentiated by colour-blind people. Avoid black ropes as 'Watch me on black' can be confused with 'slack'.

Which Dynamic Rope do I Buy?

Any UIAA-approved climbing rope will do the job, but some do certain jobs better than others. Some have characteristics that make them better for sports climbing, others for bottom-top roping or climbing walls, whereas others are better for traditional routes. Consider the following when buying a rope:

- What is the sell-by date or manufacturer's date?
- A 60m single rope is useful for sports climbing.
- High IF ropes are more durable.
- Is dry-coating necessary for sports climbing?
- Zero sheath slippage makes the rope more durable but less soft to handle.
- Is weight really important?
- Some manufacturers make ropes with an extra thick sheath for climbing walls, for example Beal Wallmaster.
- Which is best – a single or two-half ropes best?
- A low IF reduces the force on runners.
- Dry coating makes the rope more pleasant to use in wet conditions.
- Sheath slippage makes the rope more resistant to cutting over an edge and the rope softer.
- Thinner ropes and lower IF ropes stretch more.
- For lots of abseiling, ascending or tyrolean traversing a single 10mm or 11mm low-stretch rope is best.
- A flexible low-stretch rope is better for frequent tying and untying of knots and abseiling.

Life of a Rope

Manufacturer's guidelines for the life of a rope have always been ambiguous and remember that a rope can be trashed on its first outing.

Guidelines are aimed at recreational climbers using the ropes for leading. They give no guidance on the effect of repeated small falls and make no reference to the effect of aging on falls over an edge. They do not distinguish any differences in usage between sports, adventure and mountaineering usage. They also do not examine the effect of bottom/top-roping on the subsequent ability of a rope to hold a leader fall.

Research by the German Alpine Club (DAV) came to the conclusion that a rope used for sports or normal climbing cannot break in a normal fall, but its ability to hold a fall over an edge (1–5mm) is dramatically reduced with time. They also concluded that the UIAA rope test should more clearly represent real climbing;

> **Typical Guidelines**
>
> - **Black Diamond (ropes made by Beal) 1996:** 'As a rule of thumb – climbers who use their ropes occasionally (holidays); 2–4 years. Average use (weekends and holidays): 2 years. Intensive daily usage (guides, professional climbers): 3 months to one year.'
> - **Edelweiss 1996:** 'Impossible to define but we do recommend you replace your rope after five years because of material aging.'
> - **Edelrid 1996:** 'Multiply the number of feet climbed by 0.33 and then the number of feet abseiled, lowered and jumared by 1.66. Retire a 10mm rope when it has reached 5,000–15,000ft, an 11mm between 36,000 and 63,000ft. Opt for lower numbers if it is a smaller diameter rope.'

that it should be dynamic and carried out over an edge because this is the only factor to consider when examining rope breakage (when a rope passes over an edge the fibres on the outside of the curve stretch more than those on the inside, therefore the load is not on a full rope).

The DAV also states that a rope used for bottom-roping should not subsequently be used for leading when there is a chance of the rope running over an edge (climbers currently using their rope for climbing walls take note). For bottom-roping, DAV used the rope until the sheath broke or it became too stiff to use (DAV does not advocate keeping ropes until they are in the same state). The DAV also concluded that a rope which has sustained many small falls should not be used in a situation where an edge fall is likely.

In spite of the discrepancies, both manufacturers and the UIAA err on the safe side. Use common sense, monitor a rope's use, look after your ropes and check them for wear and damage. As they get older or have taken falls, reduce their exposure to situations where they can be cut over a sharp edge. Relegate them to top- and bottom-roping or abseiling where the possible IFs are less.

Gentle use of a rope can result in a much longer life for it, and allowing the rope to rest for fifteen minutes after a fall can double the number of falls the rope can take before needing to be retired. After a fall, tie onto the other end so that the stressed end can recover.

Low-Stretch Ropes

Low-stretch ropes are distinguished from dynamic ropes by their high breaking strength and very low stretch. Low-stretch ropes have a limited ability to absorb falls; they are tested to take a fall less than factor 1, but should not be used as a climbing rope. Direct falls with a factor of 0.5 and falls from heights of 5ft (1.5m) can result in serious impact forces on the falling person and the whole safety chain (slings are also low stretch, so do not clip in and climb above them). Some manufacturers market a low-stretch top-rope for use on climbing walls, but unless it is in the hands of someone experienced the 'catch' is not as soft.

Low-stretch ropes are designed for industrial use, caving or abseiling/ascending. The latter are generally lighter and a bit less sturdy. They can be bought in 9mm, 10mm, 10.5mm, 11mm and 11.5mm diameters, but climbing instructors usually require 10–11mm.

Low-stretch ropes that are continually under tension are particularly susceptible to damage from sharp edges. The use of rope protectors increases their lifespan. Low-stretch ropes which have sheath slippage can cause critical malfunctions by blocking abseil and ascending equipment; high sheath slippage also makes ropes wear faster. Before using a low-stretch rope some manufacturers recommend that the rope is soaked in water to reduce the risk of sheath slippage and left to dry slowly, but this results in a shrinkage of approximately 5 per cent.

Miscellaneous Ropes

Beal and Edelrid manufacture a 'Canyoning' rope that has a polyamide sheath for abrasion and heat resistance, but with a polypropylene core to make the rope light enough to float. It is useful for sea-level traversing/coasteering.

Care of Ropes

Most ropes do not die from old age, they die from misuse. Dirt and salt shortens their life due to internal and external abrasion. The best way to keep a rope clean is to use a rope bag and to avoid stepping on the rope.

Ropes can be washed at temperatures below 40°C in a tub or washing machine. Flake it out inside a loosely woven sack or 'daisy chain' it (see Chapter 6), but do not spin-dry because abrasion against the drum can damage it. Do

---

A Rope's Main Enemies

- Acids, even the fumes from the battery of a drill, are particularly insidious because they can damage a rope before there is any visible evidence of change.
- Recent research has shown that UV does not cause dangerous degradation – a rope, half of which was exposed to sunlight for eight and a half months, showed no difference holding a fall over a 10mm edge when compared to a section of rope not exposed to UV light. The sheath protects the core from the damaging effect of UV. UV does degrade the sheath, so do not leave ropes drying in the sun or on the back seat of a bus.
- Solvents, even those in marker pens, destroy nylon so be careful about marking the middle of a rope (Beal manufacture a marking ink).
- Alcohol, petrol and other hydrocarbon solvents do not affect nylon chemically and a little petrol is not a disaster. Oil/diesel, however, attracts dirt and bleach damages (oxidizes) the nylon.
- A study by the German Alpine Club showed that urine is bad for rope.
- Keep the rope off concrete floors until they are fully cured, which can take years, as these contain corrosive chemicals.

---

not use top-loading washing machines as the rope may force the lid off. Use pure soap flakes or Beal rope cleaner as laundry detergents strip the oils from the fibres. Rinse out any residual detergent from the washing machine beforehand. Add softener to the wash cycle in hard water areas where the chalk may crystallize out, causing the rope to stiffen.

Salt crystals can stiffen the rope, therefore when working in the sea air, regularly dip the ropes in a barrel of clean water and occasionally pull them through a 'Dobi washer' (a tube with bristles inside). Wet ropes should not be left in rope bags, but dried in a cool room and (not in a drying room or airing cupboard).

Inspect your ropes regularly. Damage can be felt by running the whole length of the rope through the hands with slight pressure. Any soft or hard areas are a sign of damage.

Kink-Free Ropes

All ropes are made kink-free. However, kinks are introduced when the rope is pulled over any diagonal feature, such as any belay device that is not truly symmetrical, passage through a figure of eight, climbing across an arête and by certain coiling methods. It is best to avoid abseiling on a new climbing rope until the sheath and core have been allowed to settle into each other by normal climbing. Kinks can be removed by running the entire length through the hands several times, or by hanging the rope down a cliff and allowing the kinks to twist out. An alternative method is to 'daisy chain' it (*see* page 192, Coiling Ropes). To reduce kinks it is important that the initial uncoiling of the rope is the exact reversal of the manufacturer's coiling. The easiest way to do this is to insert your hands through opposite sides of the rope coils and uncoil it by tipping the rope hand over hand.

Accessory Cord

Accessory cords are 2–9mm diameter brightly coloured ropes on reel. They are useful for prusiking, slinging hexentrics and wedges, replacing fixed slings and so on. They are mostly low stretch and under no circumstances should you use 9mm off a reel for climbing purposes. If you come across any tape on accessory cord, examine it carefully because it may be the point where two ends of rope have been joined for the purpose of putting it onto the reel.

Dyneema is used for accessory cord and most commercially available nuts are threaded with it. Dyneema is polyethylene (same material as used for plastic bags) and was first made by a Dutch company that licensed its manufacture to an American company, which call it Spectra. Weight for weight it is much stronger than nylon and therefore smaller diameter cord can be used. It is, however, slippery and manufacturers recommend a triple fisherman's knot. Do not use 5.5mm Dyneema accessory cord for prusiks because of its low melting point. There is also a hybrid cord called Gemini, which is a mixture of Spectra and Kevlar (carbon fibres). Kevlar is very strong but it has minimal extension under load, therefore its shock-absorption qualities are low compared to nylon and it is suitable only for low-stretch loading. Also, repeated bending can weaken it.

WEBBING (TAPES) AND ROPE SLINGS

Webbing/tape was originally used to batten down gear on boats during World War II, and

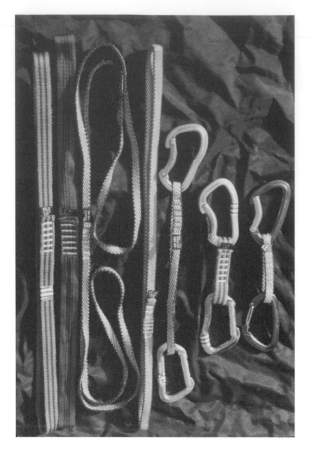

A variety of slings from DMM and Wild Country.

has since become an essential part of any climber's kit to create slings of varying length. Slings are used in many ways: for prusiking, running belays, linking anchors and so on. Tape comes in flat or tubular construction. Tubular tape is supple but flat tapes are tougher and more durable, plus they fit through thinner gaps.

A large number of parameters, such as the yarn, twist, number of warp yarns, picks per cm and so on, have to be balanced to produce slings that are lightweight, abrasion-resistant, supple, knotable and able it to cope with the large forces applied in a climbing fall.

Webbing can be knotted or sewn to create a sling. Knotted slings have the advantage of being cheaper and they can be untied and used as threads. However, they can come undone, especially in the heavier, stiffer tapes, with deadly results. Although knotted slings can have advantages, sewn slings are neater, stronger and do not come undone. Knotted slings are not CE-approved.

Slings made from accessory cord can be used in the same way as tape slings. They are less susceptible to being cut, although they can roll off rounded spikes or boulders, but they are not as thin and are therefore difficult to get behind tight flakes. For emergency threads to escape or provide protection carry one loosely knotted 7mm cord.

Spectra versus Nylon

Slings are made from nylon or Dyneema – each has its pros and cons. Amazingly, webbing slings made from Dyneema are, weight for weight, ten times the strength of steel and they can therefore be manufactured thinner than nylon slings of equivalent breaking strain. They are therefore lightweight, durable (800 per cent more abrasion-resistant than nylon), have high cut resistance, are extremely strong and have low water absorption, therefore retaining full strength when wet. The disadvantages are that they are slippery and have a low melting point (145°C). Dyneema slings should not be used where a heat build-up is possible, for example in fixed slings used for abseiling and prusiks. Dyneema tape is not available on spools because it does not hold knots well, so do not cut and retie stitched Dyneema slings. It is not possible to dye Dyneema and so coloured nylon is woven into the sling to make it more attractive.

Nylon slings have better energy absorption properties than Dyneema slings. Nylon's melting point is higher at 250°C, but it is more susceptible to attack by acid and when wet its strength is reduced by 10–20 per cent.

Sling Types

There are a variety of sling types: extenders (round slings), quick draws, dog bones, shock slings, snake slings and daisy chains. Slings can be made in any length, but the standard 'single' sling is 120cm and the 'double' sling 240cm. The width of slings varies from 12mm to 26mm.

Extenders
Extenders come in a variety of lengths and widths. Keep the diameter of slings small when using lightweight krabs so that the load is placed over the back bar and not the gate.

Quick Draws/Dog Bones
These slings have the central portion stitched to create one (dog bone) or two (quick draw) loops. This keeps the krabs in the correct orientation for clipping, although it becomes more difficult to turn the krab around. Quick draws can be made from extenders by using short extenders and rubber bands placed at one or both ends to hold the krab in place.

Shock Slings
Shock slings are designed to rupture stitching in a controlled manner. They supposedly reduce the IF and could be useful on marginal gear where the consequence of failure is serious. Their usefulness is limited to short falls of about 16ft (5m) and a fall factor 0.5. An equivalent amount of energy would be saved if a climber reverses about 1m before falling off, thereby reducing the fall factor. Another alternative is for the belayer to pay out a little rope as the climber falls off (*see* page 107).

Snake Slings
These slings are called rabbit runners in the USA. They consist of a single strand of webbing with a stitched loop at either end. They are used for threading or for extending on big roofs. They are easy to take off the body during a climb and do save weight. They are not made by any European manufacturer as there is no CE standard for the product.

Daisy Chains
Known as chicken slings in the USA). These slings consist of a loop of webbing sewn into lots of small loops along its length, to facilitate clipping a krab at any point. They are very useful as a 'cow's tail' and for aid climbing. Be careful not to clip into two of the loops because the krab is not then attached to the sling if the stitching breaks.

Care of Slings and Life Span

The care of slings is the same as for ropes, but inspect the stitched area. If it is furry with thread ends protruding, retire the sling (furring itself is not a problem). Discard slings with nicks, however small. Throw away any that have been found, as their history is unknown. Unlike ropes, where the major component of their strength is the core, tapes can be seriously degraded by UV and therefore any *in situ* tape should be viewed with suspicion. Lyon Equipment gives five years as the conservative estimate for the lifespan of textile equipment, but this can be reduced by wear and tear.

FOOTWEAR

The early pioneers wore boots with the soles covered in nails, bearing exotic names like Tricouni, clinker and mugger. Clinkers and muggers were soft and moulded to the rock, but the famous Tricounis were hard and moulded the rock to them, causing severe erosion of soft footholds, as anyone who has climbed on the Milestone Buttress in North Wales can testify. They were supposedly great on wet rock but weighed 2.25kg.

Climbers used nailed boots until the 1930s, although Colin Kirkus did make a quantum leap and placed broad rubber bands around his plimsoles in the 1930s. In 1939 a new rubber was invented by the Italian mountaineer and indus-

trialist Vitale Bramani, hence the name 'Vibram'. Initially these boots were designed for the Italian military but soon became popular with the British Army when it was realized how quiet they were to walk in. During the 1950s some climbers started using a boot with a suede upper and a lightweight cleated sole called the *Kletterscuhe* or Kletts, which were imported from Austria. Similar boots with rope or string soles called Scarpetti in Italy and Espadrilles in France were also used.

The earliest boots that would be recognized as rock boots by today's climbers were developed jointly by Pierre Allain (PA) and Emil Bordenaulin (EB) in the 1940s. By the mid-1960s the choice had been increased with RDs by René Desmaison and Hawkins Masters, but by 1979 the EB had become the most popular rock boot in the world. The development, in France and Spain, of new rubber compounds that offered superior friction led to a new generation of boots, and the boot of the early 1980s was undoubtedly the Boreal 'Fire' named after a stunning rock spire in the Riglos climbing area of northern Spain. Its domination was short-lived, however, and by 1984 La Sportiva, Calma and then Five Ten made their own versions of sticky rubber. Today, climbers have a choice of more comfortable, more colourful and lighter rock boots.

Choosing a Rock Climbing Shoe

Climbers rarely fail on routes because they have the wrong make of shoes on their feet. The average climber adapts their climbing to the characteristics of whatever footwear they have and the most important factor in performance of a rock shoe is that it fits the foot.

A balance has to be struck between stiffness, which provides edging ability, and flexibility, which provides smearing, and there are shoes for every type of rock from limestone to grit to granite cracks. In reality, climbers have different styles of climbing and there are few climbs in the UK that use just edges or smears, so one general boot will often do the job. However, if money is not an issue and you climb a variety of rock types a few pairs may give you the best option for the rock type.

Climbers have traditionally worn boots by forcing the foot to fit the boot, but modern climbing shoes like '5.10' are constructed on anatomically correct lasts (the frame that the

A variety of top rock boots from 5.10.

shoe is built on) that are contoured to fit a foot, thus eliminating painful undersized boots. There are two basic lasts – traditional, which is modelled on a relaxed foot, and cambered, which creates shoes that are more curved to concentrate the weight onto the big toe. The latter is not as comfortable for all day use, but it does provide a more precise feel on the rock. However, the comfort and fit of a rock shoe ultimately depends on the shape of the foot and whether the big toe or the middle toe is the longest.

Boots protect the ankle in cracks, but shoes provide more ankle flexibility and are lighter. Beginners tend to scrabble with their feet, quickly destroying lightweight slippers, therefore an all-round shoe is probably their best choice.

Unless you are performing at the highest standards, the friction differences between boots can largely be ignored. Most climbing soles are not made from rubber at all, but thermodynamic rubber (TDR), a petroleum-based synthetic. Surprisingly, climbing rubber performs best in every way when cold, so don't heat them up before climbing.

Care of Rock Footwear

It is pointless paying the earth for sticky rubber only to start climbing with mud all over the bottom, so take the time to clean them prior to climbing. Look after them – stuffing them in a rucksack can deform them, especially if left in there for weeks. Remove any salt water that can rot the stitching and corrode eyelets. If they get wet, stuff them with paper and allow them to dry slowly away from direct heat, but do not leave them in direct sunlight as the sole may come away.

With the exception of 5.10 'Stealth' rubber, TDR oxidizes and the surface of the sole hardens. If they have been left for months without use they can be rejuvenated using a wire brush and wiping with alcohol.

Rock boots can be re-soled and the rand (rubber around the outside of the shoe) replaced (see the Appendix for addresses), and they can also be made stiffer or softer. Rock shoes should be repaired before the rand requires repair, but be aware that re-randing often changes their shape. If this does happen they may reform to the foot; if they do not they can always be returned to be redone.

Alternative Footwear

It is unrealistic either to expect outdoor activity providers to have a ready supply of rock shoes, or for first-timers to invest in expensive rock boots. However, for anything more than taster sessions you are doing a disservice to your students if they do not use rock shoes.

While walking boots are a sturdy alternative to rock boots and protect delicate feet, they are heavy, cumbersome and require a lot of skill to use. Old training shoes, preferably cheap plimsoles, are better, but wear extra socks to make them fit snugly. Emphasize *old* trainers, because you may not be popular with parents if expensive trainers are ruined. The downside of training shoes is the pronounced lip that protrudes and bends over when used on small holds. Nevertheless, the lightness and extra sensitivity that trainers provide far outweigh the cons, plus trainers have less impact on the environment than walking boots.

Advice for Fitting Rock Boots

- Warm them for 5 minutes to allow the foot to adapt, preferably without socks, to give more sensitivity.
- If a boot is still uncomfortable after four weekends, it is too small.
- Undo the lacing all the way down so that the foot can reach the front easily and centre the tongue when the foot is in place.
- Do not flex the shoe from toe to heel, as this will damage it. Instead, put the foot into a well-tightened boot, place it on a hold and flex the ball of the foot backward. It should give with little resistance, like a good running shoe, without the foot moving around.
- A well-fitting shoe should be able to stand on a small edge without too much strain in the foot and without the shoe deforming.
- Buy the smallest size that will accept the foot without doubling up the toes or the arch, will not allow it to rotate and will not allow any heel lift.
- Shoes stretch more widthways than they do in length and unlined shoes stretch more than lined ones. Seriously tight shoes will only stretch more.
- They can be stretched by putting them on, then immersing in water and wearing them for a few hours. They can also be shrunk in hot water.

Some of the clothing worn by the UK's climbers in the 1980s.

CLOTHING

Today's rock climber more closely resembles a gymnast than the bearded, tweed-clad climber of yesteryear, and instructors should have a good knowledge of specialist clothing to give advice to students who want to buy their own gear, for example, do they really need Gortex? There is not the space in this book to discuss all the fabrics and designs available, but companies like Lowe and Stone Monkey provide a wide variety of well-designed technical clothing for the outdoor enthusiast and instructor.

Avoid giving general advice to students, such as 'wear warm clothing'. The best clothing systems are based on layering, as this allows the student to put on more when they feeling cold and remove it when necessary, or to cover up if the sun is at a burning temperature. Synthetic fabrics dry more quickly and maintain a degree of warmth when wet. Advise students to avoid shell suits (which tear easily), tight-fitting trousers and baggy tops. Wearing a belt can interfere with the harness. Extra gear should be considered necessary if venturing to climb in the hills, including woollen hats and gloves for cold days. A waterproof jacket should be carried even on sunny days, as it can double as a windproof. Shorts are acceptable, but novices are likely to go home with bruises and scratches and some harnesses are not comfortable with shorts. Instructors should carry spare clothing such as a fleece, lots of gloves and bobble hats, even on relatively warm days.

HELMETS

There is no doubt that wearing a helmet reduces the chances of head injury, especially on lower grade routes, where a fall is more likely to end up on a ledge. Rock climbers have readily embraced all new methods of making themselves safer with the exception of the helmet.

As an instructor you have little choice, there are few instances where you can avoid wearing a helmet. With the advent of the new lightweight helmets e.g. Petzl Meteor there is no excuse for not wearing a helmet all the time. Only an inexperienced climber would ask about wearing a helmet, so the answer would be 'yes wear one' until they are able to make the decision for themselves.

Some Facts about Head Injuries

- A stone falling free reaches 100mph.
- A 5kg stone falling 2m produces an impact force of 1,800KN.
- The human skull is only capable of withstanding 1,000KN without injury.
- The impact of even a small pebble is enough to cause serious injury to a climber not wearing a helmet.
- Recent evidence suggests that even minor blows to the head can cause significant injury.
- Once brain tissue is injured there is little that modern medicine can do.

However a helmet is not always necessary. When instructing on a climbing wall, novices can wear one on the first session or two because they are often nervous, not used to falling and often swing around banging themselves but in subsequent sessions, as long as the students are confident about falling off they can climb without helmets.

Design and Fitting of Helmets

Broadly, helmets work in two ways. The first type has a harness that holds the shell away from the head and the other uses a foam lining that fits directly against the skull. When a rock smashes onto either type the shell dampens the initial impact by bending or delaminating. Beyond that either the cradle absorbs the remaining energy or the foam lining shatters to absorb the impact.

Helmets are designed primarily for protection from falling rock with the result that most are of limited use in a fall when a blow to the side of the head is likely.

They are manufactured from a number of materials. Those made of fibreglass are sometimes heavy, uncomfortable and cumbersome and if they are lightweight they do not survive continued abuse by novices. The lighter plastic helmets, made of fibre reinforced thermoplastics, are preferable for all day wear by younger students who have weaker neck muscles. Children are more willing to keep them on their heads as they are also less sweaty and more stylish. Avoid dark, heat absorbing, colours although ventilation is far more important than colour in cooling the head. If money is not a problem and you want lightweight consider buying carbon fibre/kevlar helmets because they provide the greatest absorption of force for a given weight.

A loose fitting helmet is as good as no helmet at all and an outdoor centre may have to buy a variety of makes for over large and extra small heads. To fit correctly the helmet should not flop over the eyes or expose the front of the skull to a falling rock. Considerable time can be saved by using harness based helmets which are the easiest to adjust. Those with foam linings are generally the most difficult to adjust with the exception of the Petzl Meteor.

When advising a student what to buy for themselves get them to consider whether they are likely to wear a balaclava, water proof hood, a head torch or glasses and to wear a rucsack when trying them on.

Life-Span of a Helmet

Most manufacturers give the life-span of their 'plastic' helmets as five years and glass reinforced fibre helmets much longer. This does seem a conservative estimate but it is difficult to assess a well looked after climbing helmet's ability to absorb forces by visual inspection.

HARNESSES

Climbing pioneers simply tied the rope around their waists and set off up the crag, adopting the philosophy that the leader never falls. The swami belt that followed offered little more either in comfort or protection as it was simply a 1 or 2in tape wrapped round the waist a few times.

Purpose-built waist belts appeared during the 1960s and the development of leg loops in the 1970s gave us the sit harness. Continental climbers had been using chest harnesses for years, primarily for crevasse rescue, and when someone combined the two the full body harness was born.

Modern sit harnesses are featherweight, comfortable and stronger than necessary. There are models for sport, traditional, winter/alpine climbing and dedicated outdoor centre use. A broad division is made by virtue of their buckling system. There are those that rely on their

---

Sit versus Full Body Harness

In the face of medical evidence showing the importance of an injured climber remaining in a semi-upright position the UIAA have refused to recognize the sit harness. The UIAA standard only allows the use of full body harness or a combination of chest and sit harness. However, they hinder the ability to rotate and pivot during a fall which limits the chance of having the feet and legs impact first, thereby absorbing some of the force. Petzi have also shown that a full body harness whips the climber back upright very quickly.

It is generally considered that sit harnesses are adequate for rock climbing, but full harnesses are useful for pregnant women (reduced pressure on the stomach), and aid climbing, jumaring and large or small students without a pronounced hip.

The modern Petzl Meteor is a delight to wear.
Climber: Gareth Richardson.

and rely on a swami-like tie at the front. The latter are in theory safer, but they are more time-consuming to put on and have not become popular.

During 1995 the BMC reported concern over slippage of a harness's webbing through the buckle. For this to occur, the buckle must be held at an angle of 90 degrees long enough for the webbing to slide out. It is very difficult to recreate these conditions. Nonetheless, it has happened, so leave at least 4in (10cm) of tape sticking out of the buckle and check it frequently.

Lifespan and Care of Harnesses

Check to see if the tie-in loops, buckles and sewn joints are cut, worn or abraded. Common sense will tell you if the harness needs replacing. Treat harnesses in the same way as a rope and do not throw them to the bottom of rucksacks unless they are in a bag.

The UIAA states that 'all harnesses should be discarded after serious falls, i.e. fall factor 1 with a UIAA dynamic rope' and recent recommendations from manufacturers have suggested that harnesses be changed as frequently as a rope. Petzl recommend a shelf life of five years.

buckle for safety when tied into the rope, and those that do not require the buckle to be fastened for the harness to be safe. There are also a few harnesses that do not have a buckle

---

Choosing a Harness for Personal Use

- It should be easy to put on with no unnecessary buckles, joints or pressure points (Women's harnesses have a different size relationship between leg loops and waist belt and are longer between the crutch and the waist belt.)
- The force of a fall is taken predominantly by the leg loops, with the waist belt performing a stabilizing function. Choose one, with broad leg loops and a padded belt.
- Put it on and do a few leg bends; if the leg loops bind to the thighs, the harness is too tight, and if they droop it is too loose. There is a real danger of a testicle being trapped in an overlarge leg loop.
- Hang in it to see how it feels. The attachment point should be at least as high as the waist to avoid tipping backwards.
- Arguably, the most comfortable harness for rock climbing does not have adjustable leg loops, but has the leg loops and waist belt linked by an abseil/belay loop. If there is no abseil loop, consider linking them with a semicircular Maillon Rapide instead of a screw-gate krab.

- To test the racking take your arms in the air and try to take gear. Is it in the correct position? Most harnesses are racked for right-handed climbers, so if you are left-handed consider buying one with an adjustable racking location. Sports climbing harnesses generally have fewer gear loops. Climbers with short legs may prefer the gear loops hung from the top of the harness to prevent the gear clanking into the knees. Gear loops close to the front allow the selection of the correct gear as it can be seen and reached more easily.
- Velcro tabs or plastic grippers allow fast access to a single piece of gear, but they do increase the chance of gear falling down the cliff.
- Aid climbing may require a 'haul' loop on the back. These loops are not designed to take the forces generated in a fall.
- Releaseable bum straps allow the wearer to go to the toilet.
- Before buying the latest lightweight krabs to save a few grams, weigh the harness and change that instead.

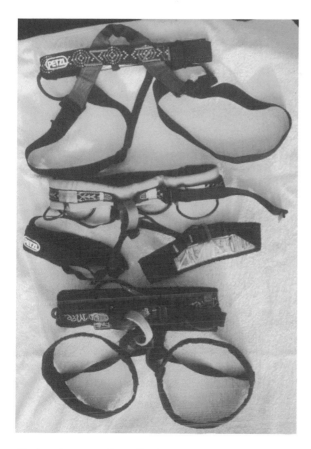

Modern harnesses from Petzl.

breaking strain of 1,800kg. The aluminium krab came later, being invented simultaneously by Pierre Allain in France and Bedain in California. Today's aluminium krabs weigh around 43gm and have a breaking strain of circa 2,000–2,500kg.

Most are now made of aluminium alloys and a few of steel. Aluminium's biggest drawback is its softness, which means that krabs can be damaged when clipped through steel bolt hangers and pegs. Steel krabs are heavy and expensive. They are too heavy for normal use but handy when krabs are going to take a lot of wear and tear, such as bottom-roping and on the first bolt of a sport climb.

Krabs come in different sizes determined by the diameter, for example 9mm (no longer manufactured as they do not achieve CE 7 KN breaking strain with the gate open), 10mm, 11mm or 12mm. In cross-section they can be oval, round, T-shaped or a variation on these.

Interesting Fact

Weight for weight krabs are amazingly strong – scaled down to 1gm they would hold a climber's body; scaled up to 1lb they would hold over 25 tons.

KARABINERS

Karabiners attach the climber to the rope and other parts of the climbing 'safety chain'. They were called Snaplinks in the early days, Mousquetons in France and Biners in the USA. Climbers in the UK have settled on the term 'krabs' from the German karabiner.

Steel krabs were invented in Austria circa 1910; they weighed up to 240gm with a

The load-bearing portion of a krab is the back bar and they are only effective with the gate closed. Their strength across the minor axis is considerably lower and with the gate open, a krab must have a minimum breaking strain of 7KN. Krabs are arranged on quick draws with the gate opening facing down and in a different direction to the krab at the other end of the quick draw. This apparently keeps the load over the back bar and make it easier to clip the climbing rope into the krab.

Open-Gate Karabiners

There are four main shapes of open-gate krabs:

- **Oval krabs:** These are best suited to aid climbing because their shape holds more gear in an orderly fashion, especially pegs, and they do not shift around in pegs when aiding. On the downside, they are heavier and weaker.

2000 UIAA Standards for Karabiners

- The portion where the rope runs must have a radius of at least 4.5mm.
- Minimum 15mm gate opening.
- Can accommodate two 12mm ropes without interfering with the gate mechanism.
- It must withstand forces of 22KN and not deform at 14KN.

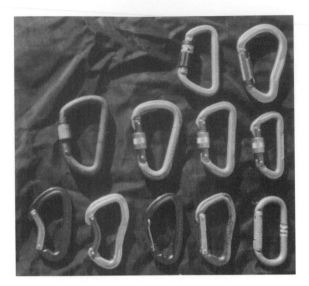

A variety of open gate and locking krabs.

- **D shaped krabs:** These concentrate the load along the back bar and less on the weaker gate area. They are fine for the top krabs on quick draws – the one that clips into protection – and general use, but they are heavier and typically have less gate open space than Asymmetrical Ds.
- **Asymmetrical D krabs:** These are narrower at one end and bring the forces closer to the back bar. They are the most popular choice for the krabs on quick draws.
- **HMS krabs:** The HMS stands for *Halb Mastwurf Sicherung* or half-securing knot, that is Italian hitch. They are large, pear-shaped locking krabs that were originally designed for use with the Italian hitch belay. The *klettersteig* is a large asymmetrical D krab, sometimes confused with the HMS, but this does not work as well with an Italian hitch.

Gates

The gates on krabs can be straight, bent or wire. Straight gates are applicable to any climbing situation, while bent gates make clipping the rope easier but conversely make unclipping the rope harder, particularly when the krab is not free to rotate, such as when clipped directly into a bolt.

There is the chance that the gate can be opened during a fall because the krab vibrates when a rope slides over it or when it is knocked against the rock in a fall. This is especially likely with those krabs that have a weak spring, for ease of opening. A krab with an open gate is often 50 per cent weaker than when closed and can therefore fail completely. Wire gates help to overcome this problem because their lower mass resists opening due to whiplash. They are also ideal for winter climbing because the gate does not freeze up.

Most gates stay closed because they have a notch and rivet to act as a stop, grabbing the gate under load. At somewhere around 20KN the body of the krab stretches to engage the notch, at which point the krab cannot be opened. Most krabs can be opened under body weight loading which is important for aid climbing. There is one other unique gate system, the 'key-lock' mechanism which has no notch. This has advantages in that there is no rivet to fail and nothing to snag on wires and slings, but it does have the drawback that if the krab is used for storing wires care has to be taken that the wires do not all come off when one is removed.

Locking Karabiners

A locking krab must be used for ropework where failure of a single krab is catastrophic (see Chapter 6). Locking krabs are mostly large so a number of ropes can be clipped into them. They come in D-shape, offset-D or Pear-shape (HMS). There are many types of locking devices: screw-gate, auto twist locks and spring-loaded twist locks.

Screw-gates are the most trouble-free and can be operated easily with gloves. However, the gate can unscrew when vibrated and conversely can lock up so tight that it cannot be undone. Ideally there should be ample space for lots of ropes or slings.

Autolocking krabs have a spring mechanism to lock the gate automatically, but conversely some designs can unlock themselves when a rope passes over them. To overcome this some have a mechanism that locks the gate after it has closed automatically, for example, the Petzl ball lock.

Autolocking krabs also have the disadvantage that they are difficult to use with mitts or thick gloves.

The Maillon rapide is not made for climbing but is very popular with cavers. These are available in stainless steel and galvanized versions. They are found on many sports climbs and

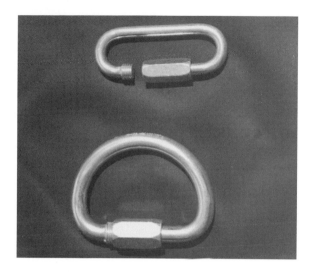

Mallion rapides.

semi-circular ones are sometimes used instead of screw-gate krabs for linking the leg loops and waist belts of harnesses together. They are extremely strong and offer a less expensive alternative to steel krabs for permanent lower offs. Beware that there are non-CE approved ones available for linking fencing and so on – these have not been tested for climbing use.

Two useful innovations are a plastic sleeve called the Belay Master created by DMM that clips to a screw-gate krab to prevent accidental opening of the gate and keeps the krab positioned correctly on the harness when belaying, and a locking krab called the 'Link' (Troll equipment) for rope to harness attachment. In the latter, the lower end of the krab is rectangular so the abseil loop sits correctly and there is a semi-permanent pin, which can be driven across this to lock the krab and the abseil loop. The pin is tapped into place with a hammer and removed with a pair of pliers. It does eliminate the chance of the harness loop putting a three-way load on the krabs. The pin can be fitted in seconds and also eliminates krab loss.

Lifespan and Care of Karabiners

Black Diamond stated in *Climbing* magazine that 'if stored in a dry environment (salt water speeds up the oxidation process on aluminium) a krab could last 100 years', but also said 'There is no way to know whether dropped hardware is safe without doing expensive analysis'. The CE recommend a 10-year life. Usage of old krabs

must depend on careful inspection and knowledge of its working life. The safe ethic to employ if in any doubt is replacement. If you do decide to retain a krab, for example for cleaning krabs on aid pitches, mark it clearly.

Aluminium is particularly prone to oxidization (corrosion), which leaves a white powdery dust. Instructors who are active on sea cliffs should take special care to rinse their gear frequently in fresh water. Sticking gates can be cleaned in kerosene, wiped dry and then sprayed with silicone spray. Wild Country recommends WD-40, but use this sparingly as it attracts dirt. To release a stuck screw-gate try undoing it under a load or in desperation use a pair of pliers. If it is stuck due to salt water, soak it in hot water and spray with WD-40.

BELAY AND ABSEILING DEVICES

At the turn of the century climbers brought up their second by passing the rope around a spike of rock or boulder. Termed 'direct belaying', this was more comfortable than the indirect methods of waist and shoulder belays. The first mechanical belay device was the Sticht plate (pronounced shtisht) designed in 1968 by Fritz Sticht who wanted to climb with his 6-year old daughter but realized that a waist belay would be pointless. The early Sticht plates were simple slots in a piece of metal; since then, many other belay devices have arrived on the market, all working along similar principles.

There are also locking devices that use a 'camming' action to jam the rope and some devices that use a combination of braking methods. All the belay devices discussed can be used for abseiling, apart from the Yates Belay Slave and the Petzl Stop (not a belaying device), although they all kink the rope to differing degrees.

Belay tubes and plates are divided into those that grab the rope and those that have a smooth action (there is no CE test for belay devices and all the frictional differences are subject to my anecdotal evidence rather than hard facts). Those that grab stop the rope more quickly, but do make paying out the rope more difficult, while those with a smooth action allow the rope to move easily but require greater vigilance to hold a fall. With any belay device the braking ability is affected by the diameter and state of the rope being used.

All belay/abseil devices have a smoother action when used with a round-bar HMS screwgate krab, the wide end closest to the device. An HMS krab allows the ropes to sit equally over each slot and makes belaying with half-ropes easier. Attach all belay devices to a short length of cord (some come supplied with a thin cable in place) to prevent the belay device travelling along the rope.

Purpose Built Abseiling Devices

The figure-of-eight descender is the device most frequently used for abseiling. However, it puts one twist in the rope for every 3m abseiled because most climbers abseil with the rope positioned down one side of the body. Keeping the brake hand directly below the figure-of-eight with the rope between the legs does reduce the twisting effect. The figure-of-eight has advantages when taking young people abseiling because it is one of the cheapest, smoothest, most controllable and durable abseil devices, with no parts to break or jam. However, because of its twisting effect on ropes consider another device for multiple double-rope abseils. Figure-of-eight descenders have a tensile strength of approximately 40KN, but when worn to half their original thickness they should be replaced immediately.

The Petzl Stop is an autolocking single rope descender that does not twist the rope. Squeeze the red handle to descend – the harder it is squeezed the faster your descent. Let go of the handle during the descent and you stop. The speed of descent is regulated (as with all descenders) by the braking action of the dead or tail rope, the handle is for back-up safety only. A krab clipped through its frame jams the autolock and allows it to be used as a conventional abseil device. It can be loaded without removing it from the harness, reducing the chance of dropping it. Those who spend a long time abseiling may find it useful. Its disadvantage is that it can only be used with single ropes and is useless for belaying.

Belay Plates

Belay plates are divided into those with a spring and those without. The spring provides a smoother action and prevents the plate jamming against the krab. This makes it easier to 'lock off' one rope and pay out the other when using

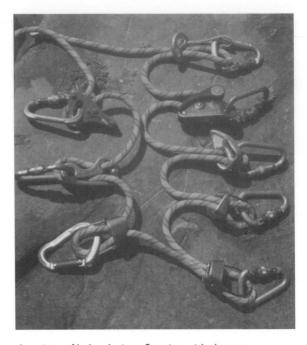

A variety of belay devices. Starting with the top right in a clockwise direction: Salewa Sticht plate, Petzl Gri Gri, Wild Country Raptor, Wild country Vario controller, Black Diamond Air Traffic Controller (ATC), Salewa Tubus, Wild Country Single rope Controller.

half-ropes. However, the spring can become tangled in other equipment that is hanging from the harness and sport climbers have reported that the spring forces the belayer to use more energy when holding a climber in tension after a fall. However, they are still popular because they are a good compromise between the more grabbing plates and the slicker tubes.

Belay plates can be used for abseiling, although this generates heat and on longer abseils a sudden stop could conceivably damage the rope sheath. The virtual indestructibility and durability of plates are plus points, as is the fact that it is difficult to load them wrongly. The grabbing nature of plates is disconcerting to a beginner when paying out the rope but it does make it easier for them to hold a fall.

Belay Tubes

The first tube-like device was The Tuber, designed by Jeff Lowe in 1988. It offers two friction opportunities depending which way it is used: the advised method is to have the wide end against the krab for belaying and the narrow end for abseiling. In practice, there is not a lot of difference when a HMS krab is used to avoid jamming. The larger mass and the fins dissipate heat, although the latter are mostly a marketing ploy. The internal bar can wear and earlier models produced sharp edge so examine them carefully before and after use.

Many other variations have appeared since the Tuber, with the main difference being their wider aperture. They all provide sufficient locking to stop a fall while also allowing one of the ropes to be pulled through when the krab is flush against the device. These features are useful when using furred-up ropes on climbing walls and belaying with double ropes. Tubes do not grab the rope like belay plates nor do they kink the rope as much, but be aware that when used with smaller diameter ropes continuous vigilence is required to hold a significant leader fall. Abseiling is also harder work.

The Salewa Tubus has two grooves that add friction in the braking mode and when abseiling, but these do not affect the belaying action. The DMM Bug has thicker walls to dissipate heat and slightly smaller holes than the others. The Variable Controller is a wedge-shaped twin slotted, tube-like device that offers two friction options. The Raptor (not manufactured anymore) is probably the most unusual tube-like device. Loading of the live rope causes an HMS krab to slide along a slot, trapping the rope (it is not an autolocking device).

Autolocking Belay Devices

The Petzl Gri Gri has a cam like a seat belt on a car which pinches the rope when loaded, stopping it immediately. The benefits are three-fold: it takes no strength to hold a fall; the Gri Gri stops falls automatically; and it does not twist the ropes. It has become standard equipment for some sports climbers, but because it stops a falling climber without any assistance the temptation is for the belayer to pay less attention to the climber.

However correctly the device is used, the Gri Gri is not recommended for adventure climbing and hard aid climbing because it stops the rope without any dynamic element, thereby transferring all the force generated to the runners, climber, belay anchors and belayer. Because there is no dynamic element there is also more chance of the belayer being lifted up in the air. It is the heaviest and bulkiest of the belay devices,

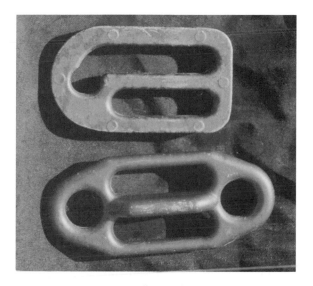

A New Alp Magic plate and a Gi Gi.

does not work on icy ropes and cannot be used with double ropes.

The most useful autolocking devices for an instructor/guide are the New Alp Plaquette 'Magic Plate', the Gi Gi and the multi-functional Petzl Reverso. The first two resemble a stretched belay plate. They can be used for belaying a leader or second and for abseiling, but come into their own when used as a belay plate (on a direct belay) for bringing up two seconds simultaneously. When the climber falls, the krab that is clipped through the ropes jams against the plate, stopping the rope. This can make it difficult to take in when one climber's weight is on the device – the Gi Gi is easier than the magic plate. It is also difficult to lower the fallen climber unless they can get their weight off the rope (Chapter 6 shows a method for doing this). The Petzl Reverso is a belaying device that can be used for belaying the leader or second on single or double ropes. It can also be used as an autolocking device. I predict it will be standard on many instructors' harnesses.

Other Belay Devices

There are a few devices that do not fit into the previous categories. The Wild Country Single Rope Controller (SRC) consists of two slotted plates connected by three pins. It is a friction plate, but also uses the trapping action of the connecting HMS in a slot to hold a fall (it is not an autolocking device). Pulling the smaller end

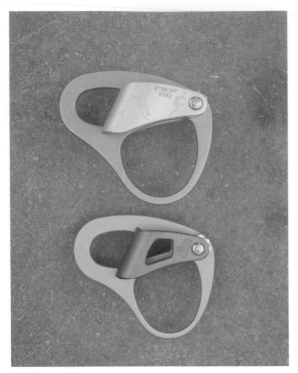

Petzl Reverso.

results in a progressive release of the rope, which can be confidence-inspiring for lowering heavier climbers and abseiling. As its name suggests, it can only be used with single ropes and for it to work correctly it should be used with a round bar HMS krab.

The Camp Yo Yo is very similar to the SRC, with the exception that it has a lock to prevent rope slippage after a fall has been held. The locking slot, however, makes the accidental locking problem worse when belaying a leader.

Which is Best?

They all stop a falling climber when used properly.

When bottom-roping on 'taster' sessions or outdoor education courses, the Italian hitch works well (see Chapter 6). On starter climbing courses where the students need to practise belaying on a bottom-rope, any device will do. The Gri Gri is the best of the self-locking devices when supervised carefully, but be careful when lowering students because the device either grips the rope or it doesn't. The SRC is a good alternative for bottom-roping.

As soon as novices start to belay a leader the choice becomes more crucial. All un-sprung plates tend to grab at the rope in a novice's hands. The Salewa Tubus, with its grooves, is my favourite, although the Variable Controller is also good. The ATC and Bug are slicker and best used with more experienced belayers.

For guiding two students the Petzl Reverso is best but the Gi Gi and Magic Plate also do a good job. By the time students are being introduced to double rope technique they should be sufficiently competent to use any of the devices.

PEGS AND BOLTS

No subject is likely to wind up a gathering of climbers more than the subject of bolts and fixed gear. This is the technical side of the argument.

Pegs

The first pegs were placed in 1909 by Pierre Blanc and Charles Mead on the Campanile Basso in the Dolomites. They were used even before the invention of the Krab. The rope was attached to the piton with short lengths of string or passed directly through the ring. All pegs were made of iron until after World War II, they were soft and malleable and once driven in they were permanent fixtures. The catalyst for the invention of hard steel pegs was the ascent of long routes in America. In 1947 John Salathe forged the classic hard steel 'Lost Arrow Piton' from the axle of a Model-T Ford. This was a major breakthrough, changing the face of big wall climbing because it allowed pegs to be reused and therefore less had to be carried. Most modern pegs are made from 'hard' chrome-molybdenum steel as this provides a better holding power, but soft steel pegs may still be found because they are cheaper. Titanium pegs are available from Eastern bloc countries; these do not rust but are only durable for one or two placements.

Pegs are less strong than natural elements or many artificial placements. A new, well-fitted soft steel peg only holds 5–10KN in a transverse crack and 2–5KN in a longitudinal crack. A new well-fitted hard steel piton holds 10-20–KN in a transverse crack and 5–10KN in a longitudinal crack. For information on placing pegs see Chapter 6.

The design of pegs has changed little in the last twenty years. They can be divided into two types – blades and angles.

Blades

Blades are flat sections of metal with either a welded eye attached or a bent section with a hole. They come in various lengths and widths, but the thinner blades are not CE-approved and are available for body-weight loading only. There are various types of blades:

- Lost Arrows and Kingpins fill the 4mm to 8mm size (thickness at the eye end).
- Knife blades, invented in the early fifties by the American Charles Wilts, are wafer-thin horizontal pegs tapered to a sharp flat end. Their offset eye promotes torque and holding power
- The RURP (realized ultimate reality piton) is a 2cm paper-thin rectangle of metal with a cable attached. These fit in tiny cracks and when opened up aid possibilities on big blank-looking walls.
- Birdbeaks are 2–4cm long pieces of steel with a protruding downward pointing blade at one end.
- Angles are pegs bent to form a V profile. They come in a wide variety of sizes from baby ones of 1.5 cm, through standard angles of 2cm, to massive 15cm ones called Bongs. Z pitons or Leepers fill the dimensions of large Arrows up to standard angle. The extra bend provides greater grip and surface contact than conventional angles. This is important on soft rock. They are also used for stacking pegs. Bongs are really large angles but modern nuts and friends that are easily placed in wide cracks have removed the need for them.

Placing Bolts

- The rock should be sound.
- Bolts should be placed at least 10mm away from edges on another bolt.
- The hole should be at right-angles to the rock and the correct depth. A piece of tape around the drill bit helps to keep the depth constant.
- Blow all the dust and debris from the hole using a flexible pipe and if possible a brush.

Bolts/Hangers

Bolts are not a new invention. They were in existence as far back as 1925 when Rossi and Wiessner used them to cross an overhang on the south-east face of the Fleischbank. The use of

LEFT A variety of pegs.

BELOW The perfect peg!

bolts made it possible to scale any rock regardless of how steep or blank it was. Probably the most extreme use of them came with the ascent of El Capitan in 1970 where 330 expansion bolts were placed.

A large and moral issue surrounds bolts and bolting. It is avoided by this author and what is written here does not condone the placing of them. Any instructor placing bolts, for use with students, should consider the liability issue and ask themselves whether they have the training and experience to place them, plus the ability to test and maintain them.

A bolt describes the section placed into the rock and the hanger is what the krab is clipped into. Bolts are often trusted without thought, but they can and do fail, either by breaking, pulling out or destroying the rock around it. Bolt breakage can be eliminated by using a bolt with a shear strength of at least 2,300kg and placing them correctly. In hard rock the bolt or hanger generally fails before the rock crumbles, but the failure of the rock is a real concern in medium or soft rock. Bolts broadly fall into two categories.

UIAA Strength Requirements for Bolts

- 15KN axial strength.
- 25KN radial strength.
- Hanger eye should have a radius of 2mm.

Mechanical Bolts

These are held in place by the pressing action of the bolt against the rock. When the pulling power overcomes the friction the bolt can pull out.

The main types of bolts are outlined here:

- **Nail drive bolts:** For example, Petzl Long Life. A nail is driven through the centre of the bolt, expanding the anchor at the back of the hole. These are the best bolts for hard rock. They are easy to place, tamper-proof strong and corrosion free. They are of no use in medium or soft rock.
- **Sleeve bolts:** These are the next best thing in medium to hard rock. They are tapped into a hole of the correct length and then tightened with a wrench that pulls a cone into a sleeve. There are two types – avoid the ones with external threads as they are weaker.

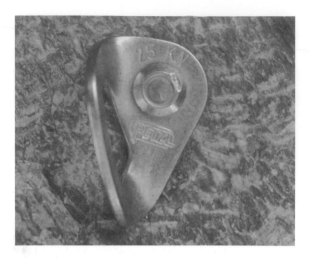

A mechanical bolt.

- **Wedge bolts:** These have a threaded shaft and nut, and use a small clip on the tip of the bolt to expand and grip the rock. They have the advantage that the hole cannot be drilled too long, they are easy to place, tap in and tighten, and they also tighten themselves when loaded. The big drawback is that there are many brands and they are of erratic quality. The strongest are Petzl and Hilti. They are not as dependable as sleeve bolts and they are difficult to remove. The threaded portion attracts and accelerates corrosion.
- **The Raw:** This used to be the best before portable power drills became available. It is easier to place on the lead, but it can shatter the rock and does stress-fracture over time. It can also rust and become unreliable. Only use these if you have big wall aspirations.
- **Drilled angle pegs:** These are dangerously weak in straight pulls, but are surprisingly strong when drilled at a slight downward angle and with the eye down. They loosen very quickly with age.
- **Bolts to avoid:** You should avoid torque bolts that require a specific torque to tighten them, drop in bolts, stud bolts and self-drill bolts where the bolt is the bit of the drill. After the hole has been drilled a cone is then placed in the bit and the drill hammered home. These can be bombproof but are often left unfinished as they are difficult to drill. The latter two were once very popular and constitute 90 per cent of dicey bolts.

A glue in bolt.

Glue-In Bolts

The only anchor for soft rock is a 'glue-in'. These use a glue which penetrates the rock, and forms a chemical coupling. With the correct glue, the bolt can be as strong as the rock, plus the glue fills any fractures; they also age better. However, undersize the hole or fail to clean the dust and they can be incredibly weak. Mechanical bolts are favoured for hard to medium rock because of the cost of 'glue-ins'. They are also difficult to place, require a power drill, and take a day to cure precluding their use on the lead. More importantly, the effect of glue-in anchors is more difficult to erase.

The glue systems come in two styles:

- **Cartridge glue:** This dispenses like tooth-paste. To use this glue, drill the hole, fill it with glue, run a bead of glue down the bolt shaft and then twist in the bolt.

- **Capsule glues:** Like cartridge glues, and capsule glues are two-part glues, activated when the components are mixed. Unlike cartridge glues, capsules encase the glue and hardener in a single glass vial which are inserted in the bolt hole like a suppository. On overhangs a piece of cloth around the end can stop it falling out. Shoving the bolt in the hole and rotating it around breaks the vial and mixes the components. There is zero waste and no dispenser. The disadvantage is that the bolt should be spun with a power drill to ensure that the glue and hardener mix. With threaded rods this is no problem, but with eye bolts like the Petzl ring the bolt needs to be turned twenty-five times, a prac-tice Hilti and Bosch warn against.

There are two choices of bolts, ½in threaded rod and eye bolts. For soft rock threaded rods are stronger as their extra length provides more contact area. In medium and hard rock either bolt suffices. Stainless steel rods are available for sea cliffs. The only bolt hanger that works with ½in threaded rods is the Petzl Coeur P38150. Others have to be drilled out to make them fit. Eye bolts allow the rope to be threaded directly through them for retreat without slings, but beware of sharp edges on the inside. Because they are made of one type of metal there is no chance of galvanic corrosion (electric currents built up between different metals). Petzl make Collinox and Ring bolts, DMM make a similar one called the Eco Anchor. Beware of cast-iron industrial bolts because they are not made to a high enough standard.

NUTS

The development of removable protection has mirrored the advances in climbing standards.

Prior to the invention of metal chocks climbers used slings, pegs or knots jammed in cracks, and before that nothing. During the 1950s climbers brought chockstones from Wales to Derbyshire because granite gripped better in gritstone cracks. The impetus for the next devel-opment came from Joe Brown who had the bright idea of jamming a large metal nut from the Snowdon railway into a crack on Cloggy. This led to all sorts of ironmongery being jammed in cracks for protection, the bicycle crank wedged in Kaisergebirge wall on Clogwyn y Grochan being a good example. The problem

Interesting Fact

Most nuts are designed with a complementary thickness to width ratio, that is the wider profile of a rock seven is the same as the narrow profile of a rock eight, but below half an inch this does not occur.

Breaking strengths of nuts

Rock	KN.
0–1¼	2
½ – ¾	4
1	7
2–10	12
On Dyneema	
7–10	12

of machine nuts was the thread inside which had to be filed down and the obvious answer was to make an artificial nut, specially designed for climbing. In the early 1960s Paul Seddon probably made the first nuts with his T-shaped Parba nuts. The first manufactured nuts were from Troll and Peck. The original Troll nut, called a spud, was merely a wedge of aluminium alloy drilled with a single hole that could be threaded. This basic idea was extended and Troll produced the first nuts made from alloy hexagon bar, with two holes drilled in it so that the bar could be used sideways or crossways.

John Brailsford designed the first nut that would not look out of place today and Clogwyn Climbing Gear took on the manufacture of the famous double tapered Moac nut. Although the impetus and ideas behind the development of alloy nuts came from Britain, manufacture soon spread to America. During the late 1960s Yvon Chouinard brought protection into the modern era with his purpose-made metal chockstones setting the stage for every imaginable shape to appear. There have been P, T, V and Z shapes; hexagonals and hexentrics, cams and cogs. Those that remain have withstood the test of time.

Care of Nuts

- Regularly inspect the wire for broken strands.
- Replace rope every few years.
- Wash if exposed to salt water.

In 1979 Mark Vallance invented the first curved wedges, known as Rocks. The theory is that most nuts are placed in cracks where the sides vary and the curved nuts offered more placement options and greater security. When placed and yanked the curved nut cams on the convex side and rotates into the best position. Those with too much curvature are prone to sticking, but may hold in places where less curved ones do not. Those without a flattening

of the curve at the top and bottom are also more prone to sticking. The rounded edges increase purchase in marginal edge-contact placements. A further innovation is the use of unequal faces to improve performance in flared cracks, most companies offer this on the narrower faces, e.g. DMM Peenuts.

Nuts fall into three categories: wedges, micro-nuts and camming nuts (for example, Wild Country Rocks and DMM Wallnuts). The difference between nuts is a matter of personal preference, as all of them work. They differ in

DMM Wallnuts and Peenuts.

degrees of hardness. Softer nuts bite better into the rock, but harder ones are more resistant to pulling through the rock. Nuts are mostly made by moulding or hot-forging rather than cutting them from bar stock, allowing them to be sculpted three-dimensionally with scoops and cut-outs. The thickness of the wires can affect performance; thicker wire is more convenient to use for those placements just out of reach but may lift out easier, whereas soft wire stays in the rock but is more difficult to place at full stretch. Rocks can also be bought on Dyneema or cord – they have the advantage that they can be placed deep into cracks and a sling attached directly to the cord to extend them, plus they do not necessarily require an extender to stop them lifting out.

Micro-nuts were introduced in the late 1970s by the Australian, Roland Pauligk, who invented the RP. In hard rock the softer micro nuts can deform and pull out, but in soft rock the brass micros have a better bite than harder nuts which can shear through. Most micro wires fail at the krab end of the wire because their narrow diameter weakens the wire; a 5 to 10 per cent increase in breaking strength was observed using a 12mm krab as opposed to a 10mm.

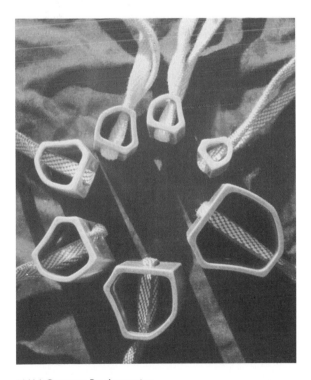

Wild Country Rockcentrics.

Camming Nuts

The original passive camming device, the Hexentric, is over twenty-five years old. It is lighter, less expensive and offers a stronger placement than moveable camming devices.

Hexentrics can be wedged along their widest facet or cammed in four different placements. Hexentrics have also sometimes been used as an emergency belay device, but although they may be strong enough they are not designed for that type of loading geometry, plus the edges may be too sharp. Wild Country has made them sexy again with the development of Rockcentrics, a hybrid of hex and rock shape. These can have a wire cable or cord attached. When adding your own accessory cord the knot can be hidden inside the larger hexes to prevent it becoming stuck in cracks.

Lowe's Tri Cams are another camming nut that often work where nothing else will, such as in small pockets. It can be used like a wedge or flipped into a camming position for parallel cracks and can be the best bet for horizontal cracks. It is, however, unstable, can fall out if not well seated and is sometimes difficult to place with one hand. The smallest sizes are most useful (see Chapter 6 for a diagram).

Sliding nuts also come into the category of camming nuts, in that they all work on similar principles: a small spring-loaded wedge slides against the larger wedge. They can be round, flat or triangular and some can be separated to form two wedges. Climb Tech has designed one that fits in ⅜in and ½in drilled holes. They are easy to use and are supposedly as strong as the rock they are placed in. The ½in model holds approximately 16KN. Climb Tech sliding nuts may become an important tool in areas where bolts are banned because of environmental impact. This does, however, miss the point that it is the drilled hole that is the problem. They are invaluable for aid climbing (see Chapter 6 for a diagram).

SPRING-LOADED CAMMING DEVICES

The first moveable camming device was invented by Greg Lowe in 1967, but it was difficult to use. In 1978 the American, Ray Jardine, designed the Friend. They are undoubtedly one of climbing's greatest inventions, allowing the protection of cracks that were once the preserve of pegs or stacked runners. Wild Country was

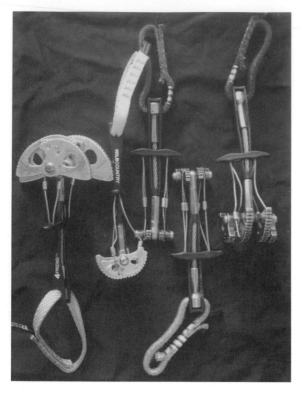

Wild Country technical Friends and Offset
Friends.

born to manufacture them, but the patent could
not cover the cam design which occurred as a
result of a mathematical formula and centred on
the trigger bar, resulting in many copies during
the 1980s with different trigger bars. There are
many variations on the basic theme and they are
collectively called Spring-Loaded Camming
Devices (SLCD) or Active Camming Devices
(ACD).

The cost of conforming to CE regulations has
decreased the variety available in Europe.
Nevertheless, there are rigid stemmed or cable,
centre cabled or U-shaped, one axle or two, fat
cams or thin cams, three cams or four, matched
or offset cams, bar triggers or rings. Does it
matter? Unfortunately it does. All the units have
pros and cons. Oddly enough, no single manufacturer (Wild Country produces the broadest
range) has cams to cover all sizes of cracks, from
fingertip size to off-width, so a mixture is
inevitable.

There are three and four cam units in the
smaller sizes, with the three cam units usually
having wider cams to provide the same surface
area. The lack of a fourth cam sacrifices some

strength and stability because only one cam is in
contact with the rock. The width differences of
the device are not important unless you are into
hard aid climbing and want to protect narrow
peg scars. The narrowest are Aliens, indispens-
able for hard, clean aid climbing.

There are three basic stem designs: rigid bar,
centre cable and a U-shaped cable. Nearly all
modern SLCDs have flexible stems. Rigid stems
are more durable, whereas flexible ones are
more useful in horizontal placements. However,
a tied-off rigid one may last longer and transmit
the load to the cams in a more predictable
manner when placed correctly. Cable stems are
narrower than rigid stems so they fit better in
cracks where the crack narrows at the entrance;
they are, however, more difficult to place but the
recent addition of a plastic/nylon frame to Wild
Country's flexible stems has improved their ease
of placement. SLCDs that have a single finger
trigger are difficult to use when climbing with
gloves or mitts but they do allow you to reach
further, which can be useful on desperate
routes. Most climbers tend to go for three cam
units for aid climbing or thin cracks and four
cams for everything else.

SLCDs are manufactured from 6061 T-6 and
7075 T-6 aluminium. The former is softer and
supposedly sticks better; the latter is harder,
stronger and longer lasting. The teeth on the
cams help to create friction with the rock by
pressing through softer layers and grabbing
irregularities in the crack. The smallest cams do
not have teeth as that would reduce the contact
area.

Black Diamond Camalots, Wild Country and
HB have stops on the cams that prevent them
opening in reverse, which is useful if the placement opens up behind, there is a chance that the
forces in a fall could open them up fully so that
they only work as a nut wedged into place.

SLCDs with small cam angles generally have
more holding power but less range of fit and visa
versa, but they are all around 13–14 degrees.
Camalots have two axles, giving a greater range
of expansion, but the downside is that they
are heavier and the range is not that different to
Friends. Wild Country have introduced Offset
Friends for aid climbing where only one side of
the cam is used. They have two small cams and
two larger cams on opposite sides. They do
work in parallel cracks as long as the correct size
is used and the small cam is not in too large a
placement. One advantage is that they are easier

to remove from cracks because only the larger cams bind and two cams are easier to release than four. They are worth considering as a second set and may be vital on some desperate routes.

SLCDs are not magic – they have to obey the laws of physics. It is therefore worth considering what happens when you fall onto one. In a perfectly smooth-sided crack, the SLCD sits in the crack held by the smallest of forces generated by the spring. When a force is applied, the cams rotate into the rock. If friction is lost they may come out; however, if friction is high enough the device will lock and transfer the forces through the cams to the rock. The total forces applied to the rock is, on average, four times that applied to the rope. In our less than perfect world, cracks are not smooth and parallel, and as the crack becomes more flared the forces generated become even greater (depending on the rock type, they can hold in flared cracks of 30 degrees). This can make it difficult to recover the device but, more importantly, it can also break the rock or snap the flake it is behind.

Care of SLCDs

Clean them regularly because the moving parts clog up easily. If they do jam, place just the head into boiling water and work the cams until they free. use detergent to get rid of oils, let the unit dry and lubricate sparingly with WD-40 oil (as recommended by Wild Country), graphite or silicone spray. Check cable cams and sewn slings for wear.

Slings can be renewed, wires can be changed and seized cams can have a new spindle. Black Diamond sells a kit for refurbishing the wires on Camalots. SLCDs with a tight plastic sleeve preventing air getting to the cable may trap water inside increasing the chance of corrosion and preventing any inspection of the cable.

ASCENDERS

An ascender is a mechanical device that clips onto the rope. The main types available in the UK are made by Jumar, Petzl, Gibbs and Wild Country. Most are left- and right-handed with the exception of Jumar's. When weight is added to one a toothed clamp grips the rope preventing it from sliding down but it can still be slid upwards. The most important component of ascenders is their teeth. Long, sharp ones grip frozen and icy ropes, although the teeth can chew up the rope. The easier the cam action of the ascender, the easier it can come unclipped from the rope. Therefore choose one with a strong cam action. An important safety feature is a hole in the ascender frame that allows the top of the ascender to be clipped around the rope, making it impossible for it to pop off the rope accidentally.

If you are doing a serious amount of ascending on fixed ropes a pair with a handle make life easier. Wild Country has produced some very light and small ascenders: the Ropeman for 10–11mm ropes and Ropeman 2, which covers the full range of ropes from 8.5–11mm. They do not have a handle which makes them less useful for long ascents, and

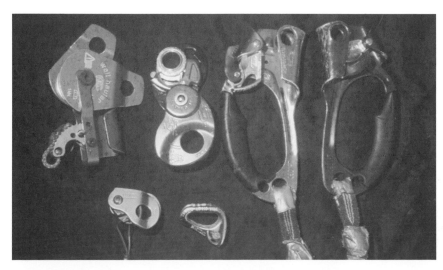

Ascending and hauling devices. Clockwise from the top left: Petzl Wall Hauler, Petzl Mini Traxion, Pair of Petzl handled ascenders, Petzl Ti bloc, Wild Country micro ascender.

they can be difficult to put on and take off fixed ropes, so for serious mountaineering their uses may be more limited. This said, they are excellent for emergencies, replacing prusiks, and do grip anything, even though manufacturers give a standard cautionary comment for use on icy or mud-fouled ropes.

Petzl has just introduced one of the lightest ascending devices, known as the Tibloc. These work like magic when placed with care, but unless the correct size krab is used and they are placed properly they can damage the rope's sheath.

Petzl makes a swing-sided self-jamming pulley, the Mini Traxion, which can also be used for ascending. This works best when combined with a handled ascender. Petzl also makes a specific chest ascender, the Croll. It has a twisted attachment point that keeps the device flat against the chest and an elongated hole for the attachment of shoulder straps. All mechanical ascenders have the drawback that they cannot be released under load.

SOLO DEVICES
Top-Roping

There are a number of devices used to protect a solo climber on a top-rope. The most common is the use of an ascender, for example, the Petzl basic. The way of clipping into the rope is shown in the accompanying diagram. If the rope will not run through easily, weight the rope with a rucksack. The smoothest device is the Mini Traxion from Petzl, a new concept in pulleys that has an anti-return clamp to stop the climber on a top-rope.

Leading

Ascenders were not designed for solo climbing and the Petzl shunt was designed to protect abeils. There are, however some purpose-built designs for solo climbing. Rock Exotica makes the Soloist and SoloAid, although unfortunately neither of them is CE-approved. The soloist requires you to feed the rope through, it does not require a chest harness, it locks in an upside-down fall and is smaller and lighter than the Soloist. It is generally preferred for aid climbing. For top-roping you need to weight the end of the rope; for leading the free rope is best carried in a rucksack so that it can feed out. After a fall you may have to stand in a prusik to take your weight off the device. Always back-up the device by tying figure-of-eight knots into your harness.

Chalk.

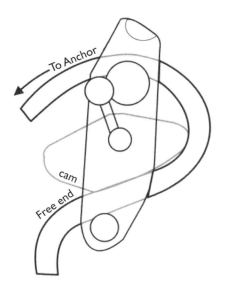

A Rock Exotica Soloist.

CHALK

Climbing chalk is actually magnesium carbonate, a white powder first introduced to climbing by the American John Gill, who borrowed the idea from gymnasts in the early 1960s to help him grip the rock. When it was introduced into the UK the climbing community was divided, resulting in the formation of the 'clean hand gang' spearheaded by Pat Littlejohn, and at least one of the original gang still do not use it. It has, however, been accepted by the majority of climbers who find its use both calming and helpful.

Soon after loose chalk had gained acceptance the chalk block appeared. Made by allowing chalk to settle, compressed into a large block and then cut into smaller pieces, it gave chalk a new feel. Texture is the key characteristic of any chalk – if the grind is too fine it feels slippery; if it is too coarse it drops off the fingers. Chalk dust is non-toxic but chalk particles can transport viruses and a recent inno-

vation to combat the overuse of chalk in climbing walls is a bag of stocking-like material filled with chalk called a chalk ball. It can be fitted with a drawcord to make it refillable. It is not so useful when having to chalk-up frequently. If it is cold put a chemical hand-warmer into the chalk bag.

To overcome the environmental impact of white marks everywhere, Powergrip produces chalk in three colours: tan, white and grey. However, you can make your own coloured chalk by adding dried mud and other things like powdered sand to the mix.

Another invention to help overcome the impact of too much chalk is Grrrip an airy powder that is an astringent and mops up oils in the skin. The hydrophobic (water hating) effect is amazing, but unfortunately it does not have much grip and chalk will not stick to it. Another new addition is Mega Grip, a liquid containing an anti-perspirant and grip enhancers, which may be useful as chalk does stick to it.

CHAPTER 6

ROPEWORK AND SAFETY SKILLS

Clear and simple ropework makes climbing safer, more enjoyable and could prevent a non-serious fall turning into a complicated rescue. Learning a safe system of ropework is surprisingly easy – the difficult part is how and when to apply it on a climb, because ropework techniques only become skills when they are used at the correct time and in the correct place. As an instructor, you are a role model, so try to engender a respect for safe practice by not cutting corners and only using techniques and equipment that the students are likely to use in their own climbing.

This chapter is not a beginner's guide to climbing, but it does answer many of the questions that students and novice instructors ask on climbing courses. It examines many of the skills that you may want to consider when teaching rock climbing. The chapter on equipment (Chapter 5) contains much complementary information that is not repeated here.

KNOTS AND HITCHES

Instructors need to be familiar with a range of knots and hitches so that they can choose the best one for a given situation. What is the difference between a knot and a hitch? A hitch must be tied around something else for it to exist, whereas a knot is tied in the rope itself. Practice them in the dark and in poor weather conditions until they become second nature.

Knots and hitches should be pulled snug but not overtight, because the tightening is part of the process of absorbing the energy created by a fall. However, as a knot or hitch tightens, it draws any slack rope into itself and if the tail sticking out of the knot is too short, it may disappear. Therefore all knots should be tied so that they leave a tail at least ten times as long as the diameter of the rope, for example 11cm in an 11mm rope. If in doubt, tie a stopper knot after tying the main knot.

A turn in any knot reduces its strength, so the sharper the turn the weaker the knot. In fact,

---

Essential Knots and Hitches

- Figure-of-eight on a bight.
- Rewoven figure-of-eight.
- Overhand knot.
- Clove hitch.
- Italian hitch.
- Double fisherman.
- Tape knot.
- Half hitch.
- Full hitch.
- French prusik.
- Double figure-of-eight on the bight.
- Bowline and improved bowline.
- Slippery hitch.
- Klemheist.
- Lark's foot.

---

any edge, for example, a krab, reduces the strength of a rope. This is because the fibres are squashed on the inside of the bend and stretched on the outside. However, rather than worrying that a figure-of-eight knot reduces the strength by 21 per cent, a bowline by 23 per cent and a clove hitch by 35 per cent, it is more important to understand their uses and abuses. Nevertheless, to keep a knot or hitch at its maximum strength tie it so that it looks neat, or in rope speak 'dressed'.

Figure-of-Eight on a Bight

Once called a 'Flemish bend' this knot was introduced when smoother kernmantle ropes first appeared.

Useful but Not Essential Knots

- Sheet bend.
- Alpine butterfly.
- In-line figure-of-eight.
- Bowline on the bight.
- Running half-fisherman's with a stopper knot.
- Rewoven overhead knot.

Figure-of-eight on a bight.

- It is difficult to adjust when tied.
- It is difficult to undo after loading; to make it easier to undo after loading, clip a krab into the centre of the knot.
- A variation is the figure-of-nine, which is less likely to tighten on itself (It takes an extra turn before putting the bight of rope through the resulting loop).

Rewoven figure-of-eight

- The knot is used for attaching the rope to the harness because it is easy to see if it is tied incorrectly.
- It does not easily come loose and it is good at absorbing the forces generated in a fall.
- It is difficult to undo after loading.

The rewoven overhand is sometimes used as it creates a small, neat knot, especially when it is rewoven in a doubled rope.

The Bowline

The bowline is useful for attaching the rope to trees and threads and can be tied one-handed. There is some dispute whether the end of the rope is better on the inside or outside of the loop, it possibly had something to do with the direction of the twist in old hemp ropes. In reality as long as the knot is a bowline and it is finished with a double stopper knot it is okay.

- The bowline is easy to untie after a fall.
- It is difficult to see whether the knot has been tied correctly and is therefore not recommended for use with novices.
- It can work loose if not under continual loading.

Rewoven figure-of-eight knot.

Bowline with stopper.

Overhand Knot on a Bight

This knot is ometimes used in place of an Alpine butterfly or figure-of-eight.

- It creates a smaller loop in a sling or rope.
- It is difficult to undo after being loaded unless it has been tied in a bunch of ropes or slings.

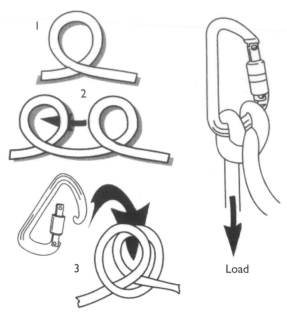

Clove hitch.

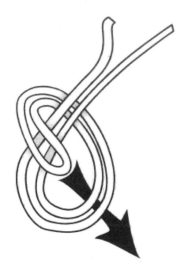

Overhand knot on a Bight.

Clove Hitch

This is an easily adjustable hitch for attaching ropes and tapes to krabs.

- It can slip when subjected to a 5.5KN force, although this may be an advantage because it absorbs some of the force and equalizes the belay system. However, it should be avoided for single attachment points when ascending fixed ropes or abseiling. When tied in the end of a rope, it should be finished with a stopper knot.
- It can be difficult to undo after loading.
- It can work loose, but pinch it tight and it will not magically leap out of a krab.
- Ideally it should be orientated in the krab so that the loaded rope is next to the back bar and not the gate.

Italian Hitch

The Italian hitch is sometimes called a Munter hitch, half-ring bend, karabiner hitch or half-mast belay. Its invention in 1973 is credited to the Swiss climber Werner Munter, but in fact it had been used for many years by dock workers moving heavy loads. It is really a half clove hitch as its German name halbmastwurf sicherung (HMS) indicates.

- The Italian hitch is simple, light and easy to use.
- When used in conjunction with an HMS krab it is a useful knot for belaying and lowering moderate loads.
- For lowering on steep terrain or lowering two people, the Italian hitch can be doubled, that is placed through the krab a second time.
- Be careful that it does not untwist the locking gate as the rope continually moves through the krab.

Double Fisherman

This knot is referred to as the Grapevine in the USA.

- It is commonly used for tying two ropes together, for tying the ends of cord together on protection and joining the ends of soft tape together (do not use it with flat or stiff tape).
- When tied in soft tapes it is impossible to undo.

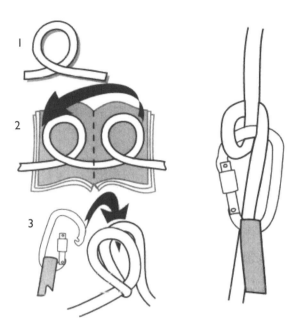

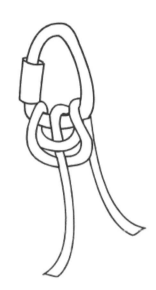

LEFT Italian hitch. *RIGHT* Doubled Italian hitch.

- Make sure that the two portions of the knot fit into each other.
- A reef knot tied first in the middle of the knot makes it easier to separate the two ropes after use for abseiling.
- A triple fisherman's is used for tying Spectra, Gemini and Dyneema cord.

Double fisherman.

Tape Knot (*see* p. 142)

This is also called a water knot or ring bend.

- The tape knot is used for tying tapes or ropes together.
- Do not stitch or tape the ends down because in obscure situations the knot can move and fatal accidents have occurred when climbers have not noticed that only the stitching is holding the tape together.
- It is most easily tied in soft tapes.

Half Hitch and Full Hitch (Stopper Knot)

- These are useful for finishing some knots. See the bowline for a full hitch and attaching to trees (page 154) for the half hitch.

Slippery Hitch/Mule Knot

- This is a useful hitch for tying off belay plates as it is easily released. See tying off a belay plate (page 150).

The Lark's Foot/Girth Hitch

When used incorrectly this knot creates a sharp angle in the sling, resulting in a pulley effect

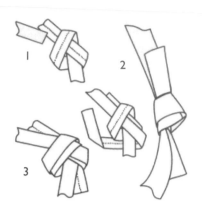

FAR LEFT Tape knot.

RIGHT Improved knot.

and concentrating the forces at the edges of the tape.

- This knot is, however, useful when tied without the acute angle for attaching a sling to a tree, tying off a peg, putting a sling onto a harness and securing a foot loop when prusiking.

Double Figure-of-Eight and Bowline, on the Bight

These two knots serve the same purpose.

- They create two loops (sometimes referred to as 'bunny ears'), adjustable to differing lengths. It is a good idea to keep something

Double figure-of-eight on the bight.

Lark's foot.

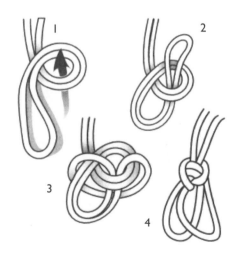

Bowline on the bight.

clipped to both of the ears as the knot can slip.

- Their main use is for looking after two people on an abseil and for linking two anchors at a belay.
- The same thing created with an overhand knot can come undone unless both ends remain clipped into something.

The French Prusik (Marchard Knot)

The French prusik is called the Marchard knot by most other European countries.

- Chapter 7 covers prusik knots in more detail, but this is the most useful one for protecting abseils.

The Alpine Butterfly

- This is an elegant knot used for tying into the middle of the rope and for equalizing anchors (see page 168).
- It is also useful for isolating a piece of damaged rope.
- It has the advantage over the figure-of-eight or overhand in that it directs the force through the knot and does not distort it.

In-line Figure-of-Eight

- This knot has similar uses to the Alpine Butterfly in that it directs the forces through the knot.
- It is useful on belays for equalizing anchors and attaching two people to the rope for climbing or lowering.

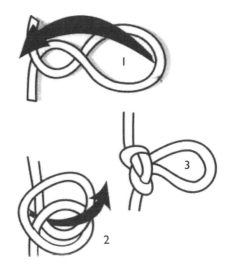

Alpine butterfly.

Sheet Bend

- The sheet bend's main application in climbing is to create a chest harness called a 'Parisian baudrier'.
- It is also used for linking slings or ropes of different diameters but not a mixture of materials and for tying tape to make a sling.
- It can work loose when it is not loaded.

SINGLE-PITCH CLIMBING

Before delving into the safety skills and ropework required to climb a single-pitch route it is worth looking at the term 'belay'. The term is of

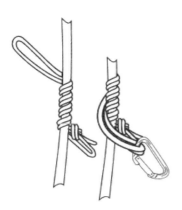

French prusik.

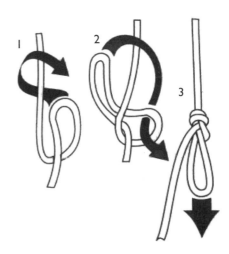

In-line figure-of-eight.

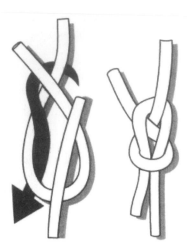

Sheet bend.

Clear and simple ropework makes climbing safer. The author on Fernhill E2 6a, Cratcliff, Peak District.

nautical origin, borrowed and amplified beyond its original meaning by the rock climber. Originally it was used to describe the tying of knots to the ship's superstructure and was often used to keep sailors busy. It is used by climbers in so many contexts, as a verb to describe the bringing up of a second (belaying) and as a noun to describe how a climber attaches to anchors at a stance (belay).

Preparation Before Climbing

Preparing a climbing rack prior to climbing is vital so that the climber knows where the protection is and to prevent it becoming tangled (see 'placing protection' for more information). Arranging gear is a very personal thing but here are some ideas:

A well racked climber will stay calm in a crisis.

- More than eight nuts per krab can become tangled.
- Carry sizes one to three on one krab, five to six on another and seven to ten on a further one.
- A bandolier (chest sling) is useful when lay-backing because it is easier to switch the gear to the side away from the rock. However, on overhanging routes the gear hangs behind the body and on slabs the gear can obscure the feet. They are also useful when swapping leads on multi-pitch climbs.
- Distribute protection equally on either side of the harness to aid balance, with larger protection at the back.
- Protection that is racked closer to the front of the harness enables the climber to see the gear more easily and can help to keep the weight over the feet on desperate slabs.

Two methods of shortening slings.

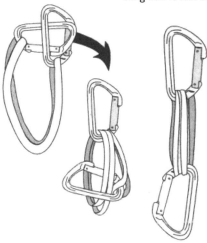

b) Unclip the lower krab and clip it into any loop of the sling and it will extend.

a) Putting twists in 60cm or 120cm slings enables them to be carried on a harness without fear of slipping into them.

- Ensure that spare screw-gates are not done up prior to climbing.
- Rack the gear away from the wall when laybacking.
- Carry a few longer extension slings (extenders), because quick draws are designed for sports routes, which often go in a straight line. Slings of 60cm can be placed over the head/arm, but they can then be difficult to remove.
- 120cm slings can be placed double over one shoulder and the ends clipped together. Make sure that a twist is put into the sling to stop the krab falling off when it is removed from your shoulder.
- SLCDs can cause problems for novices because they are difficult to place and to remove.
- For single-pitch climbing, avoid cluttering your harness with a knife, jumars or cleaning rags; keep them in an accessible rucksack or a bumbag.
- Carry a nut key even when leading because it is useful for poking nuts into, and for cleaning mud out of, cracks.

Instructing Tip

Novices often have trouble clipping and unclipping krabs. Therefore show them that when the gate is opened it traps equipment at one end. The unhinged end of the gate should be facing the rope or equipment to unclip or clip it.

Tying In to a Harness

To distinguish the rope ends for discussion purposes, the end of rope that the climber ties into is the 'live end' and the end that runs through the belay device the 'dead end'.

Tying in is a serious business – get into the habit of checking each other before climbing, concentrate and do not let anything or anyone distract you. The rewoven figure-of-eight is the most reliable method for attaching to the harness because it is easier for novices to focus on one method. It is also easier for the instructor to check, being a difficult knot to tie incorrectly.

First, tie a single figure-of-eight in about an arm's length of rope (slightly less in a 9mm rope). Then take the end of rope 'down'

A Typical Rack for a Novice

- Five sets of quick draws (i.e. ten krabs and five short slings).
- Five extension slings (ten krabs and five × 50cm slings).
- Two 120cm slings.
- Two 60cm slings.
- One set of wires 1–9.
- One set of Wild Country Rockcentrics 5–9 (possibly 10 if on grit).
- Two spare open-gate krabs.
- Four screw-gates.
- Two HMS krabs.
- One nut key.
- Two belay device.

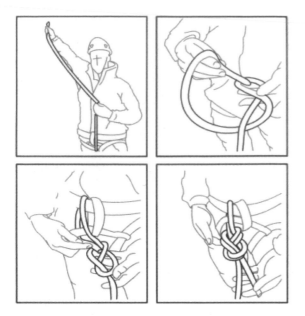

Tying in.

through the waist belt and through the leg loops (if you are then distracted part-way through the process you are at least likely to have tied into the waist belt) and then re-thread the figure-of-eight. When falls are likely, such as on sports routes, take an extra turn through the harness before reweaving the knot; the rope will then tighten on the turn around harness and not the knot. There are some harnesses where the method of attachment is different to this, although the principles are the same in that you link the waist belt and leg loops, for example Wild Country Alpiniste and DMM Alpiniste. If all else fails, read the instructions.

Anne May semi direct belaying at the top of Stannage Edge.

Correct tying in creates a loop of rope called the 'central loop', which is just big enough to put a clenched fist through. If the tail out of the knot is too long, tie a stopper knot close to the figure-of-eight; this does not contribute to the strength of the knot but it does ensure that enough tail has been left. An alternative is to tie an overhand knot in the single strand that makes up the tail. This will prevent someone clipping into the loop created by a stopper knot. Beware that finishing off a figure-of-eight by tucking the tail back into the knot can loosen the knot.

The growth of climbing walls has increased the number of climbers attaching themselves to the rope via a krab. This method of attachment is not suitable for lead climbing, because a fall could result in a cross-loading of the krab. In fact, there are few, if any, situations where attaching a climber to the rope with a krab is recommended.

The Improved Bowline
The improved bowline is a useful alternative for tying in when sports climbing or on a climbing wall with experienced students because it is easy to undo.

The improved bowline.

Tying into a Chest and Sit Harness
The chest harness has two uses: it keeps the climber upright in a fall and it prevents the harness from being pulled off when used by students with little hip definition. When tying into a chest harness the forces are distributed primarily to the sit harness and the chest piece keeps the climber upright.

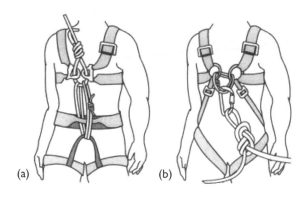

Attaching to: (a) chest/sit harness; (b) body harness.

Tying into a Body Harness

A body harness consists of leg, waist and chest sections sewn together so that the loads are distributed between the upper and lower sections. They should be fitted so that the tie-in point is relatively high, but take care to ensure the force is directed to the legs. A poorly fitted body harness can direct too much force to the back and chest. If you are tying in with a krab use a sling to link the attachment points to prevent cross-loading of the krab.

BELAYING

Belaying is a basic, but vital skill. Poor technique can be compensated for when concentrating, but if concentration lapses, poor technique may result in painful burns at the least and a dropped climber at the worst. Practice on both sides of the body. Whether the belayer sits or stands will depend on the height of the anchors, this is discussed further under 'Creating a Belay' (page 166).

Belaying Using a Plate or Tube Device

Belay plates and tubes hold a fall by pulling the device closer to the HMS krab, forcing the rope into a Z shape and increasing the friction between the device and the rope.

To hold a fall, keep the rope in a Z position. To pay out the rope, bring the live and dead ends parallel (in this position the belay device is redundant as the rope is only passing round a krab), and pull the live rope through. When changing hands, always have one hand on the dead rope throughout the changeover.

Belay devices are most easily used with an HMS krab, the wide end towards the device. This maintains a smooth belaying action and improves the braking action. Keeping the wide end towards the device can be difficult, but the DMM Belay Master, a plastic clip, keeps the krab in the correct position.

Take care when using half-ropes or wet ropes with belay devices designed for use with single ropes, as they provide less braking ability. In addition, keep the rope running cleanly through the belay device without any twists because this further reduces its ability to arrest a fall.

Tips for a Good Belayer

To help the leader concentrate on climbing it is an advantage for them to have confidence in the belayer.

- Do not rummage in your rucksack or smoke. Stay focused on the leader, pre-empting their movements and attempts to clip protection.
- Position yourself so the rope runs cleanly and does not wrap around the leader's legs.
- Pay out the correct amount of rope, so that you do not pull the climber backwards, and avoid large loops of rope on the flow between you and them.
- Keep the ropes tangle-free by loosely feeding them onto the floor with the leader's end on top of the pile.

- Consider the direction in which a leader fall will pull you.
- Position yourself close to the cliff to keep the runners in place and to ensure that a fall will not pull you into the cliff face.
- When the route is running straight up a steep cliff, stand up to belay because it is a more comfortable position to absorb the forces created by a fall.
- If the leader falls while climbing over an overhang do not be tempted to pull the rope tight, as this will only increase the chances of them slamming into the cliff below the overhang.
- Rope burns from belaying are rare, but gloves may be a good idea until the skills have been learnt.

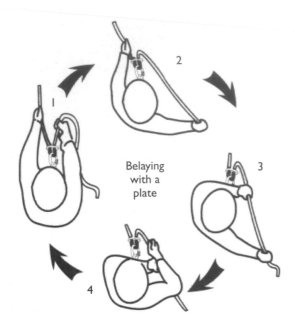

Belaying with a plate

The mechanics of belaying with a belay plate or tube.

Belaying a leader on Pool Wall, E5 6b, Lawrencefield. Note how the belayer has belayed below the ledge to prevent him being pulled into the pond.

Belaying a Leader

When a climber falls, the force that the belayer receives depends on how much friction is created through the protection placed as the climb travels up the cliff. It can vary from the belayer not even realizing the leader has fallen off, to a considerable force slamming the inattentive belayer into the cliff. However, as long as the belayer is attentive, do not anchor them to the ground or the cliff, unless one of the following applies:

- The leader is more than 50 per cent heavier.
- There is a drop that the belayer could fall off or something dangerous they could be pulled into, such as an overhang.
- The climb starts at the base of a sea cliff and is threatened by waves.
- There are boulders to stumble on.

The reason for this is that the upward movement of the belayer during a fall helps to absorb some of the forces and having freedom of movement allows the belayer to move out of the way of falling objects. In one set of tests most belay devices kept the load on the top piece of protection to about 4.5KN while the Gri Gri averaged

---

Direct and Indirect Belaying

Direct and indirect belaying describes how the forces created in a fall reach the belay anchors:

- A direct belay transmits the forces directly to the belay anchors. In its simplest form a direct belay is a rope taken around a boulder relying on the friction against the boulder to hold the fall. An Italian hitch or belay device, attached directly to the belay, is also a direct belay. It has the advantage that the instructor is free to move around, and lowering, sorting hoists and holding a fall are easier. It should not be used to belay a lead climber.
- An indirect belay transmits the forces to the belay anchors via the belayer. In its simplest form waist belaying is an indirect belay because the belayer absorbs the forcest first. It has the advantage that the body absorbs some of the forces and the belayer can feel the climber's movement.
- The belay system used by most climbers is a semi-direct belay because the forces are transmitted directly to the anchors, but by changing position, the belayer can also absorb the force.

9.8KN. If the belayer jumped into the air while catching the fall the force on the top piece dropped to 3.5KN. Also an attentive belayer can save a climber from hitting the ground by taking the rope in and running backwards. However, this increases the forces on the top runner by adding the belayer's weight to the force created by the falling climber and results in a more jarring fall for the climber.

Belaying a Second

The ideal belay at the top of a climb puts the belayer sideways to the anchors with the ropes coming along one side of the body and into the harness (*see* page 166). To ensure that the brake arm is free to move and lock the belay device in the event of a fall, it is better to have the belay device on the same side as the ropes. If this is not possible, it may be more difficult to hold a fall because the belayer's body is then in the way of the braking arm. Belaying can also be compromised by a second who climbs too fast, so tell them to slow down rather than compromise the belaying action.

Belaying with a Figure-of-Eight Descender

Descenders can be used in the abseil or belay plate mode. Both are effective although they do twist the rope, especially when used for lowering from a sports climb. A further way to use it is 'sport mode'. This method reduces the friction and allows rapid feeding of the rope to the leader, but it has a low holding power and is not recommended. In addition, there is also the chance that the figure-of-eight can jam against the gate of the krab.

There is an obtuse way of using a descender that has some serious drawbacks. The method creates an 'auto-locking' device, but there is the possibility that the rope can come off the small end of the descender. A quick draw clipped from the small hole to the harness

Direct belaying with an Italian hitch.
Climber: Trevor Massiah.

helps to prevent this happening, but it does not always lock automatically and although it is a nice rope trick it has few, if any, real applications.

Belaying with an Italian Hitch

The advantage of the Italian hitch is that there is sufficient braking power no matter where your hand is – the hand does not have to be moved to the proper position to hold a fall. It is useful for belaying a second or a leader, but not when there is the likelihood of a big leader fall because the rope slips quickly and can be difficult to hold. Wearing gloves would make it safer. Furthermore, when used with the hand in front

sports mode

belay plate mode

autolocking mode

A variety of ways of using a figure-of-eight descender for belaying.

it stops the climber rapidly and transmits more of the force to the belayer and when used for lowering it can kink the rope.

The action is the opposite of a belay plate and the hands are kept in front of the hitch at all times. This means that as long as you are in front of the Italian hitch it is not necessary to be close to it.

Belaying with an Autolocking Device

There are a number of devices which, at first sight, seem to solve the possible hazards that occur when a novice starts belaying. They are all useful for bottom-roping and sports climbing, but because they stop the fall much quicker they transfer more of the force generated in a fall to the climber and protection, so should not therefore be used for traditional climbing. Chapter 5 looks at the devices in detail.

When using the Gri Gri, most of the problems arise through misuse rather than problems with the design. It is possible to load the rope in wrongly and drop the climber; if this has been done just use it like a normal belay device. It is also possible to drop the climber too quickly by squeezing the release arm too far and failing to hold the rope like a normal belay device. There is also a small chance that the belayer can be pulled into the cliff with the device jammed in the open position. In addition, the rope jams easily if the belayer is not paying attention, which is very annoying for the leader if he is going for the 'gripper' clip. To eliminate many of these problems, hold the dead rope as for other belay devices, or, if you are careful (although Petzl do not recommend it) hold the autolocking mechanism down with the thumb.

Falling Objects

Should anything fall down the crag, do not look up to see where the rock is coming from, as it is likely to be closer than you would wish. Instead, when you hear a shout, run in towards the cliff. Falling objects do not normally fall straight down the rock face, but bounce out a few feet.

Lowering

Students may be uncomfortable with the idea of being lowered, therefore a smooth and steady descent is preferable to a jerky one. It is easier and more comfortable to lower directly from the belay anchors.

Lowering.

Belay devices are designed to feed rope through easily and can therefore be difficult to control on a lower. It may also be possible to incorporate the terrain into the lowering system to add friction, but beware of sharp or abrasive edges. Alternatively, take the dead rope through a krab behind the belay device or add an Italian hitch to a krab behind the device.

The brake best suited to lowering is the Italian hitch. To minimize rope twist, feed the rope hand over hand into the hitch so that twists do not gather in the pile of unloaded rope. To increase the friction, double the hitch.

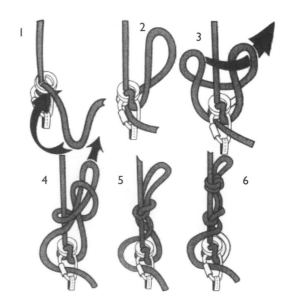

Tying off a belay plate in front of the device with slippery hitch and full hitch.

A back-up should be considered when the lower is in an area of loose rock and the instructor could be hit or it is cold/wet, making holding the rope difficult. Prusiks are added below the belay device, not to add friction to the lower but for safety. A French prusik can be used or a klemheist attached to a sling that is linked to a krab via an Italian hitch. For added safety tie the end of the rope into the belay anchors, then if all else fails the student will only fall a rope length. Two students can be lowered by tying one into the end of the rope and the other into an isolation loop created using an overhand knot, an Alpine butterfly or an in-line figure-of-eight.

Tying off a Belay Device

Tying off a belay device may be necessary when you need both of your hands free to do other things. There are a number of methods for locking the rope, but with all of them hold the dead end of the rope with the whole hand during the locking-off process – do not fiddle with just a few fingers. Keep the belaying hand close to the device and use the other hand to do the knot tying.

The easiest method is to take a bight of rope through the krab and then secure it in front of the plate with a slippery hitch, although the resulting large hitch can get in the way when creating a pulley. Do not tie off the belay device by just tying a slippery hitch in front of it because it may then jam against the belay device when loaded.

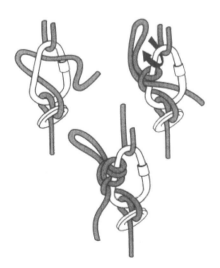

Tying off a belay plate on the back bar of the krab.

A preferable method is to pass a bight of rope through the krab and tie a slippery hitch around the back bar then secure it with a half-hitch. This method is difficult when using a DMM Belay Master.

Tying an Italian Hitch

To lock off an Italian Hitch, pull approximately 60cm of rope forward and secure it with a slippery hitch and a half hitch around the live rope.

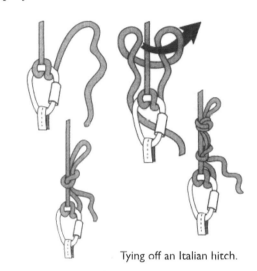

Tying off an Italian hitch.

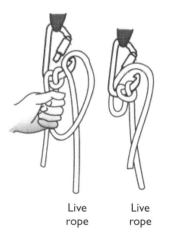

Turning an Italian hitch into a clove hitch requires the live rope to be unloaded.

Live rope   Live rope

Waist Belay

A high degree of judgement is required to determine when the waist belay is appropriate, because it is uncomfortable on the belayer should the climber fall (gloves and a long-sleeved shirt will prevent rope burns). It may be appropriate when the loading on the belayer is low, and when there is significant friction elsewhere in the system, for example rope runs

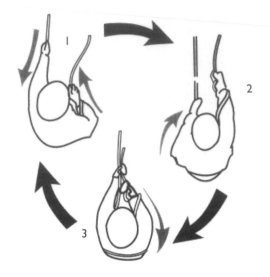

The mechanics of waist belaying.

around a boulder or speed is important. It is very difficult to hold a leader fall with a waist belay.

The rope is best taken around the waist by slipping it over the head and not by stepping into it – this prevents the rope being pulled downwards and under the feet. A twist around the arm holding the dead rope increases the friction and holding power (do not put a twist of

Waist belaying when tied into the front of the harness.

live rope around the live arm because it becomes untwisted very rapidly during a fall).

The technique for waist belaying is that the dead hand is pushed forward while the live rope is pulled up. The hand on the dead rope is brought back to its starting position by grabbing both ropes with the live hand, in front of the dead hand, and sliding the hand on the dead rope back towards the waist. Using this method means that the dead rope is never released. If the climber falls, the hand on the live rope does very little, but the hand holding the dead rope must be brought across the body. Passing the live rope through a krab attached to the front of the harness prevents the rope coming over the top of the head in the event of a fall.

The perfect belay for waist belaying is set up with the ropes from the anchors attached to the back of the harness. This means that the belayer is always facing in the direction of the fall and the ropes cannot be ripped from behind the belayer. However, waist belaying is possible even when attached to the anchors, via the front of the harness. In this situation the live rope must be on the same side as the ropes from the anchors, so that a fall twists the belayer's body into the belay. If the live rope is on the side away from the belay, a fall will twist the belayer away from it with disastrous results.

If you are wearing a rucksack you can put the rope over the sack by keeping both arms straight as you lift the rope over your head. A rucksack can prevent the waist being compressed, although it does compromise the rope handling.

Shoulder Belaying
Shoulder belaying is easy to use, but open to catastrophic error when done poorly. To use it, stand sideways, with knees flexed to absorb some of the load. The live rope passes up the side of the body under the arm, across the back and over the opposite shoulder. It may be appropriate when low loads are anticipated for short periods of time and in a downward direction. Try not to lean forward, although this is difficult when you want to watch the student.

PLACING PROTECTION

Historically, protection placed whilst leading was called a 'running belay', hence the use, in the UK, of the name 'runners' to describe any protection placed while leading.

Shoulder belaying. Note the way that the left hand holds both ropes while the right hand slides back up the rope. Climber: Trevor Massiah.

Practise choosing the appropriate gear and placing it quickly at ground level; discover what works and what does not, be creative, tug them to give you an idea of their holding power, but be aware that a tug does not recreate the forces generated in a fall. Placing protection is not simply a matter of choosing the right gear for the right place – the climber must also consider the effect a fall has on the protection (*see* page 162).

Sound Rock

There is seldom a perfect placement and choosing sound rock is not as easy as it first appears, especially when leading a climb. Here are some points to consider:

- Scan it visually, looking for cracks that create a loose area.
- Place one hand on the rock and bang it with the palm of the other hand. If a vibration is felt through the hand on the rock, try to kick or pull the rock.
- When pulling, be careful that it does not suddenly come out and disappear over the cliff edge with you hanging on to it.
- Look for soft rock and crystals inside cracks that could wedge a runner but snap easily in a fall.
- Sea cliff limestone and slate provide the least reliable of all runner placements, because the rock has a thin, easily crushed, weathered layer. Granite is a harder substance and provides placements for protection that are generally more reliable.

How and When to Place Protection

There are a number of reasons for placing protection:

- To reduce the length of a fall due to fatigue, loose rock or a slip.
- An instructor may place protection to aid a student or make following the route easier.
- To reduce the fall factor.
- To protect the rope from sharp edges or loose rock.

Here are some general points to consider:

- Identify possible placements before leaving the ground. Keep vital protection for the crux. Down-climb if necessary to retrieve protection that may be needed higher up.
- On single-pitch routes climb 180–250cm (6–8ft), then place a runner at waist or eye level. By the time the runner is at foot level, a ground fall is possible so place another. The distance between runners can become greater, the higher you go.
- Do not focus just on looking above your head – also look sideways and downward.
- It is much easier to place protection at rest places, so do not wait until you need protection.
- Place protection before and after the hard moves especially on a traverse.
- Consider the consequences of a fall. Are there any ledges that could be hit? What happens if the top piece of protection comes out?

- Do not rely on a single piece of gear on sea cliffs unless it is perfect.
- Place a good nut instead of an SLCD, but understand how to place SLCDs correctly.
- Be suspicious of all fixed slings, stakes, pegs and bolts.
- Worry about the quality of the rock, not the strength of the equipment.
- Do not blindly trust well-worn runner placements – they may not be as good as wear and tear suggests.
- Place/clip gear at waist level when laybacking or on sports climbs, otherwise you will become pumped if you keep placing it high. You are also are less likely to fall with a mouth full of slack trying to clip bolts.

Natural Protection

Nature provides some of the best protection, which only requires the simplest of equipment such as a sling.

Spikes/Boulders

The strongest and fastest way to place a sling is simply to loop the sling around or over natural protection. Slings looped over spikes are fine for a downward pull, but are prone to lifting off. Use a slip knot/trucker's hitch to reduce lifting. If this is not possible, hang a large hex from the sling. A rope sling may be better on sharp edges but it has the tendency to roll off rounded boulders. If a large boulder or block is used, make sure that it cannot tilt over and cut the sling.

To avoid excessive forces at the edges of the sling make sure that it is long enough to go around the spike/boulder or tree so that the angles created in the sling are kept to less than 120 degrees. In addition, to prevent a sharp edge severing a sling place the stitched portion over it – this presents a double thickness of tape. Roll the tape back and forth to ensure it cannot come off the spike. A sling doubled over a spike means that the forces generated in a fall are distributed over four strands and not just two. If the sling is large enough a knot in a doubled sling will create two slings.

Threads

Threads can potentially take a pull in any direction, making them one of the best runners available. The obvious way to place a sling puts the force onto the neck of rock that forms the thread, so make sure the rock is solid and has no

A sling held down by a Rockcentric.

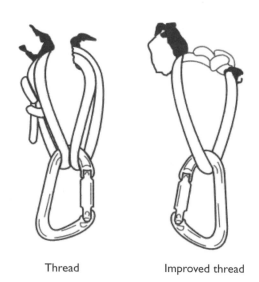

Thread   Improved thread

Using slings in threads.

Round turn and two half hitches around a tree.

sharp edges. Do not do a lark's foot around the neck of the thread because this transmits all the force to the rock neck. If the neck is suspect, a better but more difficult way is to thread a sling with a knot in it and clip the two ends together, or thread a sling through the hole, tie an overhand knot and pull the knot back into the thread tunnel. In a fall the strain is then on the knot and not the rock neck.

In situ slings should be examined thoroughly. Pull the threads through to examine the hidden portion; replace them even if this means you have to abseil prior to climbing the route. Wired runners or protection on rope can also be used as threads.

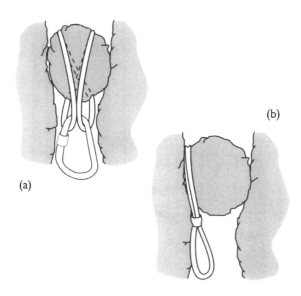

(a) A twist in the sling will stop it falling off the krab should it pull through one side of the chockstone. (b) Lark's foot on a chockstone.

Chockstones

The biggest danger with a chockstone placement is that it may lift as you move past it, or if it is not seated in the crack it may move when loaded. Attaching to it via a lark's foot around the point of contact between the chockstone can jam the chockstone in place in some circumstances.

Trees

Avoid trees if you can, but if you do have to use one, try to ensure that it has vigorous growth and a deep, well-developed root system. Trees and bushes are also more brittle in cold weather. If the tree is used regularly pad it out each time (do not leave the padding in place) and keep the pull close to the ground to decrease the leverage. Tie into it using a sling that is looped, or lark's footed, around it. Alternatively, tie into it using a round turn and two half hitches.

Artificial Protection

The development of artificial protection, with its cams and wedges, is a testament to Man's inventive ingenuity, but an even greater test is the ability to place them.

Placing Nuts/Wedges

Nuts and wedges are, in theory, the simplest protection to place after a natural runner. Here are some tips for placing nuts/wedges:

Wild Country rock in a crack.

Nuts placed in opposition (stacked wedges). This has been superseded by SLCDs but may still prove useful in some situations. Tug on the correctly orientated one and then clip into it. Clip the two wires together in case the wedge falls out. In large cracks, consider stacking a wedge and a hexentric, and in desperation a peg and a nut.

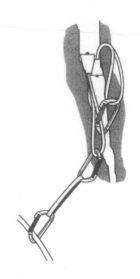

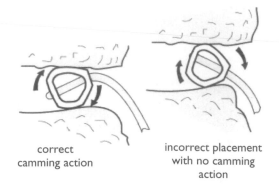

correct camming action

incorrect placement with no camming action

Correct and incorrect placement of a Wild Country Rockcentric.

- Hard metals are more resistant to ripping but softer ones bite into the rock more easily.
- Most modern wedges have curved faces so that they can pivot over the convex face and the concave side levers against the other side of the crack.
- With small nuts the force generated by a fall is transmitted to a smaller area of rock, increasing the chances of the rock breaking. Therefore place the largest nut that fits properly and make sure that the maximum surface area is in contact with the rock.
- Make sure the nut is not balancing on just a few crystals.
- Place protection deep into the crack because the rock is more likely to break on the outside of the crack. However, take care not to embed the protection so deeply that it cannot be retrieved.
- Examine the crack carefully – does the constriction become narrower so that even if the nut moves it still cannot come out?

Placing Passive Camming Devices
Passive camming devices are most useful in the larger sizes where the camming action is more pronounced.

Hexentrics (Hexs)
These are more reliable than spring-loaded camming devices (*see* below), they can be used sideways as a wedge, they fit into pockets and are useful in vertical and horizontal placements. However, be careful using them when the crack is inwardly flaring, as they may move backwards and proper camming action is then lost.

Tri-Cams
These have a curved top from which runs a tape; when loaded, this forces the nut to cam into position. They are especially useful in pockets and slots. It takes practice to place them one-handed and it may need a tug to seat them in place. They can also be used as a wedge.

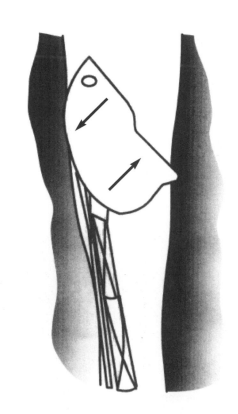

A 'Lowe' Tri-Cam.

Tips for placing SLCDs

- Avoid placements where the cams are fully open or tightly closed. They work best within 10 to 50 per cent of their expansion range.
- Avoid cracks that widen, as they become deeper.
- For optimum holding power align the cams evenly.
- Cramming too large a SLCD into a small placement makes it difficult to remove.
- Check the placement of SLCDs after a fall because they can rotate.
- Camming devices have one pair of cams pivoting inside the other creating a wedge shape. For horizontal placements, the cam is therefore more stable with the wider pair of cams at the base.
- Flexible stemmed SLCDs are better in horizontal placements because the stem can flex over the rock. However, even flexible SLCDs still work best when aligned in the direction of force.
- In horizontal placements rigid stemmed SLCDs should be placed so that only a small amount of the bar is showing or they should be tied off.
- Beware tying off a rigid SLCD in front of the triggers because in a fall it could be pulled back, releasing the cams. It is better to fit rigid Friends with a second sling through one of the holes designed for making the device lighter.

A tied-off rigid Friend.

Correct and incorrect placement of Wild Country flexible Friends:

(a) cams too small;
(b) cams too wide;
(c) Friend not in line with the direction of pull;
(d) correct placement.

Placing SLCDs

Once considered cheating, spring-loaded camming devices are now found on most climber's racks. However, because they are held in place even in poor placements they can give a false

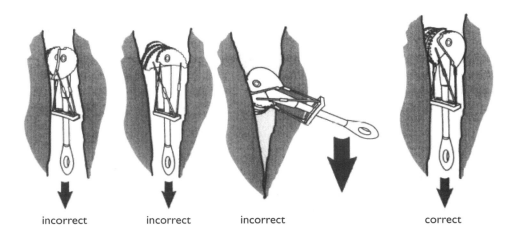

incorrect   incorrect   incorrect   correct

sense of security. The moral of this is to take care when placing SLCDs. If all the cams are in contact with solid rock and the stem is in the direction of any forces applied they work well. The grip on most rock types is enough to make the cams work, although they do not function as well on wet limestone, iced rock, on limestone with a soft calcite layer or on dirty or lichenous rock. It is for this reason that most cams have teeth so that they can attempt to bite through the unstable layer to the rock underneath.

Spring-Loaded Wedges

These are commonly called Rock 'n' Rollers, Balls and Sliders and they work on the stacked wedges idea (*see* 'Placing Nuts', page 156). Owing to a sliding taper, they fit a range of cracks. They work like magic in narrow, shallow parallel cracks, particularly slate, but the placement is only as good as the purchase on the rock and the holding power is reduced when fully extended.

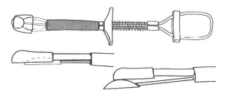

A spring-loaded wedge.

Share the load by equalizing micro-wedges with a krab and a sling.

Sharing the Load

Clipping into many micro-nuts individually may not prevent them breaking in a fall (*see* 'Forces', Chapter 5). When each protection piece is poor a single stronger piece can be created by connecting them together. If you cannot tie a knot with one hand, use the self-equalizing method described for slings (*see* page 168). However, if one comes out the other will be shock-loaded. The breaking strain of thin wires can be increased by 5 to 10 per cent if a 12mm krab is used instead of the more popular 10mm krab.

Multidirectional Protection

The force generated by a fall can exert a sideways or outward pull on the protection (see 'Attaching the Rope to the Runners') and simply moving past slings can lift them from marginal spikes. Friends can invert and walk sideways and nuts placed in vertical and horizontal placements can lift out. Protection that

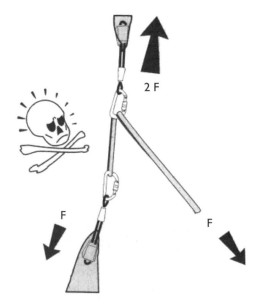

Avoid this method of placing runners in opposition because it creates a pulley and increases the forces on the top runner.

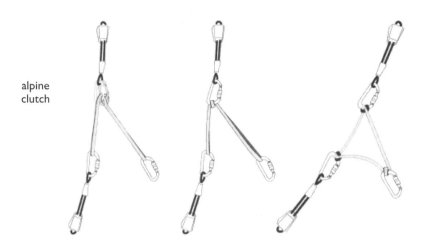

alpine clutch

Linking protection in opposition. The same method can be used for vertical and horizontal cracks.

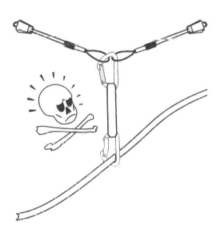

Take care when using this method of equalizing wires in a horizontal crack as it can load the krab across the gate.

can take a pull in any direction is therefore going to be better. Obvious types of protection which can take a pull in any direction are threads, trees and to a lesser degree bolts and pegs. However, multidirectional protection can be created by linking protection in opposition to each other.

Vertical Opposition
Place one wedge facing down and one facing up and link them together using the methods in the above diagram.

Horizontal Placements
Protection can be linked with a single krab, but this can expose the krab to a three-way loading which could cause the krab to break. Use the same methods as for vertical opposition.

Improvised Protection
Belay devices or krabs can be jammed into cracks and threaded, but their safety is doubtful. The best improvised protection is a jammed knot. To jam a knot, select a nice hourglass constriction in the crack and using a nut key poke in the largest knot that can fit. Keep the

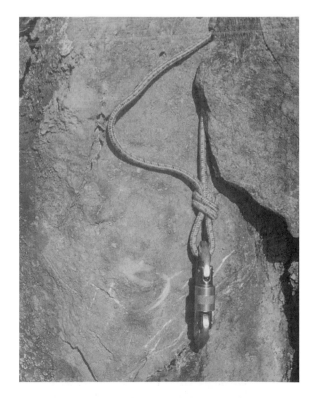

A knotted sling jammed in a crack. Note the knot tied in the bottom of the cord to keep any force closer to the rock.

Linking two wires to reach further.

knot large and flaccid, and after it is placed, pull down hard to draw the knot up tight. If the knot is the correct size, it will not pull through. It is possible to use slings or rope, even bootlaces. If the knot is close to the outside edge of the crack, tie a knot in the strand of sling closest to the cliff – this will keep the weight closer to the cliff.

Linking Two Wires Together to Reach Further

When the placement is out of reach, try linking two wires together to allow it to be reached. The stiffness of the wires will dictate how far away it is possible to reach.

Removing Protection

Do not yank runners to remove them, especially micro-wires because it can damage the wire close to the nut. Use a nut key to loosen them and try to remove them the way they went into the rock.

Do not move SLCDs back and forth because they can walk into the crack. If they have been placed too far in and the trigger bar cannot be reached, hook the bar using two wires or Wild Country's special nut key with hooks. If the SLCD has a single finger trigger ring, hook the

trigger ring with the nut key pick. You can also try hooking the holes in the cam itself.

To prevent a piece of gear being dropped clip the quick draw or extender into the gear loop of the harness before you remove it from the rope.

Fixed Protection

Fixed protection is anything that has been placed and left. Treat it with caution unless its history is known. If you are in any doubt replace it with new protection.

Pegs

With the advent of modern protection, there is a limited need for pegs, but this has meant that the art of placing them and assessing their security is disappearing.

A perfectly placed peg should slide one third of the way in before hammering and should go all the way up to the eye when hammered. Do not force the peg to fit the crack, choose one that fits the crack. A well-placed peg has a rising ringing sound as you hammer it further into the crack. A dull 'clunking' sound usually means poor rock or a marginal placement where the

Would you trust this peg?

Tips for Placing Pegs

- Soft rock requires a soft peg and hard rock a hard peg. A hard steel peg is better when the crack is straight internally. A soft peg is better when the crack curves internally.
- The ideal peg placement should make an acute angle between the rock and the direction of the force exerted.
- Bend soft pegs that protrude to decrease the leverage.
- In a vertical crack make use of any variations in the rock to hold the piton in place; a narrowing above and below the peg is ideal to prevent the peg pivoting out.
- The eye of the peg is best placed sideways in vertical cracks and downwards in horizontal.
- In roof cracks place the longest one possible and place them with slight horizontal inclination to reduce the odds of total failure should they slip.
- A peg placed in a three-way corner is almost impossible to remove.
- When using angles place them so that there are three points of contact.

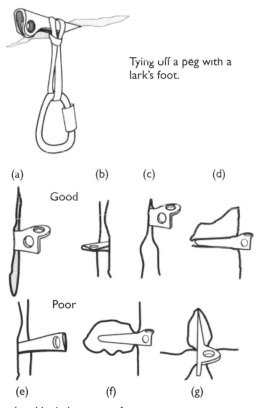

Tying off a peg with a lark's foot.

Good and bad placements for pegs:

(a–d) good placements;
(e) angle with only two sides in contact;
(f) a poor peg;
(g) a poor peg that can pivot out.

Toit du Fix at Saussois – a 7B bolted route.

peg is not in contact with the rock. Angle pegs can be overdriven which spreads the sides and reduces the holding power.

If it has not been possible to hammer the peg all the way in because the crack is shallow, stop hammering when it has bottomed out to avoid loosening the peg. Then tie it off using a slip-knot, lark's foot or clove hitch on a sling (do not use bulky rope or cord – the best is Dyneema/Spectra). The clove hitch will not come off the peg, although it does not put the load close to the rock, so use it when security is the priority rather than reducing leverage. The slipknot comes undone but puts the load closest to the rock, so use it on poorly placed pegs. Stacking pegs is described in Chapter 8.

Without a hammer it is difficult to test a fixed peg, but a reasonable test is to hold a krab loosely in two fingers and tap it on the peg. The sound it makes will indicate whether it is safe.

Removing Pegs

The removal of pegs can seriously damage the rock. Knocking the peg back and forth the full length is the quickest way but also the most damaging, so try gentler blows first. It is better to loosen the peg with predominantly upward blows because then a nut placement may be created. However, in practice, it is difficult to remove a peg with blows in only one direction. To remove it when it is loose attach a chain of krabs to it and yank it outwards.

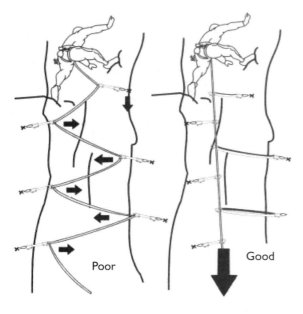

Keep the rope in a straight line.

Bolts

Because the UK has few big mountains, climbers find their adventure on smaller cliffs and crags. This book is not the place to air my personal views on bolting, but you should consider the ramifications of placing bolts to make your work as an instructor or your personal climbing more convenient (see Chapter 5 for how to place them). By the way, bolts do come out!

Assessing bolts

Bolts that do not tighten are either set in too shallow a hole or are stripped; pounding them with a hammer can only worsen the situation by bending or cracking the bolt. Beware of any bolt that is set crookedly, wobbles or is in loose or soft rock.

Removing bolts

Never chop a bolt or smash it flat. Instead, pull it out using a thin flat piton with a V cut in it and a crowbar. If it proves difficult, do not keep pulling in one direction, as you may break the bolt. If the bolt does break, punch in the remaining stud as deep as possible. To refill the hole mix some resin with rock dust or use rock coloured tube cement. To remove glue in bolts try twisting with a crowbar or cut and punch them in.

ATTACHING THE ROPE TO THE RUNNERS

Pioneer climbers simply draped the rope over spikes of rock or threaded it through pegs and behind chockstones. The next generation clipped the rope into single krabs or two krabs with the danger that the rope could twist out in a fall. Today's climbers are more fortunate that they can link the rope to protection via a quick draw or an extender (two krabs linked by a sling). These act like a hinge to prevent the protection lifting out.

Tips for Attaching the Rope to Protection

- Do not use single open-gate krabs on bolts or pegs. The krab's inability to swivel increases the chance of the rope unclipping itself. Instead, use a screw-gate on the first bolt to prevent accidental unclipping.
- A quick draw or extender placed with the krab gate down and facing out from the rock reduces the chance of the krab's gate being opened by the rock surface or by the krab banging against the rock.

Keeping the Rope in a Straight Line.

In a fall, the top piece of protection receives 50 per cent more force than elsewhere in the chain and if it is not a good one, it is nice to know that the ones below are going to stay in place. The only runner that receives a downward force is the last one; the rest receive outward pulls towards an imaginary straight line between the belayer and the leader. To prevent the likelihood of a fall pulling the runners out consider the direction that the force of a fall applies to all the runners, not just the last one placed.

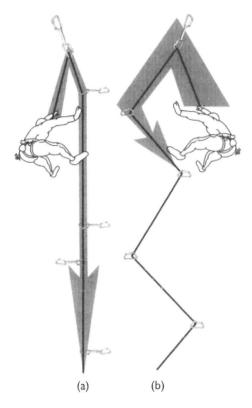

(a)　　　(b)

Keeping the ropes in a straight line better absorbs the forces generated by a fall. In (a) more of the rope can absorb the force.

If you cannot clip a wire because it is in a deep crack, replace the wire with a nut on rope and extend the nut directly with a sling. In extreme circumstances, put a sling through a wire nut, but beware that a fall could possibly cut the sling.

Compare these two photographs, which belayer would you rather be belayed by? Climbers: Danny Brown and Chris Bannister.

In addition to extending the runners to keep the rope in a straight line, the position of the belayer is important. If the belayer is standing out from the cliff during a fall, the rope has a tendency to straighten out between the belayer and the first runner. This can result in the runners lifting out and has been responsible for complete pitches becoming 'unzipped', leaving the leader hanging by the top runner alone. It is therefore an advantage if the first runner can take an upward pull because this will prevent the runners lifting out.

The direction of force on the protection becomes more difficult to assess as the route weaves around the cliff and over overhangs. Try to use placements that take a pull in any direction and consider the effect that a falling second will have on the equipment especially when traversing. It may even be necessary to end the pitch early to avoid awkward placements. Any runner that cannot be extended should be well seated or another placed to prevent it lifting out (*see* Multidirectional Protection, page 158).

Even when the runners cannot be pulled sideways, try to maintain a straight line with the rope to reduce the rope drag (friction). As the rope runs through the krabs rope drag it is at the least an annoyance and at the worst can cause a climber to fall. On overhangs it is often tempting to place a short extender to limit the fall, but rope drag over the lip of the overhang can still create problems for the climber.

Try to avoid placements that stress the krab over an edge.

Clipping the Rope

There are two easy ways of clipping the rope into a krab, depending on which way it is facing:

a) Hold the krab with the second finger or middle and clip the rope using thumb and index finger.
b) Hold the krab with the thumb and clip the rope with the index and second finger.

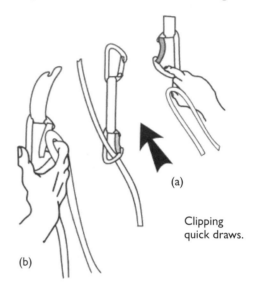

(a)

(b)

Clipping quick draws.

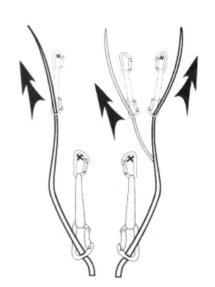

Pass the rope from the back of the krab and out to the climber, not the other way. This may prevent the rope unclipping from a krab in a fall. When climbing diagonally the gate of the krab must always be away from the direction of the climber.

Traversing Pitches

When the route traverses, protect the hard moves before and after the crux even if the ground is easy after the hard moves. This is because the second invariably removes the runner before making the difficult moves. Also consider placing protection for the second on vertical pitches that have a gradual or subtle traverse because if the seconder falls off they may swing to the side and onto steeper or over-hanging ground.

Andy Long using good double rope technique on Immaculate Arete E46a, Pordenack Point.

Take care if the route moves diagonally upwards at the end of a traverse or even on a vertical pitch because if the seconder falls during the traverse the ropes can saw along rock edges, possibly cutting the ropes.

Double-Rope Technique

A single rope is easier for the student and the instructor to use and allows the student to see the ropework techniques more clearly. However, on more difficult climbs or when the route wanders, double ropes have distinct advantages. Double-rope technique involves clipping one rope into one series of runners and the other into another series parallel to the first.

These are the advantages of the double-rope technique:

- Each rope runs in a straighter line through the protection. This advantage is lost if the ropes are crossed.
- When a climber using a single rope pulls the rope to clip into a runner above their head, they momentarily increase the potential distance they could fall until clipped into the krab. Alternately clipping double ropes into protection reduces the length of a fall should you fail to clip the protection.
- It reduces the chances of complete rope failure in a fall.
- It reduces the amount of rope needed at belays, as each rope can be used for a separate anchor attachment.
- If the belayer is paying attention to both ropes the lower impact forces generated by double ropes are distributed between two runners and two ropes. (But this may not always be the case and there is the chance of a long fall onto a single half-rope.)
- Double-rope technique can also have advantages on some traverses that reach the top of the cliff after the traverse. In this situation if the leader clips one rope into the runners, as long as the belay is above the traverse the other rope can be above the person seconding the traverse.
- Double ropes also give the option of a longer abseil should a retreat be required.

The disadvantage of double-rope technique is that two ropes weigh more than a single rope

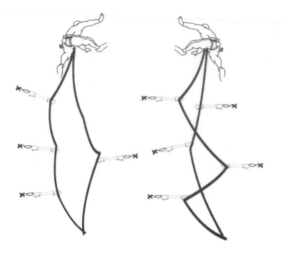

Good (left) and poor double-rope technique.

and belaying is more difficult for the student as they have to take in and pay out ropes simultaneously. There is also the distinct possibility of a large fall onto a single half-rope.

CREATING A BELAY

On reaching the top of a pitch, a climber anchors to the rock to bring up the second – that is, they create a belay. When creating belays, trade-offs and compromises are inevitable, as few systems can be arranged perfectly. Beware of becoming too complicated – the simplest systems are often the best. The ideal belay consists of the following:

- **Solid Anchors:** Search widely; do not accept the first anchors, unless they are good of course. Choose natural anchors first, then nuts and hexes, then an SLCD and as a last resort any fixed gear. Two anchors are normally a minimum.
- **Equalize the Anchors:** The phrase 'back up anchors' is confusing because the belay comprises all the anchors together. Ideally, if part of the belay fails then the remainder of the anchors take the load with no movement of the climber tied into the belay.
- **Independent Anchors:** Two smaller nuts placed in the same crack but used as individual anchors are in effect a single anchor point because if the crack expands both come out. Therefore, whenever possible, place anchors in separate sections of the cliff.

- **Tight Rope:** Keep the ropes taut to prevent the belayer disappearing over the edge. Avoid anchors a long way back because rope stretch may deposit the belayer over the cliff edge.
- **Stand or Sit?:** When the anchors are low down and the belayer is standing, the belayer can be pulled to their knees with the result that they let go of the rope. Sit down when the anchors are below shoulder height. The disadvantage of sitting is that it is difficult to give assistance to a struggling second without the leg muscles being available.
- **Communication:** It is easier to communicate with the second when they are visible.
- **Direction of Forces:** Consider which way a fall will pull the belayer and equalize the anchors such that a fall does not pull the belayer sideways or upwards.
- **What If?:** Finally, ask 'what happens if the second falls?' If the answer is nothing, then the belay is good; otherwise, it isn't.

Locking or Open-Gate Krabs?

Few European climbing books show locking krabs on belays, but in the UK there is an almost paranoid reaction to using open-gate krabs for belays. Many guides and instructors use locking krabs when working and open-gate krabs when playing. Why? This is a judgement call, but consider the following before deciding what to do:

- If the consequence of the rope coming out of the krab would be catastrophic, a screw-gate krab must be used, for example, all attachments to the harness or single anchor points.
- The chance of the rope coming out of the krab on anchor placements is negligible even if you do an Irish jig! If a clove hitch is used and you are tight on the belay, it will not magically leap out of the krab.

That said, screw-gates are advisable on all top- and bottom-rope belays because the constant movement of the system could conceivably cause the rope to come out of an open-gate krab. They are also advisable when anchoring clients on multi-pitch climbs. Avoid using a mixture of twist lock and screw-gate krabs when attaching ropes to anchors, because it is all too easy to forget that you have a mixture and not do up the screw-gates.

Attaching to the Anchors

All the methods discussed here rely on the principle of creating Vs between the harness and the anchors. The simplest way to create a belay is to take the rope around a big boulder or spike and then tie this rope into the 'central loop' (created by tying the rope into your harness) with a clove hitch on an HMS krab. This is repeated for each anchor, but with no more than two clove hitches per HMS krab.

Anchors Not Close to the Cliff Edge

Pass the rope through all the krabs attached to the anchors. Keep hold of the rope between the anchors and move to the edge of the cliff. Then pull the rope between the anchors back to the harness. Attach to each rope the central loop with an HMS krab and a clove hitch.

This method has the advantage that all the adjustments are at the harness, avoiding the constant walking back and forth adjusting knots. The disadvantage is that it uses a lot of rope.

Attaching to anchors to create a belay when they are within arms reach.

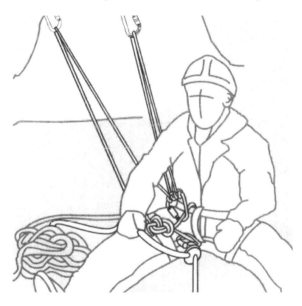

Attaching to anchors to create a belay when they are not close to the edge of the cliff.

Anchors Within Arm's Reach or When There is Limited Rope Available

Estimate how far the cliff edge is away and tie clove hitches directly to the anchors. Then link the rope to the central loop with a clove hitch on an HMS krab.

An alternative method of attaching the rope to the central loop instead of clove hitches on an HMS krab is to tie directly into the central loop with a figure-of-eight knot or two half hitches. It does eliminate a krab, but it takes more practice

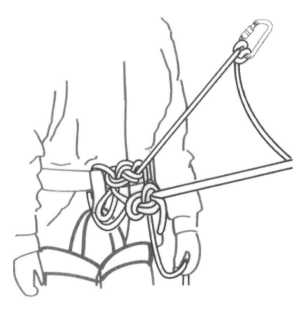

Alternative method of tying back into the harness.

to equalize the tension on the anchors. To make it easier take a step towards the anchors before tying the knot.

Attaching to Anchors When They are a Long Way from the Cliff Edge

If the anchors are a long way back from the cliff edge, untie from the rope and tie the end of the rope to the anchor(s). Return to within a foot or two of the cliff edge and take a bight of rope through the harness and secure it with two half hitches. Alternatively, tie a figure-of-eight and attach to it using a screw-gate krab. Beware that when the belay is a long way back there is a lot of stretch in the rope, which could conceivably deposit the belayer over the edge in the event of a fall.

To equalize more than one anchor use slings (*see* below), a figure-of-eight on a bight ('bunny ears') or Alpine butterfly and use the resulting loop(s) to attach to the anchors. When you have more than three anchors these methods do not distribute the load equally to all three, so it may be worth considering the order you clip them.

Equalization of Anchors with Slings

In order to share the forces among the anchors or to save rope when the anchors are far apart it may be necessary to equalize them with slings.

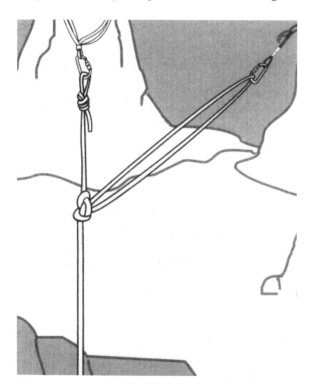

Using an Alpine butterfly to attach to multiple anchors when they are a long way back from the cliff edge.

The 'self-equalizing' system in the accompanying diagram is used when the belay anchors are strong and solid, or they are exposed to forces from varying directions, or the direction

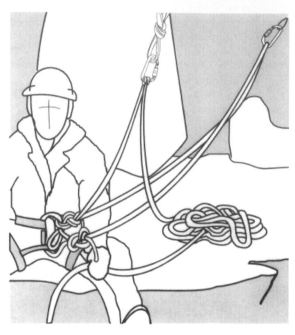

It is possible to use a combination of the previous methods.

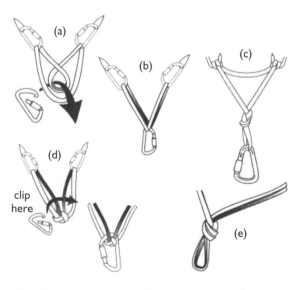

(a) Self-equalization.
(b) Two slings.
(c) Two clove hitches.
(d) An overhand knot.
(e) Two slings tied together to create an overhand knot.

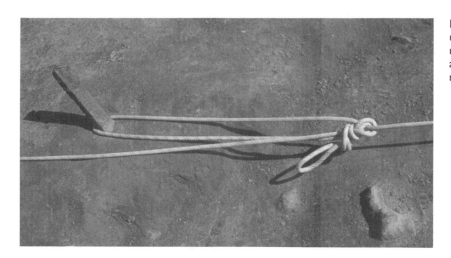

Equalizing the rope using a bowline. This method has the advantage that it does not require any krabs.

of pull is unpredictable (a rare occurrence). The downside of self-equalization is that if one anchor fails the other anchor is shock-loaded. The shock loading can be reduced by placing knots in the sling, although this seems to defeat the aim of the self-equalizing system. The self-equalizing system may have its uses on stances where the instructor needs to move around.

There has been a trend to equalize anchors with daisy-chain slings by attaching the loops to the anchors, but be aware that these are designed for aid climbing and the stitching holding the small loops together has a breaking strain of only 2KN

ABSEILING

Abseil is a German word meaning 'on rope'. In French, it is Rappel, meaning 'to recall'. Abseiling can be safe, but because it is simple to do, carelessness can easily creep in. If you abseil frequently, for example on sea cliffs, a pre-stretched abseil rope lasts longer than a dynamic rope and limits the stretching of the rope over edges.

Dave Williams abseiling in the Riglos, northern Spain.

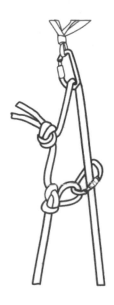

It is possible to abseil using a Gri Gri on a single and a double rope.

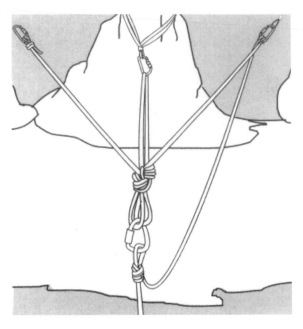

A fixed abseil station.

Rigging the Rope

The same considerations apply when setting up an abseil station as they do for creating a normal belay: solid, independent and equalized anchors. Whether the rope is fixed in place or retrieved, such as pulled down the cliff to be used for climbing, dictates the rigging method used.

A Fixed Abseil Station

This is where the rope cannot be pulled down the cliff after the climbers have abseiled. Attach the rope by a clove hitch (for easy adjustment) to one anchor, then pass it through the other anchors and pull the rope between them to create Vs. Tension the rope in the direction of the abseil and tie an overhand knot or figure-of-eight into the loops of rope. The rope is then clove hitched to the final anchor (for easy adjustment). Tie a figure-of-eight or figure-of-nine (easier to undo) in the rope to go over the cliff edge and clip it into the overhand knot using a locking krab.

If the full length of the rope is required for the abseil, equalize the anchors with a separate short length of rope (rigging rop) or slings and attach the abseil rope to them.

A Retrievable Abseil

This is where the ropes can be pulled down and used for climbing or for the next abseil. It should not be confused with 'releasable abseil', which describes the set up for group use. To allow the ropes to be retrieved, equalize the anchors with a separate short section of rope or slings. Put the abseil rope through the sling(s) or clip into them using a krab to save wear on the slings.

Joining the Ropes

A popular method for joining two abseil ropes together is to use a simple overhand knot (leaving 45cm of tail), because as it rolls over an edge it is less likely than a double fisherman's knot, to become snagged. Do not be tempted to tie two overhand knots for extra security because the second one may jam in cracks when the abseil anchors are flush with the rock. You may find it easier to pull the ropes if you have placed the abseil ropes through the slings such that you are pulling down on the rope that is exiting on the inside of the sling.

Making Abseiling Safer

Consider the following ways to make abseiling safer:

● Abseiling is often used to access or escape from a route. This means that your mind is often distracted by the storm, excitement at the prospect of the route or failure, so do not rush and make sure you check everything.

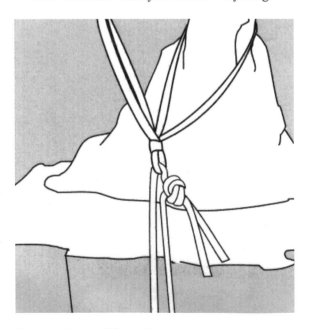

A retrievable abseil from slings.

- Make the belay station as high as possible so that the 'take-off' is easier. This will also makes rope retrieval better when the anchors are a long way back from the edge.
- The best abseil route is steep and featureless. Less steep routes provide more opportunities for the rope to snag.
- Make sure that the cliff edge is clear of loose rock and does not have any sharp edges. Use a rope protector to prevent rope wear on the cliff edge.
- Make sure that there is no one below you.
- Throw the rope down by layering the rope, doubled, across your hands (lap coiling), with decreasing sized layers. Grasp the middle and throw these down, then do the same with the end of the rope. A method that is useful when it is windy is to daisy chain the rope in a circle; this keeps the rope weighted throughout the throw (*see* Coiling Ropes, page 192).
- Always check that the ropes reach the bottom.
- If the bottom is not visible and the length of the abseil is not known, tie a knot in the end of the rope. To stop double ropes becoming tangled, tie a knot in each rope, a figure-of-eight in the rope to be pulled and an overhand in the other.
- If the rope touches the bottom do not tie knots in the ends especially when there is a chance that the rope will enter the sea because this increases the chance of it becoming trapped under a boulder. When it is windy knots in the end of the rope can also increase the chances of it catching in a crack to the side.

- Check that harnesses are buckled correctly, and tuck away hair, clothing and straps.
- Do not remain directly underneath the abseil; move to the side to avoid anything dropped or knocked down from above.
- When using a retrievable abseil separate and untangle the ropes before pulling them down and remove any knots before they become stuck at the top of the abseil.
- When the abseil ropes are to be pulled down check before the last person abseils that the ropes will actually come down. If the rope is difficult to move, extend the abseil station. To remember which rope to pull, clip an extender from the harness to the rope to be pulled. This also helps to sort out any twists.
- When retrieving the ropes make sure that they are not going to run into a crack and become jammed.

Sliding Down the Rope

The figure-of-eight descender is the choice for abseiling with large numbers of students. However, when multi-pitch climbing with students it may be better to use a single device for abseiling and belaying.

When using a figure-of-eight descender there is the small possibility of the rope lifting over the top and locking off. To prevent this occurring hold the figure-of-eight like a frying pan and thread a bight of rope through the frying pan.

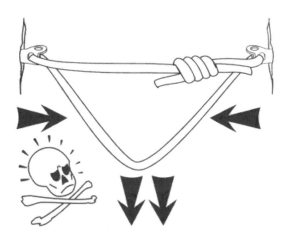

Avoid the American triangle.

To increase friction, take a wrap around the leg.
Climber: Zac Abbot.

When abseiling on a thin rope increase the friction by using the descender with the rope running through the small hole or try the 'Waddy Brake' when the thin rope is passed twice through the delay device. All devices generate friction to control the speed but some are less smooth than others. Introducing a second krab (*see* photo) can make abseiling smoother.

The ideal body position is 55 degrees to the cliff with the feet apart, knees flexed, and the heels placed on the rock to ensure they do not skid away which would result in a crash of knees or face against the rock. Smooth and controlled movements are best so do not bounce 'Rambo-like' down the cliff – it only stresses the abseil station, especially during the first few feet when there is not much rope to absorb the force. Flex the knees on the lip of overhangs, push outwards and slide quickly down the rope, or alternatively sit sideways and drop over the lip.

The upper hand only guides the rope and the bottom hand controls the rate of descent. The amount of friction at the start of a long abseil is greater than at the bottom, because of the

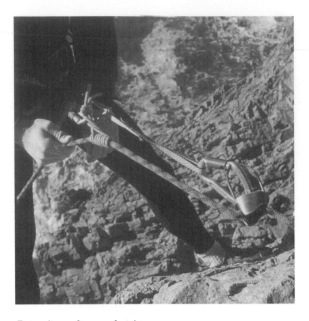

Extending a figure-of-eight.

weight of rope down the cliff. This may frighten novice students because they speed up during the descent. When the abseiler is heavy enough the rope feeds itself through the device and all the abseiler needs to do is control the speed of the rope through the device. If the abseiler is lightweight they may have to lift the rope slightly. Using the figure-of-eight in 'sports mode' (*see* Belaying, page 147) can make it easier for lightweight people, but be careful not to reduce the friction too much. To increase the friction put the rope twice through the figure-of-eight, although this also increases the twisting of the rope. Taking the rope around the waist or a leg can also increase the friction.

If the student is not strong enough to hold the rope with one hand consider extending the figure-of-eight with a sling. This will then provide enough space for both hands to hold the rope. This does, however, put the figure-of-eight in front of the face and closer to the helmet straps, jacket toggles and hair. It can also make it more difficult to get over the edge of the cliff.

When the leg loops and waist belt have been linked with a screw-gate krab, there have been a small number of failures due to the figure-of-eight descender levering open the gate. If the student has to abseil on a harness without an abseil loop, it may be better to put a sling through the leg loops and waist belt and attach the abseil device to this via the screw-gate krab.

Inserting a second krab. Climber: Babs Jongmans.

Abseiling with a shunt for protection.
Climber: Trevor Massiah.

Protecting an Abseil

When abseiling with novices a safety rope may be necessary (see Abseiling with Students, page 182), but there are alternative methods for protecting an abseil with more experienced students. One method is simply to hold the rope at the bottom of the abseil (not directly underneath). If the student who is abseiling then lets go of the rope you can pull the rope tightly, slowing the rate of descent. You must remain vigilant and concentrate on the abseiler.

The following methods of protecting an abseil are not foolproof and although they improve safety, do not trust them implicitly:

- The autolocking Petzl Shunt is the only purpose-built device for protecting an abseil. It can be placed above or below the abseil device. When placed above it is difficult to release when loaded.
- An alternative is to extend the abseil device away from the abseil loop with an extender and screw-gate krabs, then attach a French prusik from the abseil loop to below the abseil device. This has the advantage that

the abseil device takes the load and the French prusik simply holds the rope in the braked position. It also allows two hands to be used on the rope.

- An alternative system is to attach the French prusik from the rope below the device to the leg loop. This has the disadvantage that if the abseiler is knocked unconscious the body may twist in towards the harness as the leg loop is drawn upwards. This can also bring the French prusik too close to the abseil device. If you prefer this method you may want to consider attaching the French prusik to a long sling tied to the back of the harness.
- The prusik can also be attached above the abseil device, although then the load comes totally onto the French prusik knot. However, it is much easier to abseil past a knot when the prusik is above the abseil device. It is also more appropriate when abseiling with an Italian hitch.

Stopping Mid-Abseil

When stopping mid-abseil to remove a stuck runner or take a photograph, take the rope around the waist and wrap it around a leg; do not rely solely on a French prusik. An alternative method is to take the rope around the waist and tie it off in front of the abseil device with two half hitches. The diagram below shows another useful method.

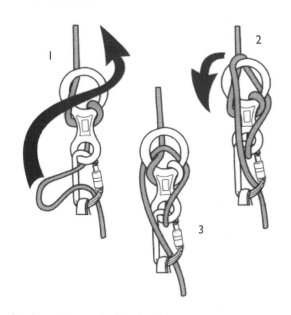

An alternative method for locking a figure-of-eight.

Stopping mid-abseil. The rope running around the
waist will add support to your back.

An arm abseil. Climber: Mark Hurst.

Retrieving a Stuck Abseil Rope
When the rope becomes stuck the first thing to
do is to pull the other rope to check whether the
wrong one has been pulled. If the rope still does
not move try pulling the rope at a different
angle. If that does not work the students can
help to pull harder, which will either make it jam
further or release it. If the rope remains stuck try
pulling heavily on both and then release the one
you do not want to pull – the recoil of the
unweighted rope may free it.

If the rope still remains stuck, things become
more serious and difficult. If both ends of the
rope are at the bottom, you can prusik up on
both ropes. If only one end is at the bottom, the
only way is to rope solo back to the anchors (*see*
Chapter 7).

Alternative Abseil Methods
The classic abseil/dulfersitz
This is unlikely to be a preference when
abseiling with students, because it is difficult,

strenuous and uncomfortable on anything but
easy slopes. To improve this abseil create a
Dulfer seat (*see* 'Improvized Climbing Harnesses', page 192) from a large sling, and take
the ropes through a krab over the shoulder and
down into the opposite hand.

The arm abseil
This is sometimes useful for descending down a
slippery or easy angled descent, when the consequences of a slip are not serious. It provides less
friction than a classic abseil.

MULTI-PITCH CLIMBING

Some students find the prospect of a multi-pitch
route daunting, but if you break the climb into
sections (a multi-pitch climb is simply a lot of
single pitches stacked on top of each other), and
take the pitches one at a time it becomes much
more manageable.

A classic abseil.

Vector E2 4b, 5c, 5b. A multi-pitch route on Tremadog, North Wales.

Preparing a Rack

Belay stances on multi-pitch climbs are a nightmare without proper organization. It is therefore important to prepare properly before embarking on a multi-pitch climb. Carry extra protection, slings and screw-gates on multi-pitch climbs because equipment may be left at the belay.

Consider carrying a small bumbag with a first-aid kit, some snacks, a small bivi bag, a head torch and shoes for the descent. Alternatively, just carry a first-aid kit taped under your helmet.

Belaying on Multi-Pitch Climbs

The same principles and mechanics apply for belaying on a multi-pitch climb as a single-pitch climb. The belaying method used – direct or indirect – is dependent on the difficulty of the climb, the terrain and the ability of the students.

When belaying a lead climber on a single-pitch climb, the belay device can be attached to the abseil loop on the harness. However, when belaying the leader from a multi-pitch stance the belay device is best attached to the top of the

---

An Example Rack for the Instructor When Multi-Pitch Climbing

- Eight quick draws.
- Five extension slings (eight krabs and five 2ft slings).
- Three 8ft slings.
- Three 5ft slings.
- One set of wires 1–9 plus some doubles 3–7.
- One set of hexentrics 5–9.

- Eight screw gates.
- Four HMS krabs.
- One nut key.
- Two belay devices.
- Two prusik cords.

More difficult routes will require two sets of wires and an assortment of SLCDs.

central loop and when belaying a second it is best attached to the bottom of the central loop. This prevents the loop becoming twisted and directs the force to the belay more effectively.

The First Runner

On a single-pitch climb the first runner is placed where a ground fall is possible, but on a multi-pitch climb a runner should be placed as soon as possible after leaving the stance irrespective of the difficulties. This prevents a factor 2 fall occurring, with the result that all the forces must be absorbed by the belayer and the anchors. Remember a short fall close to the belay puts much more impact on the anchor and belayer than a long fall a hundred feet up a pitch where the elasticity of the rope absorbs much of the force. If a runner cannot be found immediately, clip an extender into one of the anchor points. This will make not make it safer because the force on that runner is almost doubled, but it will make it more comfortable for the belayer to hold a fall.

Creating a Belay on a Multi-Pitch Climb

Try to use ropework systems that the students can use when climbing with a friend, alternating leads. The same general principles apply to creating a belay when climbing a multi-pitch route as for single-pitch climbs: solid rock; equalized and independent anchors; tight on the belay; can you see the climber; where will the force pull the belayer; sitting or standing?; and What if?

Creating a Belay When Alternating Leads

On reaching the belay stance, the lead climber attaches the rope/s to the anchors in exactly the same way as for personal climbing on a single-pitch climb.

It is a false economy to rush off on the next pitch before sorting gear. When the stance is large enough for two climbers, simply tie off the belay plate by putting a figure-of-eight knot in the dead rope; if the second falls off the ledge they are close enough for you to help them back onto the ledge. Alternatively, tie off the plate using one of the methods described earlier. If the belay stance is too small for two, clip the second into the belay using slings or their rope.

If the situation changes and the second does not want to lead the next pitch, transfer the ropes from the second to the anchors. To do this, take the second's rope under the existing anchor rope, through the middle of each one and into the anchor's krab. Alternatively, clip another krab into the protection underneath the existing krabs. The leader's ropes will then be on top on leaving the stance.

An alternative to this method is to equalize the anchors to a single point using slings. When the second arrives on the stance it is then a simple process to clip them into the slings and pull the ropes through so that the leaders end is on the top of the pile or draped across their ropes (*see* 'Storing the Ropes' below).

It is becoming popular to carry one large 240cm sling to equalize all the anchors. Americans use a rope sling called a 'cordlette'. Using a very long sling does make equalizing anchors simple, but can be a problem for the student to carry; two 120cm slings are more useful.

A hanging stance with rope running through a separate krab. Climbers Mike Rose and Trevor Massiah.

Hanging Belay

A hanging stance is required when the pitch ends at a vertical wall or when the route starts just above the sea. When creating hanging belays do not struggle with one hand – place a good anchor and take tension from the rope to free both hands, then create a belay.

If you are leading every pitch it is advisable to set up a hanging stance with slings, because changing over the ropes on a hanging belay is difficult. On a hanging belay, it is easier to let another anchor take the forces generated by a second's fall. Therefore clip the second's rope through a bombproof belay anchor or a separate runner above you. To avoid twisting of the rope as you take in, make sure that this krab is lying perpendicular to the rock.

Upward Pull on Stances

During a fall, the movement of the belayer upwards absorbs some of the force. However, it may be prudent to prevent an upward pull when there is a roof or rock spike above, or if the difference in weight between the climbers is too large. If an upward-pulling anchor is needed; consider the direction that any force generated by the falling leader is going to apply to the anchor and attach to it using the rope or a sling.

Storing the Ropes

A few seconds spent sorting the ropes on a multi-pitch stance can save minutes later on. Here are a few tips to help:

- Have a plan for the belay and clip into the anchors in a methodical fashion.
- To avoid tangles pull the ropes through so that the leader's end is on top.
- Work with the rope on the same side as the pile of rope.
- Make sure that the loaded rope does not run over other ropes.
- When there is a big ledge to belay from, simply lay the ropes where they will not be trodden on.
- On a hanging or restricted stance, stop the ropes dangling down the cliff by laying them across the belay rope(s) (between the belay device and the rock). Use progressively shorter loops to prevent them tangling in each other. Draping them over the ropes also

A hanging stance with the ropes draped across her lap. Climber: Bahs Jongmans.

makes belaying for the next pitch easier – if they are hanging down the cliff it is hard work to lift them up and through the belay device. If there is a large spike you can use that instead of the climbing ropes to lay the rope over. You will still need to make sure the leader's rope is going to flow smoothly from the top of the lapped ropes.
- On a small or a hanging stance just above the sea it is useful to have a light rope bag or rucksack for the climbing rope. Be sure to leave the end(s) of the ropes poking out of the top and ensure that the lead ends are the ends from the top of the pile.

FURTHER CONSIDERATIONS FOR SPORT CLIMBING

Sports climbs are the ultimate convenience climbs. Pre-placed bolts and a point at the top of the climb to lower off from mean that all that is required to climb them is some quick draws and a rope. However, there are a few things to consider that may make life easier for those traditional climbers new to sports climbing.

Adrian Wilson sport climbing in the sun.

Equipment

- A 10/11mm single 60m rope (many sports climbs now require this length to lower off).
- Twelve to fifteen quick draws. Count the bolts and take two extra to clip into the belay chain and sort out the lower off.
- Any standard belay device will work, but see Chapter 5 for detailed comments.

Falling Off and Getting Back to the Rock

Sports climbing means that you can push yourself close to your technical limits in relative safety. You are therefore more likely to fall off. If the leader falls off and can reach the rope running to the belayer, they can pull down on it and pulley themselves back to their high point as the belayer takes in the slack rope. If the leader is hanging in space, a technique called 'snapping' can be used, in which the leader pulls up on their rope and then lets go as the belayer simultaneously takes in. However, it is a strenuous technique which requires good teamwork.

The most effective method of doing this is for the belayer to sit on the rope, then as the climber releases the rope the belayer sits further down, takes in and repeats.

Lowering Off

The vast majority of sports climbs have a 'lower-off' point at the top, which may consist of two bolts and possibly a linking chain or sling. Before climbing, make sure that there is enough rope to lower back down. The belayer can tie a knot in the spare end or tie into the rope. If you make a mistake and there is not enough rope to lower down, tie another rope to it and bypass the resulting knot by placing a second belay device (still on the original belayer's harness) onto the rope below the knot. This is easier if there is a third person to help or the lead climber can take their weight off the rope.

UK sports climbs are often not as well prepared as continental ones, so do not expect bolts every few feet and lower offs that consist of two bolts and a chain. If the lower off is a sling, do not under any circumstances lower from the sling itself but add a krab or abseil.

The following procedure will ensure that you lower off safely:

- **Step One**: Clip yourself to the bolts using two quick draws from the abseil loop.
- **Step Two:** pull up 2m of rope, tie a figure-of-eight knot and clip it into your belay loop using a screw-gate krab.

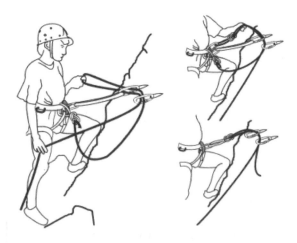

An alternative lowering system when there is plenty of rope.

- **Step Three:** Untie from the end of the rope and thread the end of the rope through the bolts or single lower point.
- **Step Four:** Tie in again.
- **Step Five:** Untie the figure-of-eight knot from the rope.
- **Step Six:** Take the tension on the rope, checking that everything is correct.
- **Step Seven:** Remove the quick draws and lower down.

If the climb is so steep that you cannot retrieve the quick draws, clip a krab or quick draw from your harness to the climbing rope to keep you into the cliff. Be careful when removing the last one because you could take your belayer with you as you swing out.

CONSIDERATIONS WHEN INSTRUCTING ON SINGLE-PITCH CLIMBS

Bottom-Roping

This has become a popular method for introducing novices. A rope runs through a belay station at the top of the cliff and back to the bottom where the climber and the belayer are situated. The climber ascends the route to the attachment point and is lowered back to the ground.

Many of the factors already discussed apply to the setting up of a bottom-rope, for example: solid rock, equalized and independent anchors and direction of pull. Try to avoid SLCDs for anchors because the weighting and unweighting of the rope may cause them to walk deeper into cracks.

A 'hitching rail' or 'rigging rope' allows a number of bottom-ropes to be created and their

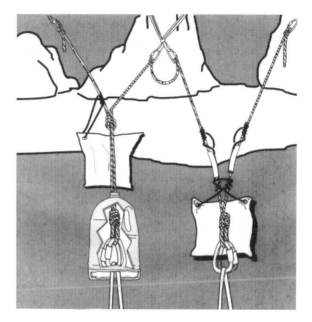

A hitching rail/rigging rope with different rope protectors.

positions changed quickly. The use of pre-stretched ropes reduces the bounce and sawing action of the rigging rope over edges. Two clove hitches on the central anchors provide an independent adjustment for each bottom-rope station. To ensure that the anchors are all equalized, tension the rope in the direction of the force applied when climbing.

It is better for the attachment point for the climbing rope to be well over the edge of the cliff. The rope can then run smoothly, its abrasion over edges is reduced and it discourages the student from climbing onto the top of the cliff. To further reduce the wear and tear on the rigging and climbing ropes, place squares of carpet underneath the knot and wherever the rigging rope runs over an edge. An alternative is to thread the rope through a plastic bottle with the bottom cut off. Rope protectors are essential even on gritstone, rounded edges can also cause considerable rope damage. A knot tied in the rigging rope above the cliff edge reduces the amount of padding required as the rope passes over the cliff edge.

Using only one anchor point, such as a tree, is not advisable even if it is bombproof, because two or three anchors forming a V-shape create a more stable attachment point, therby reducing the movement of the rigging and climbing ropes from side to side. If a long static rope is not

---

A Typical Rack for an Instructor with a Group of Students Top-and-Bottom Roping

- Eight 120cm slings.
- Four 60cm clings.
- One set of wires 1–9.
- One set of Rockcentrics 5–9.
- Up to fourteen screw-gates.
- Six steel screw-gates.
- One nut key.
- Three belay devices plus HMS krabs.
- One prusik cord or mechanical ascender.

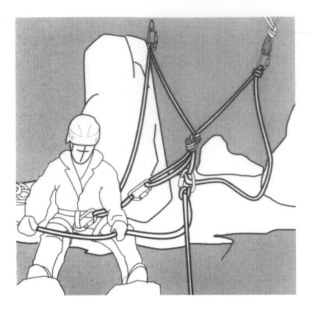

A typical set up for top-roping. The instructor here has tied into the end of the rope and the belay point via a sling.

available for a hitching rail use a short section of dynamic rope or equalized slings for each bottom-rope station.

Wear and tear on the climbing rope can be reduced by increasing the diameter of the attachment point though which the rope runs. This can be done using two screw-gate krabs (steel krabs last longer), with their gates pointing down (vibrations can undo the screw-gates) and in the same direction. Placing the krabs in opposition pushes the back bars together, increasing the friction. Petzl have developed a pulley to reduce the wear and tear on the rope, but because this reduces the friction in the system the belayers have to be vigilant and its use is not advisable with young climbers.

It is possible to set up the attachment point for the climbing rope without using krabs but with a figure-of-eight descender. It is only really useful when the rope is free-hanging because the alignment of the figure-of-eight traps the rope against the rock. This may be useful when working with students who will not leave the attachment point krabs alone, but in this case it would probably be safer not to take them climbing at all.

Top-Roping

Top-roping is when the belayer is at the top of

the crag and the climbers are attached to the rope at the bottom. It does have advantages over bottom-roping because the students get a sense of achievement getting to the top, it teaches a progression to multi-pitch climbing and avoids the problems caused by lowering people from the top of the climb when bottom-roping.

It is imperative that the instructor can see the students because there is often no protection in the climb. The belayer should ideally be directly above the climber to prevent any potential pendulums if they fall. A top-rope belay with a group must allow the instructor to escape from the system rapidly. One method for achieving this is to tie into the rope as for leading a climb then clove hitch the rope into a solid anchor, take the remainder of the rope and clip it into the next anchor and so on. Then pull the ropes to create Vs and tie a figure-of-eight or 'bunny ears' in the resulting loop. The system created is a direct belay. Using the ropework systems already shown there are many possible variations on this theme, each having its own pros and cons.

A popular way to link the climber to the rope is to use a screw-gate krab and a double figure-of-eight knot. This only has advantages when there is no responsible person at the bottom to tie the students on. Whenever possible, tie students into the rope. Troll has developed a krab called the 'Link' which traps the belay loop behind a pin, keeping the krab orientated correctly; however, each harness requires one.

Two Students Climbing Together

It is possible for two students to climb together for fun or to allow a more experienced climber to climb with a nervous one. The easiest method is to tie an Alpine butterfly, 'in-line' figure-of-eight or overhand knot in the rope three arms length from the end of the rope. The resulting 'isolation' loop' should be about 1m long. One climber attaches to the resulting loop with a krab, or preferably a rewoven overhand knot, and the other to the end of the rope. The distance between the climbers depends on the climb and whether it is possible to climb alongside each other. Each climber is independent of the other because of the isolation loop, but both climbers should avoid any slack appearing in the rope by climbing in unison.

Two students climbing together.

Belaying When Using Top-Ropes

The method used depends upon whether the brake arm can move behind the device. The Italian hitch allows the belayer to lean over the edge and still be in the correct position for it to work. Using a belay device with this system would make it difficult to keep the brake arm behind the device and therefore stop a fall. The autolocking Gri Gri can also allow the instructor to lean over the edge and belay effectively.

Belaying When Using Bottom-Ropes

An advantage of bottom-roping is that the group can be supervised more easily and allowed to belay each other from the outset. A conscientious instructor may be able to look after two or even three climbs in close proximity to each other. The belay device that is used depends on the experience of the students and possibly even the aims of the session, for example, whether the group is likely to go climbing again.

The Italian hitch requires minimal skill on the part of the belayer plus it is cheap. Always use a 'buddy system' and have at least two students holding the rope. A belay device requires more skill to operate and this sometimes leaves the climber with a slack rope because the belayer is unable to take the rope in fast enough. The coordination between the belayer and his buddy system can also be difficult to achieve especially with belay plates, which do have a tendency to jam at inopportune moments.

The Petzl Gri Gri is popular for group work because of its autolocking properties and when used properly it does teach correct belaying action. However, it is not the panacea for all the problems of belaying with novices. Preventing the students lowering the climbers too fast requires careful supervision. A prudent use of the buddy system and operating the device as if it has no autolocking properties may help to prevent any accidents.

To avoid any falling objects, position the belayer close to the cliff, and to one side of the line of the route. If they cannot be close to the

Single-pitch work showing the Italian hitch in use.

Two young people tied together to enable them to belay a heavier person. Climber: Robin Neath; belayers: Wendy, Gemma and Jago Neath.

cliff, attach them to a ground anchor or the other students.

When the belayer is much lighter than the climber attach them via a sling to another person(s). If this is not possible, attach the belayer to anchors placed in the ground such that any forces go to the anchors. Another method for belaying a heavier climber is to tie six students to the belay rope; they can then walk backwards as the climber ascends. However, this is only feasible when the bottom is large and flat. It may prove useful in some situations, but its greatest disadvantage that it erodes the ground more quickly and over a larger area.

Be aware of the problems rope stretch may create, especially when the climbers are near to the ground. Therefore, keep the rope tight during the first 1.5 to 3m of climbing. The majority of bottom-roping problems occur when lowering the climber back down. A practice lower, done under control near to the ground, ensures

that the student can be clearly instructed about what is required and can help to avoid a student refusing to be lowered.

Abseiling with Students

Here are some further points to consider:

- When the anchors are low down it may be easier for the students to sit down and slide over the edge, then start abseiling.
- An abseil should not be steep nor too long – even a grass slope can provide a good introduction.
- Overhangs on the way down make life difficult and may bruise shins.
- Ledges on the way down, big enough for the student to stand on, can also create difficulties with scared students refusing to leave the ledge.
- A large area at the top of the abseil and a flat area at the bottom allow the group to sit comfortably and wait their turn in safety.
- The students should move away from the line of the abseil to avoid falling objects.
- Shorten the abseil rope so that it is 1m off the ground; this allows the students simply to walk backwards off the rope plus it prevents the rope being trodden on.

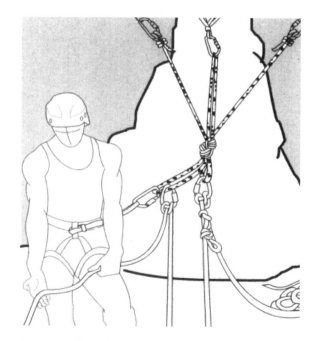

A typical releasable abseil. The instructor is in a position to see and help the novice.

A group abseil.

The ropework used when abseiling with a group is similar to that described for a fixed abseil, with the exception that the abseil rope is not, in most cases, part of the belay and is releasable (a tied-off Italian hitch or descender makes the abseil rope releasable). The advantage is that the safety rope can be tied off if a student has something stuck in the abseil device and the abseil rope can be released. The releasable abseil also allows the lowering of an abseiler 'frozen' in space and too scared to let themselves down. It also solves the rare problems of the abseil rope becoming jammed in a crack below the abseiler or a knot suddenly appearing in the abseil rope. In all cases, release the abseil rope and lower the climber to the ground on the safety rope.

A safety rope is essential with novice students, but this does not require a separate set of anchors to the abseil rope. If there is any doubt about the security of the abseil anchors, do not abseil. After all, one set of anchors is enough at all other times.

A direct belay using an Italian hitch is the simplest method for operating the safety rope. Note in the accompanying diagram that the Italian hitch of the safety rope is elongated away from the tied-off abseil rope to prevent the two jamming against each other. Tie into the belay using the safety rope or a sling, then tie the student into the safety rope before they approach the abseil and the edge of the cliff. It is possible to abseil two people at the same time for fun or because one of them is nervous. It is important that the safety rope protects both of them.

ROPEWORK FOR TEACHING LEAD CLIMBING ON A SINGLE-PITCH CLIMB

Bottom/Top Roping

Bottom- or top-roping allows the student to lead while they are dragging a climbing rope and placing gear. The instructor can then climb the route and examine the protection that has been placed. This is a useful method for looking after either a larger number of students learning to lead or just one. The bottom-rope can be belayed by a third student or by the instructor and kept as slack as the student is comfortable with, taking care it does not become tangled with their legs.

Jumaring/Abseiling

With two students you can inspect the runner placements by jumaring up a fixed rope placed alongside the route. A sling and krab running from the jumar, will enable you to clip the sling into them or into the rope below them if they get into trouble. However, a jumar is not designed to take a leader fall so move with the student.

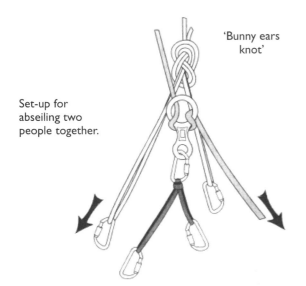

'Bunny ears knot'

Set-up for abseiling two people together.

A set-up for jumaring alongside a student.

Mike Turner jumaring alongside a student to check gear placements. Photo: Mike Turner.

Instructor Soloing

Soloing alongside can be demeaning for the student, plus it takes a great deal of judgement. Consider the implications if something goes wrong or you have to render assistance rapidly.

Abseil Preplacement

A good method when there is a high instructor to student ratio is for the student to abseil down and place the gear prior to leading the route. The instructor can then abseil and check the protection.

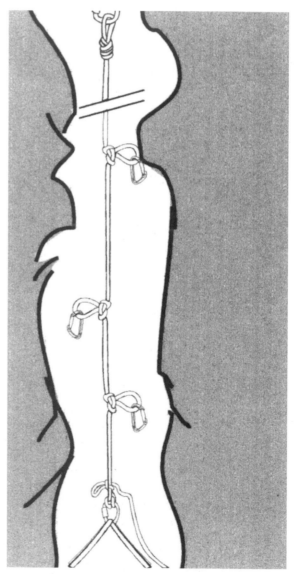

A fixed rope with loops.

Fixed Rope with Loops

With a single student, a realistic situation can be simulated by tying in-line figure-of-eight knots or Alpine butterflies every 2m, with a quick draw attached (a useful technique for those climbers who like bolted climbs). Using a Garda hitch (*see* Chapter 7) or Italian hitch, tension the rope at the bottom to remove any stretch (even if it is an abseil rope). The student can climb with one half-rope and one single rope. Clip the single rope into the quick draws and the half-rope into the protection that has been placed. This method allows the students to lead with the feeling of being above runners, but with the instructor having the peace of mind that the student is not going to pull all their runners out. If the route wanders, use intermediate runners to keep the fixed rope in position. If it goes over roofs fix it below the roof – do not just pass it through a runner.

Instructor Climbing Parallel Belayed by a Third Student

With three students, the instructor can be belayed by the third student, and so climb alongside the climbing pair. This is particularly useful in multi-pitch climbing because the students lead the whole route without the instructor going up first. However, it is more difficult to give assistance if a student gets into trouble above a runner, and it requires a route where the instructor can wander close by at all times. It can also leave the instructor vulnerable to the student falling on them.

Warning

A leader belayed *directly* from a belay equalized with slings can generate enough force in a fall factor 2 to break the sling at the knot. It is worth considering using 8/9mm rope slings for the equalization of belays. Placing a runner directly on leaving the stance or belaying semi-directly from the harness will help prevent this happening.

ROPEWORK FOR GUIDING OR TEACHING STUDENTS ON MULTI-PITCH CLIMBS

The ropework described previously is applicable for personal climbing and instructing, but there are certain techniques used when guiding or teaching on a multi-pitch climb that are specific.

Guiding two students on a multi-pitch climb. Climbers: Gareth Richardson and Paul Blinman.

Guiding Methods

These are methods to be used when the day is not about teaching climbing but about completing the route. The best systems are therefore fast, simple and safe to use.

The simplest and best method of attaching to the anchors when guiding is to equalize them with slings to create a single point belay. The students can then easily clip into the single point. It may be useful to have screw-gate krabs ready on the belay for attaching the student(s). Different coloured krabs may prevent them unclipping the wrong one when they start the next pitch.

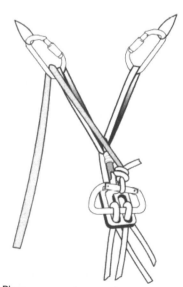

Releasing a Magic Plate.

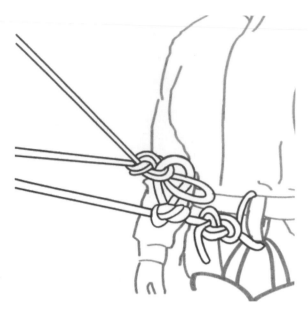

An Alpine butterfly next to the central loop. (Here the rope has been used to equalize the anchors.)

If it is not possible to see the students, set up the belay with a sling, tie into it with a clove hitch and then tie an Alpine butterfly as close to the central loop as possible. This can then be used as the belay loop. If you need to leave the belay and sort out a problem, it is a simple case of 'tying off' the belay device and untying from the end of the rope. When the clients reach the stance they can be tied into the single point on the belay as usual.

Which Belay Device?

An important consideration is what belay device to use. If you are guiding, use a belay device that makes life simple for the instructor. If you are teaching, use a device that the students are likely to use themselves.

A single point belay also makes direct belaying with a Magic Plate (see Chapter 5), Italian hitch or Gri Gri much easier. The advantage of a direct belay is that you are free of the belay system, your position can be adjusted, the student is easily held and it can simplify rescues.

Student Care and Stance Organization on Multi-Pitch Climbs
Students often experience two big stress factors on multi-pitch climbs:

- They often lose sight of the 'bigger picture' and overlook things as they become stressed about tackling the task in hand, for example, they may forget to take any medication they are on, or forget to eat and drink. It is crucial that you help them to see the bigger picture by relaxing them.
- The second is a fear of making mistakes, leading to a hesitation to act – for example, the ropes may become tangled and they do not want to sort it without instruction.

To resolve these stresses, make the students as comfortable as possible and help them to identify real as opposed to perceived hazards, and encourage them to carry out tasks without worrying about making mistakes.

Taking one or more student climbing is easy, but when guiding two students on a multi-pitch climb there are a number of different ways of using the rope.

Do not automatically follow guidebook descriptions for stances – create stances wherever proves best for the students. This may mean that pitches are shortened and sometimes lengthened. If the pitch ends at a very small ledge with only enough room for two students, consider positioning yourself above the stance in a hanging belay and bring the students to the ledge.

Effective management of students at a stance aids speed, efficiency and safety. The problems of stance organization are most pronounced when the stances are small. Consider the order of the students on the stance and their position where you will stand, where the equipment is stored and so on. Other considerations are:

- Are the clients protected from hazards such as falling rock
- If the students are going to be there a long time make sure they are comfortable.
- Does the route go left or right and which student do you want to leave the stance first?
- Can they see you?
- Which student (or both) is going to belay you?
- Where are the ropes best stored?
- Can they take their rucksacks off?
- Sometimes clipping one student in with a sling can help to keep things ordered.
- Clear briefing of the students before you leave the stance often avoids any problems.

When Should You be Belayed?

This is largely a matter of personal comfort and the demands of the route. Even an inexperienced belayer can prevent a catastrophic accident and both can belay you. Consider being belayed when:

- You are at your limit.
- Where there is loose rock.
- When you are tired.
- When you are uncertain of the route.

Consider unbelayed climbing when:

- It is more of a hindrance.
- Speed is an issue.
- The route is solid and familiar.
- The route is within personal limits.

Parallel Ropework with Two Students

Parallel ropework ('*en flèche*' or 'arrow' formation) is where the instructor takes both single ropes up the pitch. This method has serious drawbacks and only works well on routes that are straight up. It has no advantages over the following systems except when you want to bring both students up the pitch at the same time. You must not alternately clip the ropes like double-rope technique because both

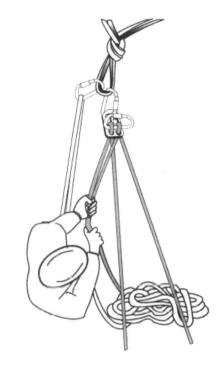

En flèche ropework.

students must be protected as the route meanders. Furthermore, two single ropes clipped into one krab can stress the gate in a leader fall, so if both students are clipped into one piece of protection use separate extenders or two krabs.

If you do decide to use this method, both students can belay you on their ropes. The students then follow the climb separately or together depending on the route' degree of hardness and the difficulty of getting back onto the rock after a fall. Students climbing together often twist the rope as they step across each other, although good communication can avoid this problem. You have a difficult decision whether to belay directly from the anchors or semi-directly. When belaying directly, the Gi Gi (not Gri Gri) is best as it is less difficult to release and lower the students back down the route (but it is difficult to set up an effective hoist). The Gi Gi makes belaying easier when the students move at different speeds. If the ropes are different diameters it is better to clip each rope into a separate krab

Series Ropework with Two or More Students

An alternative and often superior method with two or more students is to bring one student up

---

Single versus Double Ropes for Belaying a Second

Manufacturer's advice about the use of ropes is aimed at the leader and few provide advice for bringing a second up a route, although Edelrid does state that a half-rope can be used for top-roping. Many of us will privately second routes attached to a half-rope, but is this advisable and can we do the same thing with students?

There are a number of issues to consider before using a half-rope to bring a student up a route but the decision is ultimately yours.

- The chance of the rope being cut – a half-rope will be cut more easily than a single rope.
- Does the weight-saving matter and is the increased wear and tear on a thinner rope worth the sacrifice of a few pounds in weight?
- Will the increased stretch using a half-rope land someone on a ledge or projection?
- Will your belay device work as well with one half-rope?

on one rope while carrying the next student's rope (attached properly to the harness). The student can clip the rope they are dragging into the protection already placed on the route and the last student takes out the protection (unless it is straight up). The number of students you can cope with depends on the route, the stances and their experience, but it is unlikely to be more than three. The potential for inexperienced students to get into a tangle is obvious so be diligent about sorting out the ropes on each stance.

Teaching Leading on a Multi-Pitch Climb

A progressive process for teaching leading and creating belays will have the best results. First, refresh the students at ground level. You can then lead the first pitch and set the belay up with slings. Student A can second the pitch belayed by student B. At the belay, student A can place new anchors and arrange the belay under supervision. As soon as student A is safe you can take your rope off student A and they can belay student B and you. Student B can then be attached to your anchors and tied into your rope. You lead the next pitch belayed by student B and the process is repeated, with student B arriving first and setting up the belay. Take care when swapping over the ropes and positioning the students.

A progression from this is for you to lead the pitch belayed by the student, and then abseil to rejoin the students. The student can then lead the route and you can jumar up alongside. Repeat the process to the top.

MULTI-PITCH ABSEILING

Repeated abseils down a big climb require you to have a method for swiftly attaching the students to the crag. One popular method is to lark's foot a sling through the leg loops and waist belt to create a cow's tail. Tie a series of knots along it to create various length clip-in points. Alternatively, use a pre-stitched daisy chain. Here are some things to consider:

- Inexperienced students are often very slow at abseiling, therefore if time is important consider lowering the students.
- Before untying, completely tie the ropes separately into the belay a few metres from the

ends. Leave enough rope to thread them through the belay and then retie them ready for abseiling.
- If it is windy take the ropes down, loosely fed into a rucksack, with the first abseiler rather than throwing them down the cliff. Alternatively, daisy chain them in a circle (see 'Coiling Ropes', page 192).
- To safeguard the first person dubious anchors can be backed up by placing another anchor. When it is the last person's turn they make a judgement about the anchors and either remove the back-up or leave it for extra security.
- When the way down is not obvious, it may save time to lower someone down to check out the route and if it is incorrect belay them back up. If you are carrying rucksacks it may be better to hang them from the abseil device to reduce the chances of tipping upside-down.

Abseiling with Students

Instructor First
When abseiling with students on multi-pitch climbs or sea cliffs you may need to abseil first to arrange the next belay or check out the abseil. The students then abseil to you and clip into the new abseil station or stance with their cow's tail. Unless the students are very experienced attach them to the rope before leaving the stance – this is called 'stacking'. Attach the abseil device to the rope and clip this to the student with an extender using screw-gate krabs on both ends. This gives the student 'freedom of movement' and prevents them being tugged as you abseil. If they are still being pulled as you abseil, consider tying a figure-of-nine in the abseil ropes below them and clip this back into the belay; the student removes the krab and knot before abseiling. Problems do occur with the stacked abseils, such as a student getting stuck part-way down and it may be better to lower them.

It may be better not to attach the students to the belay because they may not want to leave its security. It is better to leave them sitting below their abseil device so that they do not have to climb down below it to start abseiling. If the students are out of sight and nervous you could abseil part of the way down to an intermediate ledge. The students can then abseil to join you and the abseil be completed from there. There is, however, a tendency for the first student, at

A stacked abseil from the inaccessible pinnacle on Skye.

least, to be tugged from the ledge as the instructor abseils, which may be counter-productive to a nervous student.

On multi-pitch abseils work as a team with the students. You set up the anchor and the students sort out the ropes. The students can then be attached to the abseil rope and you abseil to the next anchors, create a belay (or check the existing one) and attach yourself to the anchors via a cow's tail. Check which rope to pull and thread the end you are pulling through the anchor station and tie both into the anchors. The first student then tie abseils to the new stance. The reason for tying the ropes into the anchors is so that the ropes are not blown around, and if the top anchors fail the abseiler may have a chance of survival, albeit with a long fall. The next stage is to pull the rope already fed through the abseil station and repeat.

Students First
There is less likelihood of problems if you can lower the student(s) to the ground or abseil with

a safety rope. An alternative method, when the next abseil stance is clearly visible, is to lower the students to the next stance. They remain on the abseil ropes, but also clip into the belay. The instructor can then abseil to join them, make sure they are safe and continue.

Counterbalance Abseils

Counterbalance abseils are used when speed is important, but because of the extra forces involved care should be taken that the ropes do not run over sharp edges. They can be used in two ways:

● The Instructor and Student
  When using two ropes, tie a large knot on the side of the student and clip yourself to the student with a sling. If the student then loses control the knot will prevent the rope slipping through. Always abseil off a Maillon or a krab because the rope does move over a sling with

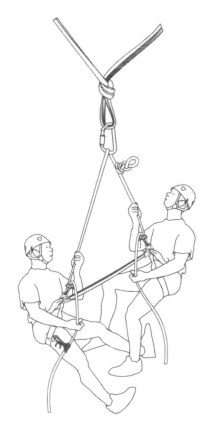

Conterbalance abseil. The left-hand person is the instructor.

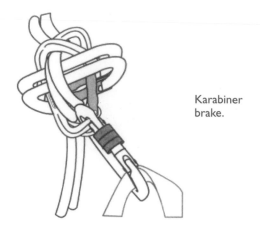

Karabiner brake.

this method. The instructor and student can be connected via a sling with this method, or with an experienced student there could be a French prusik below the abseil device.

- Two students

This can be done after the instructor has abseiled. The instructor can provide a bottom belay for both students.

Alternative Abseil Methods

There are a number of alternative methods for abseiling that can be employed if the belay or abseil device has been dropped or forgotten. If there is only one belay device the student can pull it back up after the instructor has abseiled. Another method is the karabiner brake. Always use two krabs to create the platform and be certain to reverse the gates. Be careful that the rope passes over the back bar of the krabs and

not the gate. The attachment krab must be a screw-gate or two krabs in opposition. A single krab usually creates adequate friction when descending on two single ropes, but on vertical walls or with double ropes two or even three are better. To increase the friction when part of the way down take the rope around the waist or pass it through the leg and back up to the hand.

The Italian hitch is an alternative method to the karabiner brake, although it does twist the rope, especially double ropes. If you have to use it put the Italian Hitches on separate krabs and extend one away from the other, or arrange the hitch on one krab with the ropes overlapping each other, not side by side. If this method is used the person with the abseil device should go last to remove the kinks.

Abseiling with Different Diameter Ropes

It is possible to climb with a 9mm and an 11mm by mistake, something that is more likely to happen as single ropes approach double ropes in diameter. It is also possible for sports routes to be climbed using a single rope and the second to drag an 8.5mm for abseiling.

When using ropes of two different diameters for abseiling be aware that the thinner rope stretches more than the thicker one and travels through the device faster, so the thin end is reached first. To make matters worse, if the knot is on the side of the thicker rope the knot travels down the abseil. To avoid a disaster make sure that the thinner rope is through the abseil anchor and that the ends of the rope are tied together.

Stop just above the knot

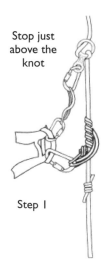

Step 1

Step 2

Step 3

Abseiling past a knot.

Abseiling on a Damaged Rope

When one of the ropes has been damaged and cannot be relied upon for an abseil but is trong enough for pulling the ropes down, or it has been isolated with an Alpine butterfly, abseil on one rope. This method can also be used for abseiling with a Gri Gri (*see* diagram on page 169).

Abseiling Past a Knot

This is used when two ropes have been tied together for accessing a big sea cliff or escaping from a route and returning to get the ropes at a later date. To pass the knot it is essential that the French prusik or Petzl Shunt is above the abseil device and on an extender. When you are close to the knot stop and sit on the French prusik, then take the belay plate off the rope and place it below the knot. The extender should provide you with enough rope to slide the French prusik down and for your weight to come onto the belay device. It is essential that the French prusik remains within reach. If you cannot release the French prusik, place a prusik between the abseil device and the knot and stand in it to release the weight from the prusik.

MISCELLANEOUS

Improvised Chest Harnesses

With large or small people, there is a tendency for the sit harness to end up around the knees or for them to finish upside-down after a fall. A full body harness or chest harness may be necessary in this situation. If these are not available, improvize using a figure-of-eight in a sling or a Parisian baudrier. The Parisian baudrier comes into its own for supporting an injured climber. However, these two methods have the problem that they only link to the front of the harness and there is still the danger that the belt can slip off the waist at the back and over the buttocks.

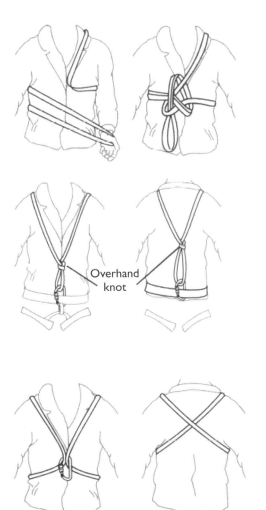

A variety of improvized chest harnesses.

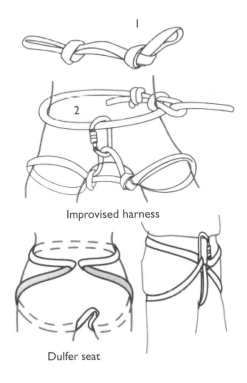

Improvised harness

Dulfer seat

Improvised climbing harnesses.

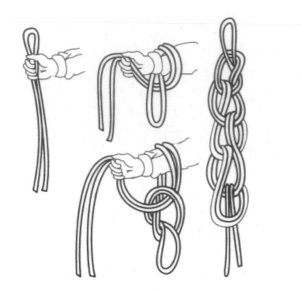

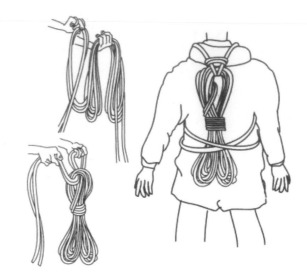

Daisy chaining (left) and lap coiling.

A full body harness can be created by lark's footing a standard sling to the back of the belt and knotting it at the shoulder blades to keep the sling in place. Bring it over the head and knot it as necessary for size, then clip it into the front of the harness. This method is comfortable, but it is not designed for lead climbing.

Improvized Climbing Harness

If we simply tied the rope around the waist, a free-hanging climber would be dead after approximately twenty minutes. The method shown in the accompanying diagram is useful with smaller people but a 120cm sling may not be big enough to make the sit harness. If that is the case make a Dulfer seat out of a sling.

Coiling Ropes

There are a number of methods for coiling ropes. Daisy chaining and lap coiling are the preferred methods because they kink the ropes less. If it is particularly windy and you want to throw the ropes down the cliff, consider daisy chaining them in a circle. First, make a loop of rope and then daisy chain around the rope, incorporating the loop into the daisy chain. The resulting loop of rope will act as a weight when thrown down the cliff but will unfurl as it goes.

CHAPTER 7

SOLVING PROBLEMS

Running or telephoning for help is not always possible when you are on a sea cliff or high up a mountain crag in a remote corrie on the Isle of Skye. Serious incidents can and do occur on Britain's cliffs and first aid is potentially life saving when administered during the first hour after an accident. In addition any delay in reaching someone who is unconscious and upside-down or bleeding could result in further injury or death. The skills in this chapter can help prevent an epic turning into a disaster, but rescue procedures are not like a fire drill – the cliff environment is always changing and the belays are never the same, so following steps ABC will not always work. The scenarios and solutions in this chapter are examples of the tools rather than the only way to solve the problems. For simplicity all the rescues are described using a single rope.

Instructors seldom use the techniques appropriate for rescuing someone and therefore regular practice is very important in maintaining proficiency.

A Word of Warning
A rope under tension can be cut very easily, therefore when practising these techniques on real cliffs with real people, take great care. If practising alone, consider using a totally separate rope so that if it all goes 'pear-shaped' the victim is not seriously injured.

ACCIDENT AVOIDANCE

With common sense, the need for a rescue can be reduced by choosing the correct route for the students and any subsequent rescue made easier by choosing an appropriate stance, a simple belay and keeping the ropes in an orderly manner. It also makes sense to avoid loose routes, routes that are too difficult for the students and routes with overhangs if there are overweight students. Keep things simple – for example, if your students cannot remove their ropes from a screw-gate krab on a stance, just get them to take the protection out of the cliff.

Serious accidents do occur but rescue procedures are not a fire drill.

Teaching Solving Problems to Climbers

One way to approach solving problems is to look at them as a series of tools that can be interconnected in a variety of ways. The most useful components of a rescue system are:

- A good belay.
- The Italian hitch.
- A system for locking the belay device.
- A prusik knot or mechanical device that grips the rope.
- A prusik or mechanical device that releases under load (autobloque).
- A pulley system.
- A lowering system.
- Look at how these can be used in and out of the system.

Remember:

- It saves time if students are clearly briefed about what to do if they lose contact with the rock.
- It is easier to give assistance on routes that are straight up.
- Choose stances that allow communication.
- Reduce the friction of the rope through runners by extending them.
- Pitches that end with loose rock inevitably put the student and/or belayer at greater risk.
- Maintain climbing equipment including prusiks in good condition.
- Create a simple and effective belay.
- Place runners that are not difficult to retrieve.
- Remove jewellery to prevent fingers becoming stuck.
- Undertake first-aid training.
- If it can happen, it will happen. Ask yourself – What If?

Prusik Cord

- 5.5 or 6mm soft, kernmantle cord is best. Thinner cord will melt easily but thicker cord will not grip the rope in wet conditions. The wider the difference in diameter between the climbing rope and the prusik cord, the more grip there will be.
- New cord is slippery, so carefully roll it around on the floor to 'rough it up'.
- The ideal number of prusik loops to carry is three, but for most situations two will suffice.
- Approx. 1.3m in length is ideal. Shorter prusiks maintain the tension on the rope better than long ones, but too short and they maintain the tension too well!
- Tie them with a double Fisherman's or an overhand knot pulled firmly and with long enough tails. The latter makes it easier to undo to use for small threads.

THE TOOLS

Prusik Knots

The term 'Prusik knot' has become the collective noun to describe friction hitches that are used to grip a rope. They essentially involve the use of small-diameter accessory cord to grip the main rope. There are many variations on a theme from the *Kreuzlem* to the *Val d'Aosta* hitches, but the most useful of these knots are described below. Some of the hitches described can be used with slings, but Spectra and Dyneema grip less than nylon and have a lower melting point. A neat prusik knot grips the rope more effectively, but keep a close eye on it as it may not grip the rope when conditions are muddy or wet.

Prusik Knots that are Difficult to Release Under Load
These hitches are used when failure to grip the rope would be disastrous. They are not easily released when a climber's weight is on them and they may remain jammed when the climber's weight is taken off them, that is they are not autoblocs.

The Original Prusik

- It can be tied more easily with one hand.
- It is easier to open and move when ascending.
- It can jam on wet ropes and may not grip at all on icy ropes.
- A krab can be inserted into the hitch to make release easier but this reduces the friction.
- Slings should not be used for this hitch.

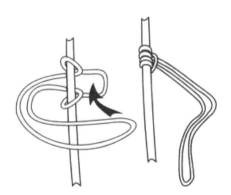

Original prusik.

The Klemheist

This is more correctly termed a French prusik but UK climbers have stuck with the use of klemheist.

- It grips the rope well and can cope with all situations where the rope needs to be gripped. More turns increase the grip.
- It can be tied using cord or tape.

The Alpine Clutch/Garda Hitch

This hitch is formed using two identical krabs that are preferably pear-shaped:

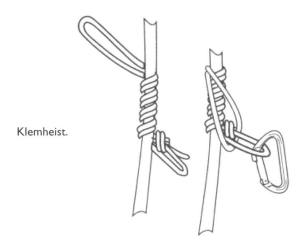

Klemheist.

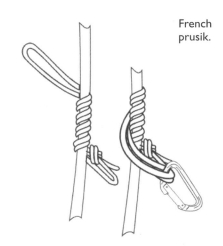

French prusik.

• When it is used as part of a pulley system it generates friction, reducing the overall efficiency. It is mainly used when there is a shortage of prusik loops.
• The krabs lock the rope so that it can only move in one direction. This is a disadvantage if the victim has to be lowered back down. The hitch can be freed by pulling on the slack rope and wedging a third krab between the original two krabs.

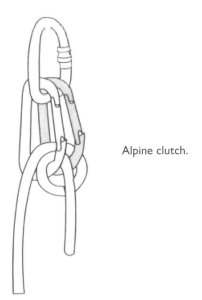

Alpine clutch.

Prusik Knots That Can be Released Under Load (Autoblocs)
These are essential in many rescue situations, but use them with care because they can release very easily.

The French Prusik (Marchard Knot)
The most important autobloc for you to remember. It is often confused with the Klemheist:

• To release it when loaded, push firmly on the end of the hitch furthest from the krab (do not pull the whole hitch).
• It can release if you grab hold of it.

Prusik Knot That Can be Untied When Loaded

Mariner Hitch
• This is a useful hitch for lowering someone past a knot when two ropes have been tied together.
• It can come undone if the tension is removed.
• An alternative to this is to use a sling/French prusik combination.

Mariner hitch.

Mechanical Devices

Ascenders with handles are *the* tools for ascending long distances, but they are too big to be useful in rescues and non-handled ascenders are too heavy (see Chapter 8 for further information). However, the recent invention of the lightweight Wild Country Ropeman ascenders means that mechanical devices are becoming as much a part of climbing equipment as a nut key. Petzl produces the lightest ascender, the Tibloc (see Chapter 5 for further information).

Ascenders do not work as efficiently on frozen or muddy ropes and they have the serious drawback that they cannot be released under load. Do not push an ascender hard up against a knot because it needs to be fractionally unloaded before it can be released.

Ascending and Descending a Rope

Irreversible brain damage can occur in five to six minutes if the victim is not breathing. Rapid ascent and descent of a rope is essential to reach an injured climber and regain the stance.

The correct distance between the prusik/ ascender and the harness is dictated by strength, agility and length of arms. It is worth practising to get this correct. With all methods of ascending a rope it is prudent to tie the rope into your harness at frequent intervals, using a clove hitch or a figure-of-eight on a screw gate krab.

Klemheist/Garda Hitch Combination
Attach a Klemheist from the rope to the harness and place a Garda hitch for the foot.

- The Garda hitch allows the foot to be raised easily by pulling the rope below it.
- It cannot be used to descend a weighted rope.

Ascending Using a Klemheist and French Prusik
Place a Klemheist on the harness and a French prusik on the foot.

- Provides grip where required and ease of movement of the foot.
- Both feet through a sling provide more pushing power, but you can ascend effectively using only one foot.

Ascending Using Mechanical Ascenders
Mechanical ascenders are used in a similar way to friction knots, but are more reliable.

- A Wild Country Ropeman rides up the rope simply by pulling the rope below the device.

Ascending with a Single Friction Knot
This is useful when prusik loops have been dropped or forgotten. Attach a Klemheist with a long sling above the belay plate to stand in, then

Ascending using a Klemheist/Garda hitch combination

Ascending using a Klemheist/French prusik.

Ascending using a single prusik knot.

move the belay plate up the rope and sit in it. This method is also useful when you need to change from prusiking to abseiling part way up a rope. Attach a belay device below the loaded prusik, take a wrap around the foot and stand to take the weight off the prusik.

Prusiking Down a Rope

This is essentially the reverse of ascending and although it requires practice it does not warrant extensive description.

Abseiling and Reascending

In Chapter 6 abseils were protected with a French prusik attached to the abseil or leg loop of the harnesss. However, if you have to descend to an injured climber and reascend to the belay, it is best to abseil with a French prusik or Klemheist attached above the abseil device. It is then a simple matter to remove the abseil device and attach a French prusik or Garda hitch for the foot to ascend.

SOLVING PROBLEMS ON SINGLE-PITCH CRAGS

Serious incidents are unlikely on single-pitch crags if you:

- Choose routes and crags carefully.
- Belay diligently.
- Remove jewellery.

Nevertheless, problems do occur whilst bottom- and top-roping on a single-pitch crag. An instructor working on a single-pitch crag can carry a sling, a prusik or, even better, a mechanical ascender, plus a few krabs. A knife should not be necessary in any rescue but tangles can happen and mistakes do occur, so a knife discreetly hidden in a pocket may prove useful.

When an incident has occurred, stay calm and take a deep breath. You will cope more effectively if you have thought through and practised solutions to all possible scenarios. If the situation is serious, stop the other students climbing and lower them down so that you can give full attention to the current problem whilst avoiding the occurrence of another.

If you decide to solo to a student in difficulty, consider the implications should you slip. Soloing is a real judgement call and many good climbers have slipped from easy climbs, some

Burbage North a good single pitch crag.

with fatal consequences. A 5–6mm cord is easily melted, so be careful if using one to protect you when climbing to a student.

Student Traversing Off-Route

Some routes wander naturally around the crag and if you are not paying attention, a student may traverse off the line of the route and face a pendulum back across the crag.

- When bottom-roping, quickly take the belay rope across to the student, who can then grab hold of it and swing back onto the route in control.
- When top-roping, drop a loop of rope from the top, so that the student can use it to regain the line of the route.

The Student Untying from the Rope

This issue is really one of prevention rather than rescue and is most likely to occur when working with 'difficult' students on routes where there is an easy escape at half-height.

Where the student is 'tied in', prevention is a simple matter of rapidly pulling the rope tight to prevent them from undoing the knot. This can also be done if the person is linked to the rope via a screw-gate krab, although it may be quicker for them to release a krab than undo a knot. If the student has succeeded in becoming detached from the rope, quickly lower a rope from above with a screw-gate krab attached and do your best to get them reclipped.

The Frozen Climber

A student frozen on a ledge through fear is not in any physical danger. If all attempts to talk them down have failed, get some coffee out and have a break. They can't stay up there for ever. When top-roping, it is risky to tie off the belay device and leave the belay, as this may present an even bigger problem if the frozen climber then decided to climb. You will rarely have to go to the help of a frozen climber, but if you do then one of the methods outlined below could be used.

The Physically Stuck Climber

If a boot or helmet is stuck, the climber can remove the helmet or boot and be lowered. It becomes altogether more serious when a finger is stuck. This can be avoided by removing rings.

When Top-Roping

Leaving the belay is the only option. Tie off the belay plate, escape the belay and use the excess rope to abseil to the victim, release the finger and continue to the ground. If you do not have enough rope to reach the person you will need to use another rope. Return to the top and lower them down. In all situations where abseiling is required use a French prusik for protection.

When Bottom-Roping

Bottom roping presents its own problems. Initially, the rope leading to the stuck climber can be pulled tight, using the rest of the group to haul the climber's weight off the jammed finger if necessary. Then tie off the belay device. At that point, there are several options available.

Option One

Send an assistant or teacher up an adjacent climb.

Student attached to the instructor's abseil device via a sling. Climber: Mark Hurst.

Option Two

The group can belay the instructor on an adjacent route to the stuck student.

Option Three

When there is no adjacent climb set up, abseil from the anchors at the top. The instructor can descend with the victim if the group below has been briefed to release the tied-off rope. If the belayers are unable to release the knot or lower correctly, the victim can be attached to the instructor via a sling from the instructor's abseil device to the victim's harness.

When there is neither an adjacent climb nor a spare rope, the climbing rope is ascended from below or descended from above. To avoid this 'worst-case' scenario, always have another rope available even if it is not used for climbing. With any of the methods for ascending always tie into the rope at regular intervals as height is gained.

Option Four

One method for ascending is to place a Klemheist onto the rope above the tied-off belay device and clip it into the abseil loop on your harness, slide the Klemheist up the rope to take the weight until another one can be placed below it and ascend to the stuck climber. Attach a belay plate onto the rope to abseil back down.

Where the rock is not too steep a similar method of ascending is to transfer the belay device already being used on the rope to the instructor, then place a French prusik above the belay device and, using this combination as an ascender go to the injured person. The French prusik automatically releases as the belay device is pulled up the rope. After releasing the stuck student, either clip them to you as described above or lower yourself to the ground and supervise the lowering.

If a Gri Gri is being used to belay, transfer it to the instructor, then attach a French prusik above the Gri Gri. Take the rope up through the French prusik so the rope can be used like a pulley to ascend to the climber (*see* the photograph on page 184).

Option Five

If ascending, and the rope causes too much pain for the victim, go to the top of the route and clip into the attachment krabs through which the climbing rope runs. Place a French prusik from the attachment krabs to the live rope and take some slack from the dead rope (ensuring that the French prusik is holding) and put an abseil device onto the rope. Once your weight is onto the dead rope, release the prusik and transfer it to protect the abseil. Once the finger is released the instructor can abseil to the ground, taking the victim with them via a sling from the descending device to the victim's harness. Alternatively, they can descend to the ground and supervise the lowering of the victim.

Stuck Abseiler

If the abseiler has something caught in the abseil device, lock off the safety rope, release the abseil completely and continue the descent by lowering. Alternatively, lock off the safety rope, release the abseil, sort out the problem and then allow them to continue abseiling.

If the abseiler has a foot stuck in a crack on the way down or will not leave an intermediate ledge you may have to go to them. In this situation, take the student tight on the safety rope, release some of the abseil rope and retie it, then use the slack abseil rope to abseil to the victim (you may be able to use excess abseil rope if the

abseil is short). Once the foot has been removed you can release the student from the abseil rope, continue to the ground and return to the safety rope. If an assistant is available they could take over the safety rope and the instructor can attach to the student via a short sling from the instructor's abseil device to the student's harness and abseil with them. If an assistant is not available and the student will not leave the ledge, the last option is to attach to the student as described above and then remove them from the safety and abseil rope. The abseil rope should be easy to remove but the safety rope requires the student's weight to be taken off the knot. As a last resort the threat to cut the safety rope may make them move more quickly. This is a rare situation which can be avoided by appropriate choice of abseil.

SOLVING PROBLEMS ON SEA CLIFFS AND MULTI-PITCH CRAGS

Rescues automatically become more complex when lowering to the floor is not an option,

El Capitan: a multi-pitch crag.

therefore, try to arrive at stances or the top of the cliff with enough equipment to effect a rescue. A minimum of two or three prusik loops, a long sling, a few krabs and a few extenders should be enough to solve most problems.

Belay anchors equalized to a single point make life simpler when a rescue is needed. The live rope could also be taken through a high krab or into the belay; this will allow a pulley system to be set up easily, but will also make an assisted hoist difficult, if not impossible.

What To Do if an Accident Occurs?

- Tie off the belay plate.
- Take a deep breath.
- Look, listen, shout for help if necessary and think carefully.
- Can a rescue be effected while still attached to the belay?
- Once out of the system do you need to go down to the student to render first aid?
- Is it quicker to go for help?
- Are there any climbers on an adjacent route?
- Is the injured climber conscious?
- Descend rather than ascend with a victim, even if it means tying two ropes together and coming back another day to retrieve them. Ascending is more difficult and time consuming, although it may be the only option on sea cliffs.

An accident will not turn into a tragedy if the question 'What happens if?' is asked at every stage in the rescue. Be especially vigilant in all rescues where a loaded rope is running over an edge.

TECHNIQUES WHILE ATTACHED TO A BELAY

When communication is difficult, beware of any situation where slack rope is paid out to the student, as it could mean they are climbing above a runner. Any solution to this problem must be rapid if a fall is to be avoided.

- Tie off the belay plate and drop a loop of rope to the climber, who can then grab hold of it and be lowered by hand or via an Italian hitch to below the runner.
- If the climber is too tired to hold a loop of

rope, drop a loop with a krab attached, which they can then clip it into their harness.
- If a loop of rope cannot be sent to the student, they can try to grab the rope above the runner, tie a knot and clip it into their harness with a screw-gate if possible, although any krab will do.

Occasionally a rogue knot magically appears in the rope. In this event, move the knot as close to the student as possible, then bring both students to the belay and remove the knot.

If the student fails to remove a runner.

- Leave it or bring the student to the stance, tie them into the belay and abseil down the rope to reach the runner, then prusik back up.
- Alternatively, the student can lower the instructor to the runner and belay them back up.

The commonest form of rescue is assisting a climber to overcome a difficult section or to get back onto the climb after a fall. A tug on the rope may be sufficient. If not, a system for hoisting may be required.

Hoisting

Hoisting is physically demanding and can cause serious back damage, so avoid it if you can. Never try to hoist without a pulley system. The efficiency of raising systems (compared to their theoretical potential) is relatively low due to rope stretch and high friction. Remember that you cannot hoist someone through the runners, so if they cannot remove them or unclip them from the rope you must escape the system and go down to remove them.

The In-situ Assisted Hoist
As the name suggests, an *in situ* hoist is where the climber in difficulty can assist by pulling on a loop of their existing climbing rope. This system is limited by several factors:

- Does the loop of rope reach the fallen climber?
- Is the victim sight?
- Are they more than one-third of the rope length away?
- Can the victim hear, understand and carry out instructions?

In situ assisted hoist.

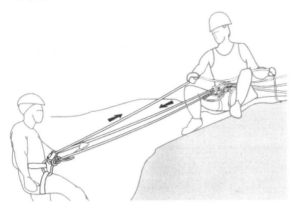

It is important that clear instructions are given to the fallen climber as to which rope to pull down on. This is a very strenuous method on steep rock. If a rest is needed push the French prusik forward so that you do not loose any height gained and lower the student until the French prusik grips the rope. Once the student has regained the rock revert to normal belaying mode.

The In-situ *Counterbalance Hoist*
This has distinct advantages:

- It works well on restricted stances where any other pulley system has a short pull distance.
- The rope comes in faster than any other method.
- If you need to go to the victim it is simple to change it over to a counterbalance abseil.

The disadvantage is that this hoist is only easily accomplished when the anchors are brought to a single point with a sling.

- **Step One:** Tie off the plate.
- **Step Two:** Attach a French prusik between the live rope and the belay anchors (if this cannot be done, attach a Klemheist to all the anchor ropes and link the French prusik to this), and transfer the load from the belay plate to the prusik.
- **Step Three:** Put a screw-gate krab on the anchor.
- **Step Four:** Take a bight of rope from between the prusik and belay plate (leave the plate in place) and clip it into the screw-gate krab. You are now in a counterbalance.

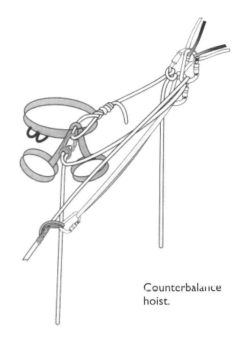

Counterbalance hoist.

- **Step Five:** Attach a second prusik to your leg loop and place it below the plate.
- **Step Six:** Lengthen your tie-in point to the anchor to give yourself enough room to move. Work yourself and the belay device up the rope towards the anchors, lean back and take the strain.
- **Step Seven:** Pull up on the live rope. Be careful, because if the student decides to help, you may shoot backwards.

The In-situ *Unassisted Hoist*
The *in situ* unassisted hoist or Z-pulley is used when the fallen climber cannot assist you to pull. It is only useful when the hoist is over a relatively short distance because it is difficult to create an effective pulley while still attached to the belay. It is, however, much quicker to remain in the belay and to help the climber gain a few metres.

This pulley only has a theoretical three to one advantage, that is for every 3m pulled the student gains 1m (for methods of improving the efficiency of the hoist see 'Escaping from the Belay' below). Note the use of two krabs on the lower Klemheist to reduce friction. A Petzl swing cheek pulley would reduce friction even further but pulleys are rarely carried when rock climbing.

When the bottom Klemheist has worked up close to the belay device it must be pushed back

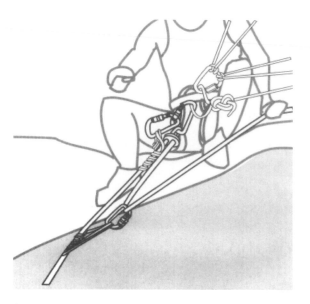

In situ unassisted hoist.

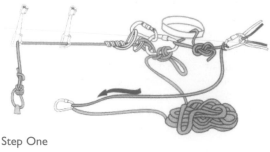

Step One

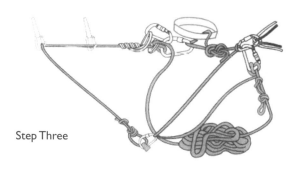

Step Two

Step Three

In situ rescue of a climber on a traverse.

down the rope. To avoid loosing any height gained, assist the French prusik to grip the rope by pushing it down before letting it take the load.

In-situ *Rescue of a Climber on a Traverse*
One possible solution is:

- **Step One:** Tie off the belay plate and attach a French prusik from the belay or central loop to the loaded rope.
- **Step Two:** Throw a loop of rope or the end of the rope, if available, to the student to clip into the belay loop of their harness. This rope can then be attached to an Italian hitch or a Garda hitch, making it easier to control when taking in.
- **Step Three:** A combination of pulling by the student and lowering of the main rope will move the student to below the belay. If the student cannot help to pull, it may still be possible for the instructor to pull and lower the student until they are beneath the stance.
- **Step Four:** The student may then be able to climb to the belay. If the student is still free-hanging a hoist is needed.
- **Step Five:** Once the student is on the stance, secure them then retrieve the rope and decide whether you are going to retrieve the runners from the traverse. The easiest way of doing this is for the student to belay you along the traverse and back to the belay.

If the rope cannot be thrown to the student or they are unconscious, you will have to escape the belay and go to them.

ESCAPING FROM THE BELAY

Escape from the belay is necessary when the student is badly injured and requires immediate attention, or when an *in situ* solution is not possible. If you are on the top of the cliff it may be quicker to run and get help. Escaping the system creates a more serious situation for the instructor as well as the injured student and care must be exercised to protect both. If the instructor is subsequently injured there can be no rescue.

Removing Your Harness

Removing your harness is the simplest way to escape from the belay and is used when a harness is not required to effect the rescue. Removal of a harness is easiest when more of the forces are directed to the belay. The tie-in method on certain harnesses such as the Wild Country Alpiniste and the Whillans does not allow the harness to be removed easily.

To simplify rescues, try to keep the belay anchors within reach. When you cannot reach the anchors consider tying an Alpine butterfly close to your central loop (*see* page 186) and use that as the belay loop. This allows you to untie from the rope without having to transfer any of the forces.

Escape When the Belay Anchors are Out of Reach

- **Step One:** Tie off the belay plate, then attach a French prusik to the live rope and a

Klemheist to all the anchor ropes (use a 240cm sling with as many turns around the rope as you can) and link the two together with a sling.
- **Step Two:** Lower the live rope until the weight is on the French prusik.
- **Step Three:** Remove the belay plate and untie from the rope (protect yourself with a sling if necessary). Leave any knots tied in the end of the rope in place.

After Step Three there are two options depending on whether you need all the rope to effect a rescue.

Option One

This option is best when you need the full length of the ropes:

- **Step Four:** Return to the belay anchor and set up a belay using slings.
- **Step Five:** Attach the live rope to the sling belay with a tied-off Italian hitch.

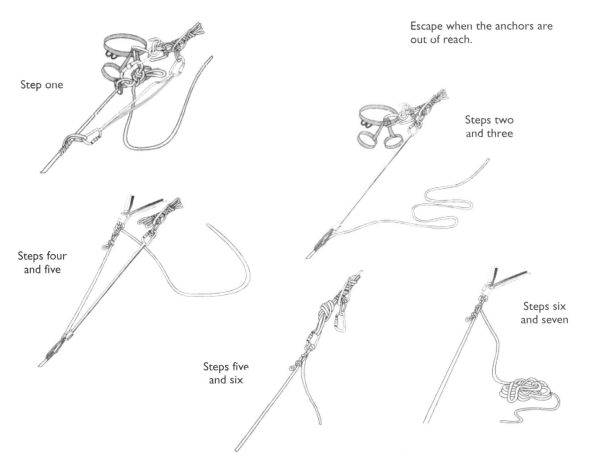

Escape when the anchors are out of reach.

Step one

Steps two and three

Steps four and five

Steps five and six

Steps six and seven

- **Step Six:** Release the French prusik and lower the live rope onto the tied-off Italian hitch.
- **Step Seven:** Remove the rope creating the belay.

Option Two
- **Step Five:** Tie a knot in the anchor ropes below the Klemheist and attach the live rope to the knot with a tied-off Italian hitch. If you cannot tie all the ropes together, tie a knot in the rope you were attached to and attach the live ropes to the Klemheist.
- **Step Six:** Release the French prusik and lower the live rope onto the tied-off Italian hitch.

When Belay Anchors are Within Reach

If the belay is set up using slings and you are using a direct belaying method:

- **Step One:** Tie off the belay plate.
- **Step Two:** Place a cow's tail on the harness and clip into the sling belay.
- **Step Three:** Untie from the rope and then release it from the belay.

If the belay is set up using the climbing rope:

- **Step One:** Tie off the belay plate.
- **Step Two:** Arrange a belay using slings if the existing belay is not made of slings.
- **Step Three:** Place a French prusik in front of the belay device and attach it to the new sling belay. If only one anchor can be reached but it is rock solid then use it, but improve it as soon as you can reach the other anchors. If the single anchor is suspect treat it as though you cannot reach the belay.
- **Step Four:** Release the live rope slowly onto the French prusik. Remove the belay device and retie the rope into the sling belay using a tied-off Italian hitch.
- **Step Five:** Attach a cow's tail from you to the sling belay and remove the climbing rope.

WHAT TO DO ONCE YOU HAVE ESCAPED

What you do after escaping will depend on how the belay is set up, how injured the student is and how much is left of the climb. The options available are:

Escape when the anchors are within reach.

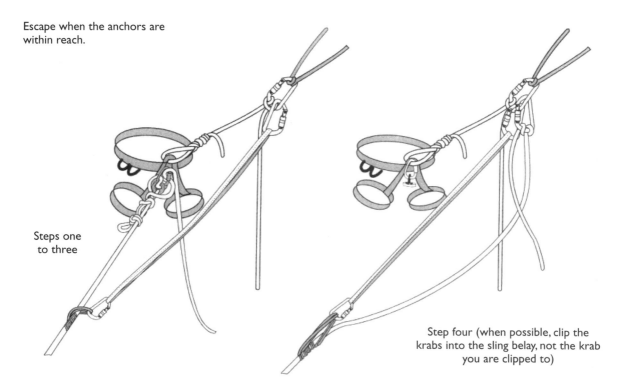

Steps one to three

Step four (when possible, clip the krabs into the sling belay, not the krab you are clipped to)

- Lower the injured student.
- Convert straight to a counterbalance abseil and descend to the injured student, apply first-aid and continue descending.
- Descend to the student and give first-aid, reascend to the belay, then hoist.

Lower

If the ground is less than 50m (165ft) away, lower the injured student to the ground (*see* Chapter 6, 'Lowering'). The instructor could then abseil and retrieve the rope later. When you have two ropes you can lower up to a 100m (330ft), but this requires you to pass a knot where the two ropes are tied together:

- **Step One:** When the knot comes close to the belay device but is not touching it, attach a French prusik in front of the belay device. Link it to a sling tied into the belay (to be extra safe you can use a tied-off Italian hitch on the sling or a Mariner knot).
- **Step Two:** Lower the weight onto the French Prusik then place an Italian hitch behind the knot.
- **Step Three:** Remove the belay device. Now release the French prusik or the Mariner knot.

- **Step Four:** Remove the French prusik and replace it behind the knot.

Lower/Counterbalance Abseil

When a full lower to the ground is not an option it may be possible to lower the victim half a rope's length to an intermediate ledge from which an escape can be made. The instructor can then abseil on the other section of rope, thereby counterbalancing the student, and set up a belay to which the student can attach. Counterbalance systems are complex, require strong anchors and equipment must be left behind. They also involve a moving rope through a krab, so revert to simpler systems as soon as possible.

- **Step One:** Lower the injured student almost half a rope length. It is also possible to abseil with the injured student instead of lowering them.
- **Step Two:** Place a French prusik onto the live rope.
- **Step Three:** Remove the Italian hitch and replace the rope through a krab. Attach the abseil device from the instructor's harness to the dead rope. The instructor's weight counterbalances the student.

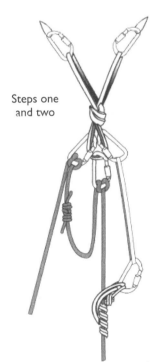

Steps one and two

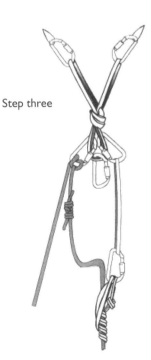

Step three

Lower past a knot.

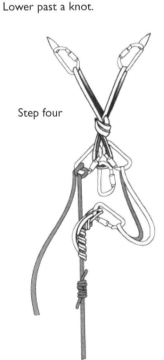

Step four

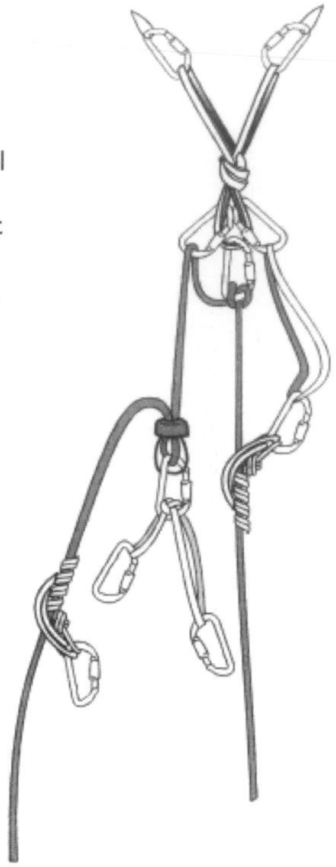

Counterbalance abseil of a victim. This diagram shows how it is possible to counterbalance abseil with the student attached to you.

- **Step Four:** Transfer the French prusik from the live rope to protect the abseil.

If there is a big weight difference between the student and the instructor an Italian hitch can be left in place. Remember to tie a knot in the end of the abseil rope.

This situation could go very wrong if you run out of rope and cannot reach the student. (Hence why it is safer to abseil with the student.) In that case, abseil until you can create a new belay, attach the student's rope to the new belay, then transfer your rope to the new belay and carry on abseiling.

If two ropes are available, the injured student could be lowered 50cm (165ft) and then a counterbalance abseil effected. The injured student can then be evacuated the rest of the way using an assisted abseil or lower.

Rescuing an Injured Student on a Traverse

If the student cannot be reached with a rope, escape the system and reverse the traverse. Belays on traverses notoriously do not direct the forces to the belay and when you escape it can affect the pull on the belay anchors. If this going to cause problems, it may be best to set up a whole new belay or add anchors to keep the forces directed to the anchors.

Protect yourself across the traverse. Be very careful using a Prusik to traverse the rope, as a slip could easily melt the Prusik. When attaching a mechanical ascender make sure that you have it set up so that you remain protected if the runners on the traverse come out.

- **Step One:** Escape the belay and traverse the rope protected by two cow's tails and a prusik or descender until above the student.
- **Step Two:** Set up a new belay.
- **Step Three:** Transfer the loaded rope to the belay.

Once you are above the student you could set up new belay, transfer them to this and hoist. Alternatively, return to your belay, dismantle it and rope solo to the new belay.

Hoisting

When descending is not an option, hoist the injured student onto the belay stance (remember runners must be removed before an injured student can be hoisted). Once out of the system it is much easier to create an efficient pulley. The actual hoist is the same as shown in the diagram on page 202 for an insite unassisted hoist. These steps follow from the methods for escaping from the belay described on pages 203–204.

- **Step One:** Place a French prusik in front of the tied-off Italian hitch and attach it to a krab in the belay.
- **Step Two:** Take some rope and put it through another krab, then remove the Italian hitch and put a Klemheist in front of the French prusik.
- **Step Three:** Attach the dead rope to the Klemheist via two Krabs or, even better, a pulley to reduce friction. Then pull. If the student is difficult to hoist, try attaching the rope to your harness with an Italian hitch and use the leg muscles to pull.

When resting or moving the lower, prusik back down the rope. Always push the French prusik forward so that you do not lose any height gained. Alternatively, replace the French prusik

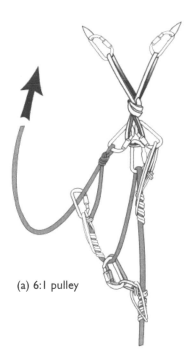

(a) 6:1 pulley

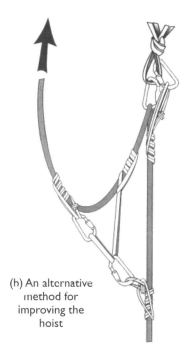

(b) An alternative method for improving the hoist

Improving the hoisting system.

with a Garda knot which does not allow any slippage backwards but does increase the friction slightly.

Improving the Hoist
The pulley system described above gives a theoretical physical advantage of 3:1. In reality, this may not be enough if your student is heavy and there is a lot of friction in the ropes. The only true method for assessing the efficiency of a pulley system is to measure the amount of rope pulled against the amount gained, for example a 6:1 pulley – less amount is required but for every 6m pulled you only gain 1 metre.

- **Step One:** From the 3:1 pulley. Tie the rope into the belay.
- **Step Two:** Attach a Klemheist to the rope and attach the spare rope to this then pull again.

An alternative method is to increase the pulley to a 6:1; however, the amount of rope that can be pulled is limited by the length of the sling.

There are many weird and wonderful ways of increasing the efficiency of a pulley, but in reality increasing it beyond 6:1 makes any rescue such a slow proposition that it is not worth consideration. If a 6:1 pulley does not work, then an increase in efficiency will not help.

Assisted Abseil

Once the injured student has either been lowered or hoisted onto the belay stance you may want to abseil with them. To increase friction when abseiling attach a karabiner brake above your abseil device.

An assisted abseil. Photo: Mike Turner.

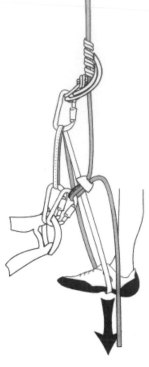

Removing a stuck abseiler's weight from the rope.

The Stuck Abseiler

There is the nightmare scenario of the stacked abseiler who becomes stuck above you. To solve this problem, ascend the rope until above the student. Then to remove their weight off the rope and release the obstruction.

Removing the Weight from a Rope to Untie the Victim

The student may be dangling on the rope and need to be transferred to a new belay, or one of their ropes may be required for a long lower, or you may want to transfer them to your abseil straight away. The most drastic method would be to clip them into the new belay or abseil device and then cut their rope. You could also use the method given above. They must be attached to something else before the knots are untied.

RESCUING A LEADER FALL

The rescue of a leader may be necessary when they have injured themselves and cannot be lowered to the floor. They may be out over the sea or at the top of the pitch. Before attempting any rescue of a lead climber the security of the top anchor must be beyond question.

- **Step One:** Create a solid ground anchor and attach to it using an Italian hitch.
- **Step Two:** Escape the belay.
- **Step Three:** Ascend to the injured student. Because the rope is tensioned it is not possible to use back-up knots, therefore use two Klemheists attached to your waist and clip into the rope with a sling and krab. Unclip any anchors but do not remove them – clip them into the rope below you.
- **Step Four:** Reinforce the top anchor or create a new anchor.
- **Step Five:** Clip the injured student to the new anchors using a Mariner knot or an Italian hitch tied off. If necessary, attach a chest harness to the student.
- **Step Six:** Connect the rope you have ascended to the anchors.
- **Step Seven:** Descend using Klemheists and remove the bottom anchors.
- **Step Eight:** Ascend back to the anchors, removing any gear on the way.

You now have a number of options.

Option One

Lower the student to the ground. If the student will end up hanging in space, you will have to convert to a counterbalance abseil.

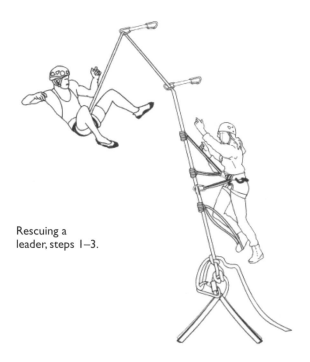

Rescuing a leader, steps 1–3.

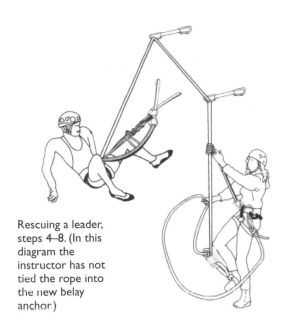

Rescuing a leader, steps 4–8. (In this diagram the instructor has not tied the rope into the new belay anchor.)

Option Two
Climb out and get help or hoist the student.

SOLO CLIMBING

If the accident has occurred close to the top of the crag, the quickest option may be to go to the top and get help. Rope soloing is the safest method to get out, but enough rope is needed to reach the top of the crag. The same system is used whether aid climbing or free climbing.

- **Step One:** Set up an upward-pulling anchor and tie the rope into it with a double figure-of-eight or figure-of-nine knot.
- **Step Two:** Tie into the other end of the rope.
- **Step Three:** From the anchor take 4m of rope, tie a figure-of-eight knot and clip it into your harness with two reversed krabs or a screw-gate krab.
- **Step Four:** Take 2m of rope from the upward-pulling anchor and tie a clove hitch.

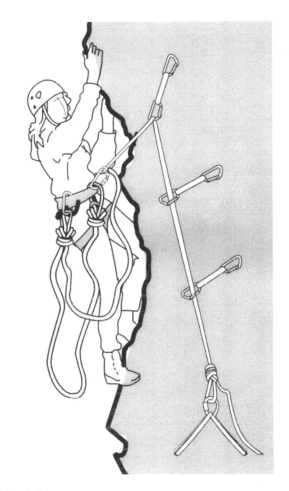

Solo climbing.

- **Step Five:** As you climb, clip the rope below your clove hitch into the placements.
- **Step Six:** When you reach the clove hitch, readjust it to pay out the amount of slack you are comfortable with.
- **Step Seven:** When the clove hitch meets the figure-of-eight take a new 4m of rope and attach it to your harness. Continue climbing as before.

CHAPTER 8

AID CLIMBING

Aid climbing is great fun, and a useful activity, especially when the weather is too poor for free climbing. It can also give students confidence in their gear placements and teach efficient rope-work. Aid climbing up trees with young people provides a safe, challenging and exciting session, and is a good alternative in poor weather when a climbing wall is not available. The beauty of a tree is that slings on branches are generally more predictable than nuts in cracks. This section is not intended as a guide to big walling, but it does provide the rudiments to run a simple aid climbing session and to take clients up an aid route.

Paul Donnithorne aiding in Zion National Monument.

WHAT IS AID CLIMBING?

Aid climbing varies from the inappropriately termed 'French Style', that is pulling on a runner to overcome difficulties, to a 'full blown' aid pitch where the climber places their weight on all the protection to the top. The former requires little specialist equipment, while the latter requires a lot of gear, some of which is unique to aid climbing.

There are two methods of aid climbing:

- Clean aid climbing where all the placements found on a normal free climbing rack are used, maybe with the exception of sky hooks.
- Full aid climbing using pegs, bolts and a variety of other equipment that has to be hammered into the rock. Full aid climbing damages the rock so use it as a last resort.

EQUIPMENT

A long aid pitch can require fifty to ninety placements. It is therefore more efficient and quicker to reduce the number of placements by reaching as high as possible.

Krabs
Oval krabs are favoured because they do not shift when weight is added to them, plus two aiders clipped into one krab sit better. Krabs that can be opened under body weight loading are better because the ropes can then be clipped in and out. Do not use your finest krabs for aid climbing because they will become tatty very quickly.

Slings
A short sling 10–20cm (termed 'hero loops' in the USA), attached to fixed gear instead of a krab allows maximum height to be gained with each step and to save the weight of carrying krabs. However, tying a sling through the eye of a peg is not as safe for stopping a fall. Slings are also needed to tie off pegs that are not fully driven in. Carry approximately three medium

The author weighed down with climbing gear on an aid pitch in Zion National Park.

and three long slings for extending the rope over roofs. Some aid climbers carry energy-absorbing slings to use on questionable placements, but these are generally too long and their ability to absorb forces debatable.

Protection
A wider variety of nuts and camming devices than normal is advisable and some aid pitches require lots of the same size. More micro-wires (DMM peenuts are excellent) and small cams are required for peg scars. It may be worth considering some of the offset Friends from Wild Country (*see* Chapter 5). Sliding nuts are also very useful.

Ropes
A 50–60m single rope is ideal for aid climbing with a spare 9mm or 11mm towed as a haul line and for abseiling. Some aid climbers carry a 'zip line' which is a 7–9mm rope, and is used for hauling more equipment, water or food when in the middle of an aid pitch. The zip line is then used to pull the haul line up the pitch. If the route requires pendulums, a third rope is required. Aid climbing punishes ropes, but do not be tempted to use old ropes. If you are guiding an aid route it may be worth considering a third rope to protect the students as they are ascending.

Étriers/Aiders
These are small four- or five-rung ladders. They should ideally be long enough to enable the climber to step from the top step of one to the bottom step of the next. Some climbers carry three or even four, but two usually suffice. Different-coloured étriers are easier to select amongst a background of tapes and gear. A grab loop on the top of the étriers protects the hands from the punishment of grabbing krabs when reaching up.

Daisy Chains
Two, preferably of different colours, are useful for aid climbing. They can be commercially bought or made by tying overhand knots every 8 or 10cm. The correct length of a daisy chain is a full arm's reach after lark's footing it to the leg loops and waist belt or just to the abseil loop.

Fifi Hooks
These are sometimes attached to each étrier, via a short sling, for clipping into aid quickly. They make it easier to retrieve the étriers from aid placements below, but can become unclipped if tension is not maintained. Open-gate krabs are recommended for novices rather than fifi hooks. A fifi hook can also be attached to your harness for ease of clipping into the gear or the daisy chains.

Mechanical (Handled) Ascenders
Essential for serious ascending (*see* page 135).

Peg Hammers
These have a flat hammer for placing pegs and a blunt pick for removing them. Wooden shafts are superior to metal as they absorb vibration. A sling allowing maximum reach can be attached to your harness.

Pegs
The use of pegs has declined in recent years because of the development of other clean methods of protection and because they damage the rock. Nevertheless, on hard aid routes they are essential. They have been examined in earlier chapters.

Malleable Protection

Sometimes called 'basheys or 'masheys', these are lumps of soft metal that are smashed into irregularities in the rock.

Bolts

These are a last-resort placement and have been covered in earlier chapters.

Skyhooks

These are hard steel hooks that come in a wide variety of shapes to grip ledges and holes. Attach the sling so that the lower end of the hook is pulled into the rock.

Miscellaneous

Nut keys for placing and removing nuts must be sturdy enough to be hammered; a sack hauler or pulleys are needed for sack hauling; cheating sticks enable the climber to reach further and clip fixed protection out of reach; leather gloves prevent wear and tear on your hands.

PLACING AID

Clean aid climbing requires ingenuity in getting the equipment to stay in marginal placements plus you must consider how easy it is for the second to remove the pieces after they have been weighted. Avoid standing too long with your face in front of an aid placement because if it pops out you will receive a face full of a rock nine, a piton or skyhook before you plummet. It may even be worthwhile wearing safety glasses.

Stacked pegs using a leeper 'z' peg.

Skyhooks are invaluable for clean aid climbing, but they can come off small edges while standing up. If they are solid, consider duct-taping them in place for protection. Hard aid pitches may involve hooking into bolt-holes, but try to avoid hammering the hooks into place because this increases the chance of them coming out and damages the hole for future placements.

The placement of pegs and bolts has been covered already in Chapters 5 and 6, but there are some peculiarities involved in placing pegs for aid climbing:

- The aid climber is more creative, especially where the crack is shallow or flaring.
- The major difference is that aid climbers balance how well pegs and bolts are embedded (for example, their ability to hold a fall) against how difficult it is to remove them. If every peg is driven into the hilt, each pitch will take half a day to lead and second.
- Excessive hammering wastes energy.
- The true art of aid climbing is stacking pegs, with its endless variations.
- With all stacking it is useful to place a tie-off around the pegs before driving them home.
- Stacked pegs are easily lost when placing them, so clip them together with a sling before hammering them in.
- Blades are generally stacked back to back.
- Avoid stacking angles one on top of another as they are difficult to separate. Leeper Z pitons (Grivel make a similar one) are very useful in stacking. A peg can also be placed alongside a nut. Clip the wedge to the peg because it can fall out when removed. Whether you weight the peg or the wedge depends on the placement.

Malleable placements, 'basheys', tend to be the preserve of the hardened aid climber. They are all suspect, only to be used as a last resort, and require a lot of practice to place securely. They are placed as you would a chock and are pounded using either the pick of the hammer or a blunt peg or chisel. Start by making an 'X' pattern on the 'bashey' using angled strokes, then pound the right and left sides. To test the placement, hit the bottom and top at a slight upward and downward angle. If the head rotates, do it again. If you can smell a metallic odour it means the bashey has cracked.

A bashey.

BASIC AID TECHNIQUE

Approach an aid climb as you would a free climb and plan ahead for the good placements, whether there is going to be rope drag and so on. Aid climbing is strenuous, so look for good places to rest.

Rack up precisely, three or four pitons per krab on one side and clean gear on the other. Make sure the hammer is accessible even if you do not think you will need it. In addition, keep your ascenders handy, especially if the pitch has an overhang – you never know when you may be left hanging in space.

There are many variations on a theme for aid climbing, but here is one basic system using two étriers linked via an oval krab to a diasy chain that is lark's footed to the harness. A fifi hook is also attached to the harness via a short sling.

- **Step One:** Place an aid piece at the furthest spot you can reach.
- **Step Two:** Clip in two krabs separately (the second takes the climbing rope). If you have placed a peg put a small sling onto it and then clip the two krabs into the sling. Do not clip the climbing rope into the piece unless the placement you are standing on is poor and the higher piece is more solid.
- **Step Three:** Clip an étrier to the krab without the rope. Test the piece with a gentle

one-footed hop or, if it is poor, ease from one étrier to the other slowly. If it is very steep you can clip yourself into the daisy chain via the fifi hook on your harness.
- **Step Four:** Remove your second étrier from the lower piece and clip it into the placement or your first étrier's krab.
- **Step Five:** Move onto the étriers fully and clip your fifi hook into the new piece of protection or to daisy chain.
- **Step Six:** Clip the climbing rope into the second krab.
- **Step Seven:** Stand as high as you can and repeat.

Aid climbing an overhang creates its own difficulties. Using a daisy chain enables you to hang from the harness in a stable position. A chest harness may be useful when the overhang approaches horizontal.

It is tempting to reach down and remove pieces from below as equipment runs out. As a general rule, however, leave every other piece in place, especially if it is your only good piece.

High Stepping

Moving onto the top step of an étrier can be unnerving, but being able to do so greatly reduces the number of placements required. The process is simple if there are handholds or the rock is easy-angled, but on steep/overhanging rock it becomes more difficult because tension between the feet and the harness must be maintained at all times. Tension can be taken via the daisy chain, but this increases the chance of pulling the protection out.

Resting

Aid climbing takes time, but try to relax and rest frequently to conserve strength. To rest, bend one leg and place it close beneath you. Your weight is then on the bent leg. You can also take some of the weight on the daisy chain. Asking the belayer to make the rope tight simply increases the forces on the placement.

Switching from aid climbing to free climbing can be a mentally difficult adjustment, so do not be tempted to do it too soon.

Creating a Belay Stance

Creating a stance when aid climbing requires a lot of thought, especially when sack hauling. Generally, the anchors are brought together to

A well thought out and neat belay can save a lot of time. Climber: Terry Ralphs; Photo: Mike Turner.

form single points. The second will probably ascend the rope, removing the gear as they go, therefore the lead rope must be secured to the belay. It may be prudent to set this up on a separate anchor directly above the second. When the second reaches the stance it is useful if there is somewhere for them to clip into so they can make a quick change from ascending the rope to aiding. If the aid pitch is short the second may aid the pitch, following the same sequence as the leader except for removing the climbing rope before stepping onto the étriers.

TENSION TRAVERSES AND PENDULUMS

Tension traverses are straightforward – the leader simply uses tension from the rope to reach another crack or hold nearby. When the gap is greater, the leader must climb up, place a solid runner, be lowered down and then run across the cliff to reach the next crack. The bombproof runner cannot usually be retrieved.

The aid sequence.

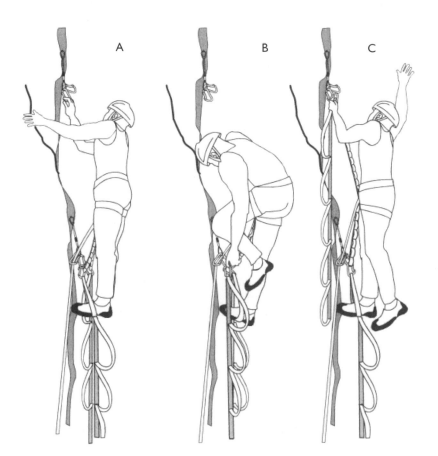

Be careful not to be lowered further than necessary. On long pendulums the leader can use an extra rope to abseil from the bombproof anchor and still be belayed on the climbing rope. The abseil rope can be left for the seconder to use.

Once the new crack has been gained, climb as high as possible before placing any protection. The higher you are before clipping the climbing rope, the easier and safer it is for the second. If the pendulum is very large, an extra rope can make life easier for the second.

HAULING

Hauling anything heavier than a pack containing sandwiches by hand can damage your back. The steeper the route, the easier it is to sack haul. To sack haul when on a ledge attach a sack hauler or a pulley and ascender to the belay (often a separate belay to the side of the first), and use your body as a counterweight to haul (see *In-situ Counterbalance Hoist*, page 201). Hauling can also be effected if set up so that the hauler can push down with their feet (a Yosemite hoist). When ascending, it is a good idea to do so in tandem with the haul bag to clear it from any jams.

A Yosemite hoist.

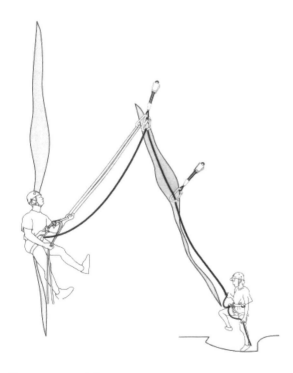

Extra rope pendulum.

ASCENDING/CLEANING AN AID PITCH

If the aid pitch is short, the second can aid the pitch by removing the placements once past them. It can also be useful on traversing pitches where ascending would pull outwards on the aid placements. For longer pitches it is a good idea to ascend the rope. There is a variety of methods.

Method One
- Ascenders can be connected to the appropriate daisy chain (left-handed on left daisy chain and right handed on the right one).
- The length of the daisy chain to the upper ascender is adjusted so that when the ascender is weighted it can just be reached by a full arm extension.
- The daisy chain to the bottom one is slightly shorter but the distance is not so critical.
- Place the ascender of your dominant hand on top.

The author ascending in Zion National Monument.

- The free end of the daisy chain is linked to an étrier. The separate connection allows you to clip into a piece of protection or anchor without taking the ascender off the rope. This is particularly useful when cleaning traverses.
- To ascend, stand in the étriers alternately as the ascenders slide up the rope.

Method Two
- A second method involves the attachment of a Petzl Croll ascender to a chest harness and a normal set-up for the leg. The best way of doing this is to use a semi-circular Maillon and a smaller oval Maillon.

Method Three
- Have your jumars set up for your arm length with slings. The advantage of this method is that your feet do not fall out of the étriers.

General Advice for Ascending

- Try to keep your movements smooth to prevent the rope sawing through on sharp edges. Let your legs and back do the work.

Mike 'Twid' Turner demonstrating the first two set ups for ascending.

- Tie the rope into your harness using a figure-of-eight knot every 6–7m, so that if the ascender fails or it has to be removed to bypass a knot or a piece of gear you do not die. If you do have to bypass a knot in the rope, clip a third sling above the knot as you bypass it.
- Traverses are best aided across (sliding the ascenders ahead of but not weighted), because of the potential pendulums between pieces when ascending. If the rope traverses a short distance or runs diagonally, clip a krab from the rear of the ascender to the rope to prevent it popping off the rope. It is important to tie off the climbing rope more frequently on traverses.
- If there is a long span of rope between placements you can lower yourself across. Thread a sling through the pendulum point and then thread a bight of rope from the harness through the sling. Clip this to a locking krab on your harness belay loop. Pull up the slack so that your weight is transferred onto the bight. Unclip the lead rope from the pendulum point and strip the krabs from the anchor. Lower yourself back into jumaring line. Unclip the bight of rope from your harness and pull it through the pendulum point.
- As you remove gear, rack it tidily as this saves valuable time at each stance. Malleable pieces are best left in place, but if you need to remove one tug it a few times and inspect carefully before using again. If the wire is stripped from the bashey take the time to clean the head from the crack so that others can use the placement.
- When you remove gear it may be a good idea to clip into it with an old sling just before it pops out, so that you do not lose it. Sitting in pegs as you hit them can also help to remove the pegs, but beware you do not receive an eyeful.

Fixing Ropes

Fixing ropes is rarely necessary unless you are on a big multi-day aid route. It goes without saying that the primary anchors should be good, but to prevent the rope being blown around pull it taut and anchor it at the bottom. If the rope runs over a sharp edge use rope protectors or 'Duck' tape to prevent abrasion.

When the rope runs over a very sharp edge, such as a roof, protect the rope by placing intermediate anchors between the main ones. The weight is then on the rope running over the sharp edge for less time. If the fixed ropes are tight and do not allow someone ascending to tie off at regular intervals, place a French prusik above the mechanical ascender and clip it into your harness. The French prusik will move upwards automatically.

Louise Thomas seconding a traverse on Baffin Island. Photo: Mike 'Twid' Turner.

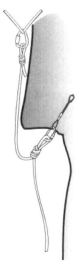

Fixed ropes.

CHAPTER 9

SCRAMBLING

Scrambling is the link between mountain walking and rock climbing, often involving the rockiest way up a ridge or tackling the deep, damp gullies that rock climbers avoid. Scrambling is potentially a very dangerous activity, requiring a high level of judgement, concentration and anticipation from an instructor/guide. Scrambling cannot be learned from this book – it involves efficient movement and demands the appropriate application of a variety of techniques generally employed in alpine climbing.

It is the ultimate test of the 'What if ?' question. What if the students fell here? What would happen if I left the students unattached to the cliff and I fell off? If the answer is other than 'nothing will happen', then choose the fastest and most appropriate course of action to avoid an accident. The efficient scrambling instructor/guide is someone who can choose the appropriate technique at any given moment and change between them quickly. They must also make judgements continuously, not only about the terrain ahead but also about their students' abilities.

Scrambles vary from the sort of terrain that an adventurous walker would encounter, such as Crib Goch ridge on Snowdon, to ascribed rock climbs such as the Parson's Nose on Crib y Ddysgyl. Scrambling takes the climber away from rock faces and into more remote and secluded areas of the hills. These routes, by virtue of their seclusion, are often sanctuaries for rare plants and animals which have escaped areas overgrazed by sheep. These areas must therefore be used with extreme sensitivity and great thought given to every footstep. Keep to the rockier ridges unless it is very windy and leave the delicate plant life between the rocks to fight for its own existence.

This section predominately examines the guiding of scrambles, but of course you may be teaching others how to become competent themselves. What you teach will depend on your students' experiences of hill walking and rock climbing.

Scrambling is the link between mountain walking and climbing.

Scrambling Grades

Grade One: Easy scrambles. Straightforward for experienced hill walkers. It may be necessary to use the hands occasionally for progress. The exposure is not too daunting.

Grade Two: This grade is more sustained and requires more use of the hands. The exposure is significant and retreat is difficult.

Grade Three: The rock becomes very steep and is exposed at times. Most people will prefer a rope and there are occasional difficult moves. The ability to abseil may be important.

EQUIPMENT

The grade of the scramble selected dictates the amount of equipment carried. It could vary from a 30m length of single rope tied around the waist, a sling and an HMS krab for grade one scrambles to a full rock climbing rack.

If you are going into the hills with the intention of using a rope, students should be equipped with a helmet and, for comfort, a harness. Each student can carry a sling, screwgate krab and belay device.

Scrambling terrain is often on wet and dirty rock. Good footwear is essential for the student and the instructor because it affects their ability to avoid/control a slip. A fairly stiff boot with no lateral twist provides a solid foundation for the foot. A pair of leather gloves is also absolutely essential to improve the grip on the rope when short-roping.

SCRAMBLING TECHNIQUES

A variety of ropework techniques and instructing skills is required to make scrambling a fluid progresssion up the mountain. The techniques used will depend on the type of terrain

Scrambling footwear should provide a stable base for the feet.

covered and will range from specific rock climbing skills to shortening the rope between you and the students for moving together. The most efficient method for guiding is with both students attached to a single rope.

Walking Terrain

A rope is not required for this type of terrain, but you must be able to 'spot' a student on a difficult step (see Chapter 2, 'Spotting'). Again,

On an isolated step it may be enough to simply 'spot' your students.

ask what are the consequences of a fall and what is the terrain like ahead? Is there more walking after the difficult step or is it necessary to put a rope on? Do you need to get harnesses out or can you just attach the rope around the student? What are the students' abilities? Are they stable on their feet? Are they climbers or walkers?

Easy Climbing Terrain

Easy climbing terrain is defined here as the sort of terrain where a slip would be serious and where spotting is no longer effective because there are many difficult and exposed steps. You must now attach the students to the rope and adopt the techniques of short-roping. Short-roping requires the instructor to be in position at all times, and ready to hold a slip by the students. If the instructor is unstable or unbalanced, the students must either be stationary or on ground where a slip is not dangerous. Short-roping is usually about moving together with the students unencumbered by protection, but occasionally you may move together, placing protection as you move.

The art of moving together requires fluency and concentration and a good body stance. When guiding you are not dragging the students up the route and you should try to achieve fluid progress without the rope coming into play. It is often the non-verbal communication that can make the difference, the eye-to-eye contact and the messages sent through the ropes that will give the students confidence.

Moving together requires fluency, concentration and a solid stance, especially on simple but exposed ground.

Here are some things to consider when short-roping/moving together:

- Always ask the question: 'Can I hold the students should they slip'?
- If there is the risk of a serious slip the instructor should try to be above the students whenever possible.
- Minimize slack between the instructor and the student.
- Develop a sixth sense so that you can anticipate the students' movements without continuously looking back. If you are doing your job, the rope should never come into use.
- On traverses, carry the rope in the downhill hand. Try to stay above the students whenever possible on a traverse. If you cannot be above the students, then the distance between you must be minimal. Whether you are in front or behind the students depends on the terrain and whether it is a descending or ascending traverse.
- Your confidence must be unquestionable. The students must see you moving confidently, sure-footedly and at an easy pace. A calm and relaxed approach will reassure them. If they sense anxiety in you they may become less confident and move more slowly.
- Safety relies on your sure-footedness, the students' ability to adopt a braced stance and tension in the rope. Keep the rope reassuringly taut but not tugging at the students.
- Try to be as close to the students as the terrain allows. The inherent elasticity in the rope makes it harder to arrest a slip the further away the students are, even when the rope is tight.
- Place the weakest student close to you so that they can be reassured. However, because they are on the isolation loop (*see* 'Attaching the Students' below) it is more difficult to keep them snug on the rope. When they are placed on the end of the rope the instructor can more easily keep the tension in the rope.
- When you come to a section where you or the students cannot maintain a stable base ask them to stop. Climb over the difficulty and then continue as before. Do not run out long lengths of rope because communication is difficult and there is more stretch in the rope.
- Any loose rock must be moved out of the way if there is the chance that the students could knock it down onto a following party.

- Avoid constantly changing the rope length.

There are a number of practices you can employ to minimize the chances of being pulled off-balance:

- Keep your movements regular.
- Keep the arm slightly bent to act as a clutch and absorb some of the initial force in a slip.
- When this is not possible, take the rope in and pay it out as your pace varies.
- Be alert for spikes and boulders around which to loop the rope.
- Look ahead for problem steps and possible belays.
- Be aware of the students' needs and anxieties as well as watching the weather and finding a route.

Shortening the Rope

If the full length of the rope is not required it can be coiled around the chest or put in a rucksack.

All useful methods of shortening the rope have one important similarity – the coils are tied off, not just draped over the head. When taking coils, make them long enough to reach the top of the harness and remember to wear coils on the outside of the rucksack straps. Three separate sets of coils allow you to drop one without the bother of retying the remaining coils. The disadvantage of this is the large number of knots at the waist.

Attaching the Students

The number of students that can be taken scrambling depends on the terrain, conditions, size and weight of the students, skill and experi-

More difficult terrain may require pitching.

ence of the students and the instructor. It is generally two for difficult scrambles.

The most versatile method is to attach one student to the end of the rope and take a few coils around the student's chest in case there are some difficult sections requiring the students to be further apart. The second student is attached two arm spans away via an isolation loop created using an Alpine butterfly or overhand knot so that the first student is not standing on the hands of the second student. Try to avoid long isolation loops that hang around their knees. Tie the student into the isolation loop using a rewoven overhand.

This method of shortening the rope makes taking separate sets of coils easier.

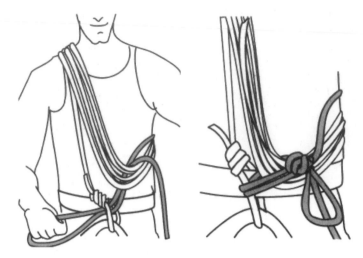

This method of shortening the rope incorporates the coils and harness into one unit. It also keeps the pull at the waist level. The length of the coils are important to prevent the overhand knot being pulled apart.

This method of attaching two students allows tension to be given to them individually or together. It is better for the first student to be on the uphill side of the rope running alongside them. To allow you to be uphill of the students when traversing, you can hold the rope between the two students.

When descending with a student of good ability it may prove an advantage to put the strongest student in front of you, although not on a separate loop, and the weaker one on the end of the rope. However, this requires very strict control to keep the tension throughout the rope and to prevent a domino effect if the first person slips. It is also useless when traversing and is difficult to use in ascent.

The V method is an alternative way of descending with two students which can also be used in ascent because it is easier to maintain tension. Problems with this method can occur when descending broken ground, as the students must take different lines to avoid the rope getting in the way of the second student. It is also difficult to use when traversing.

Holding the Rope

No Coils

When holding the rope on its own, always have the hand with the little finger closest to the students, i.e. pointing down the rope.

Taking Coils in the Hand

Take hand coils in one hand and lock them off with a final twist around the palm or lap the rope across the palm adding one final twist.

Both of these methods allow the other hand to be free but do not allow the coils to be released under tension, although this is easier with lap coiling.

Method Three

A third method of holding the rope is to take coils in one hand but to hold the rope to the students in the other. In this way, the tension can always be released if a belay is required. The disadvantage is that both hands are occupied.

Method Four

A fourth method is to tie a slip knot in the rope and hold the rope just in front of the knot. This is useful when it is cold or for those with small hands and can be combined with Method Three, making it easier to hold the rope. Using a slip knot means that the knot can be released quickly.

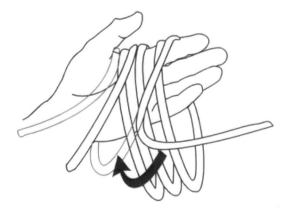

Locking hand coils.

In a short, isolated step it may be enough to take a braced stance and hold the rope in your hands. Climbers: Richard Morgan, Andy Applegate and the author.

A longer step will require belaying.

More Difficult Climbing Terrain

This can be defined as terrain where you are no longer confident that students could hold a slip while moving together. This is determined by the experience and size of the students. It can vary from a single short section of difficulty on an otherwise easy ridge to a full-blown climbing pitch.

A Short Isolated Step

The first thing to ask yourself is: 'What if I fall?' If there is any chance that you could pull the students from the ledge, then you must attach them to the rock. This can be done simply by wrapping their rope around a boulder or draping the rope between them over a spike or clipping the rope between them into a runner. Once you have climbed the difficult step you must secure the rope in some way to protect the students. This can vary from a full-blown belay to a braced stance. Keep the tension in the rope to safeguard any slips.

A Longer Difficult Step

When the section is longer or more difficult or the consequences of a slip are more serious, for example a fall would leave the students in space, consider placing runners in the pitch to protect them. You may or may not choose to be belayed by the students (*see* When Should You be Belayed, page 187). If the students are going to end up space should they fall, the belay must allow you to sort the problem out. A braced stance, for instance, would not be suitable.

A Ridge

On an easy ridge the last student on the rope can take a few coils in their hands. This gives them a few second's thought before deciding which side of the ridge to dive if someone falls. It may necessitate lengthening the rope between the students. When the ridge becomes more difficult it is more appropriate to pitch it or to move together with runners between the instructor and students.

Knot in the rope.

The lower hand should have the little finger
closest to the students.

Belays

When choosing a belay you should try to match
the seriousness of the situation to the quality of
the anchor and the distance that the students are
away from you. Apply the same factors for
choosing a belay as you would when rock
climbing – solid anchors, equalization and direction of forces, independence of movement,
tension on the belay and ability to communicate
with the students.

Four examples of belays which do not require
equipment are:

● A braced stance behind a boulder.
● If the boulder is low down, sit behind it with
  a waist belay.
● Take the rope around a boulder and waist
  belay or simply pull the rope up around the
  boulder if there is enough friction.
● Wrap the rope around the boulder a few
  times.

Braced stance behind a boulder.

Belay round a boulder.

• Place runner(s), equalize with slings and direct belay to it using an Italian hitch.

The size of the stance determines whether you are also attached to the belay. In a scrambling situation, especially a ridge, it is often difficult to work out in which direction the force created in a fall will be transmitted to the belay/belayer. For example the student may slip and pendulum sideways but be caught by a boulder or projection. If there is a traverse, make sure that you are above it or have placed runners to protect it.

When the students arrive at the stance, they can be attached by either a conventional method or by clipping the rope between them into the belay or over a spike to counterbalance them.

Descending

The method you use will depend on the size and experience of the students, plus the steepness and condition of the descent. Here are some things to consider:

When choosing these belays always evaluate the consequences for the students before taking action. The same criteria apply as in Chapter 7 as to whether the outcome could be that the student could just step back on the rock or be left hanging in space. When there is any chance that the students may have to be lowered back down, could swing into space or the climbing is difficult continue as follows:

• Place a sling through a thread, or on a spike/boulder, and direct belay to it using an Italian hitch.

• Choose the easiest line for you to protect the students, although this may not be the same as the easiest line for the students.
• Decide whether you can hold a slip or need to lower the students (Chapter 6 looks at methods for increasing the friction when lowering two people at the same time).
• Inform the students as often as necessary when you want them to stop for you to sort your feet out on difficult ground.
• Brief the students about maintaining tension in the rope.
• If the ground is difficult, teach the students to put some runners in to protect you as you down-climb to them.

CHAPTER 10

COASTAL AND RIVER ACTIVITIES

Sea-level traversing/coasteering and gorge walking are popular activities with some outdoor organisations. Canyoning has become popular on the continent where the bulk of serious river gorges exist. Gorge walking becomes canyoning when the gorge is mostly descended, where there is lots of swimming, ropes are used and specialist canyoning equipment is used. It usually requires a high level of ropework and rescue skills and an understanding of white water hazards. It also requires the students to have independent abseiling skills. Canyons are usually rigged with fixed anchors to facilitate rapid movement. On the continent of Europe International Federation of Mountain Guides Associations (IFMGA) canyoning guides are professionally trained and qualified to take students on this more technical and serious way of having fun in a river gorge. Nevertheless, some of the ropework techniques used in canyoning may prove useful to UK gorge walkers.

Sea-level traversing, coasteering and gorge walking are often seen as low-key activities, but in reality they are potentially more hazardous than climbing. They draw on skills from a wide range of more formal outdoor disciplines, and as a result they are rarely trained separately in the UK, except perhaps as in-house, site-specific staff training. Many of the skills discussed in this book are, however, transferable to coastal and river activities.

SEA-LEVEL TRAVERSING/COASTEERING

(Jean Paul Eatock)

Sea-level traversing is an adventurous activity involving groups of students moving along the base of sea cliffs. It can involve abseiling, rock climbing, roped traverses, zawn hopping, jumping and swimming. Coasteering has developed out of sea-level traversing with the aim to get wet, not to keep dry. It involves traversing,

Coasteering. Instructor: Ari Sherr.

rock hopping, swimming across zawns, getting washed around in the waves and cliff jumping. There are links to some early climbing guides for Cornwall and Anglesey where pioneers traversed the base of sea cliffs to train for the Alps or to spy out new routes. The word coasteering derives from orienteering and mountaineering and is applied here to define both sea-level traversing and coasteering.

Some Aims and Objectives for a Gorge Walk or a Coasteering Day

- Teamwork.
- Giving the opportunity for groups to provide mutual physical and emotional support.
- Self-reliance.
- Communication.
- Physical balance.
- Setting challenges.
- A journey (in ascent or descent).
- Experiencing a new environment.
- Teaching environmental issues.
- Creating an atmosphere of adventure.

Risks

Coasteering is always a serious matter, undertaken in one of the harshest and unforgiving environments on the planet, even on a sunny day with a flat sea. Serious incidents occur mostly as a result of ignorance of the sea, combined with the activity itself and the ability of the group.

Potential dangers include weather, sea and air temperature, wind direction and strength, squalls, tides, tidal height, swell size, rogue waves, coasteering location, falls onto rocks, loose rock and emergency escape routes. In addition, regular immersion in the sea wearing only a wetsuit means there is considerable risk of becoming cold and exhausted, leading to possible hypothermia. Instruction of coasteering, therefore demands the following skills and knowledge as a minimum:

- Knowledge of the sea state, rip currents, tidal height, swell size and the ability and experience to relate it to the coasteering session.
- Experience of lifesaving, including good swimming ability in rough water, use of different tows and use of a throw line.
- Use of a short rope for direct and indirect belay of a group and the ability to move confidently over steep ground.
- Understanding roped traverses and forces.
- Effective group management.
- Hands-on experience of coasteering in rough water in order to anticipate and possibly avoid sea conditions around the next corner.
- Risk management – understanding that it is a very variable environment.

Jumping and Falling into Water

Jumping into water safely depends on the confidence and ability of the jumper, the height of the jump and the depth of the water. Injury can be caused by jumping incorrectly from even the smallest height. One method of jumping to minimize the chance of injury is to look ahead (looking down can cause whiplash injury), keep your legs together and arms out to stabilize you in the air. As you enter the water, tuck your arms and keep your legs straight. Helmets can be worn to protect the nervous jumper in case they fall backwards as they jump.

Jumping.

Individual Equipment

- Helmet – most instructors wear a white water standard kayak helmet because some climbing helmets do not allow the water to drain out. The Petzl Meteor is a good compromise choice.
- Wetsuit suitable for the time of year and the weather. That means a full steamer for most of the year in the UK.
- Buoyancy aid and whistle.
- Overtrousers or shorts to protect the wetsuit from cuts and scrapes. Avoid baggy ones which impede the ability to swim.

- Pair of shoes or trainers – these will get wet, so suitable and substantial wetsuit boots may be preferable.
- Kagoul if there is a cold wind blowing or the student feels the cold. This does, however, hamper swimming ability.
- A harness is essential if a rope traverse is likely. Canyoning harnesses are particularly good as they protect the wetsuit and are simple to use.

Instructor Equipment

This is as for the individual kit, plus:

- Group shelter.
- Rocket flare and hand-held smoke flare.
- A mobile phone in some places.
- Hot drink.
- First-aid kit.

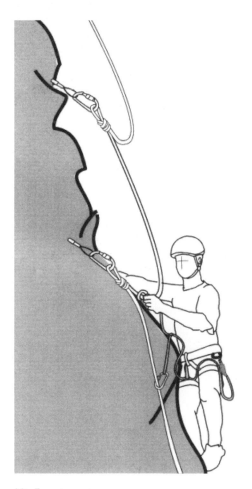

Via Ferrata system.

- Throw line.
- Rock climbing rope if the route requires it, some canyoning ropes float.
- Rock climbing kit if the route requires it.
- Knife capable of being easily accessed and opened with cold hands.
- Optional equipment – torpedo buoy for towing tired or weak swimmers, spare clothing and food.
- Fins for faster swimming.

Fixed Lines

Fixed lines are stationary ropes fixed at both ends, usually with intermediate points of protection. They can be horizontal or vertical. Fixed lines can be used when a slip has serious consequences or when you are trying to keep the students dry. They are slow to set up, but allow students to traverse high up relatively safely. Students should use two cow's tails with either a twist lock or an open-gate krab to traverse a fixed line. They can be made from webbing, but 9/11mm dynamic rope withstands abrasion for longer.

Horizontal Fixed lines

On horizontal fixed lines there should be some slack between the protection to allow ease of movement and reduce the vector forces (see Chapter 5, 'Forces'). Ideally, the anchors must be able to take a three-way loading and are best situated at head height. Try to place runners closer together where the difficulty of the traverse section increases. Only one person should be on any section of line at any time. If there are two people on a section and one falls the other may be pulled off.

Vertical Fixed Lines

The potential for longer falls is greatly increased if using vertical lines with only a krab for attachment. In some circumstances it may be useful to use an ascender, but prusiks generally slow the process down too much. Allow enough slack rope between points to form a J shape in the rope – the falling climber is then caught in the loop of the J, and the protection loaded downwards. Beware of the rope running over sharp edges. Consider using a Via Ferrata-style absorption system, for example, Petzl's Zyper if you use a lot of vertical fixed lines.

Pendulums

Pendulums can vary in complexity from using a sling to aid across a difficult section to setting up a rope above the difficulties. They can be great fun when the outcome is no more serious than a soaking.

Tyrolean Traverse

A Tyrolean traverse is used to make a crossing easier or quicker between relatively inaccessible peaks in the mountains. In the UK it is often used to allow access back across a sea zawn after the tide has come in.

Instructors frequently use it as an adventure experience, such as an exciting method for crossing a sea zawn or a river gorge. The same rules apply as they would to setting up any rope between two points, such as at a belay.

A tyrolean traverse requires:

- Multiple solid, equalized anchors.
- High anchors.
- Safe take-off and landing.
- Two releasable ropes tensioned differently.

Tyrolean traverse.

- Pulley or a figure-of-eight descender for crossing.
- Lowering /retrieval rope to assist those who are too tired.

Tensioning the rope on a tyrolean traverse can be achieved in various ways:

- The group can pull the rope. This is potentially safer because it is easier to judge how much tension is being put into the rope.
- A 3:1 pulley can be used (*see* Chapter 7).

GORGE WALKING (GHYLL SCRAMBLING)

(Clive Hebblethwaite)

Gorge walking can loosely be described as a mixture of rock climbing and caving using a streambed as the route. It provides an ideal setting for combining people with water to create their own adventure playground. A good day out depends on the instructor's ingenuity and creativity in offering a range of activities to stimulate every participant. Encourage the students to explore nooks and crannies and use their imagination as intrepid explorers discovering the unknown.

You need a good eye for small-scale bouldering problems and interesting solutions to traverses – for example, is it possible to do a whole body bridge with both feet and both hands on opposite rock walls? Be curious about what's underneath a boulder (a small tunnel squeeze perhaps), try out games (tie everyone in a line, only use hand signals and so on), and give inspiring names to different sections (The Elephant's Bottom, Turn Back Canyon, The Font, for example).

A suitable gorge provides:-

- Sufficient challenges and variety.
- High apparent risk, low real risk.
- Feels and looks like a gorge, steep sides and so on.
- Adventure factor with an element of commitment to making a journey.
- Allows for smooth rate of progress, no bottle necks.
- Selection of safe slides and boulders.
- Aesthetic aspects of water formations and lushness of vegetation.
- Escapable if conditions dictate.

Gorge walking.

The following factors make a gorge less suitable, and several of them occurring together would render it altogether unsuitable:

- Inescapable, giving an instructor less flexibility.
- Instructor's lack of familiarity with the route.
- Slow progress caused by bottlenecks on difficult sections.
- Too hard or too easy.
- Less slippery, algae-covered rocks instead of flood-scoured rocks.
- Too long, forcing a rushed day.

Success is also affected by how well an instructor fosters and reconciles the aims of self-reliance and teamwork, and the establishment of efficient communication channels early in the day, as there may be considerable water noise later on when it becomes critical. Where possible, encourage group members to help or spot each other up or down awkward steps, use communication games to test the effectiveness

of an information chain to its last link. Often the person at the back falls in or fails because they're using a different sequence of holds or they lack the vital information given to those in front.

There are some places, particularly exciting steep banks, where the consequences of a slip are not pleasant but a rope is impractical for protection. Safety is often no more than an awareness of danger so gather the group together, explain the hazard, focus them on the task and on their own self-reliance. Do not overuse this technique, however, because it then becomes ineffective. Be sure of your own judgement as to whether the real dangers are acceptable. Do not be influenced by what you have done with another group in the past nor by watching someone else lead a group in a different direction. You may also be unfamiliar with the site or have been looking elsewhere when the other group bypassed the short tricky section ahead. Your decision should be based on your group's ability, for example, whether you have younger students, a less able group and so on.

There are a myriad of objectives and as many different methods to choose from when planning a gorge walk. Some people descend gorges (canyoning), treating it as a wet activity and wear clothing and equipment similar to white water rafting, while others use mountaineering clothing and tend to set objectives to stay relatively dry.

Water Sports Approach

- Wetsuits, canoe kagouls, buoyancy aids required – these are expensive. Buoyancy aids are not used for canyoning as they hinder swimming in white water. 5mm wetsuits provide enough buoyancy and protection.
- Wetsuits provide body protection for slides and minor bumps.
- Buoyancy aids give body protection.
- Rate of progress is usually faster.
- More people moving more of the time.
- More light-hearted as less consequence of falling in.
- Water and air temperature can make this approach less pleasant.

Mountaineering Approach

- Emphasis on completing a journey.
- Teamwork more fundamental, for example, staying dry(ish).

- Greater realism involved in any pool traversing challenges.
- Individuals are more aware of 'failure'.
- Because the aim is to stay dry there is an increased chance of a slip from boulders. This can be avoided by getting the feet wet early on.
- Less specialized kit needed.

There are several pros and cons on the issue of kit, often depending on the variables of conditions, type of group, objectives and so on.

Choices of Equipment/Clothing

Walking Boots versus Wellington Boots versus Wetsuit Boots

Walking Boots
- Better for technical climbing on rocks.
- Provide more ankle support and protection.
- Good to and from gorge on steep muddy paths.
- Comfortable all day.
- Leather rots when continually wet.

Wellington Boots
- Good quality, with deep tread and a heel.
- Stay dry in shallow water.
- Warmer when wet.
- Dry quicker.
- Fall off feet when full of water or trying to swim.

Group plus instructor kitted out.
Photo: Clive Hebblethwaite.

- Can be less comfortable, e.g. sock-eating wellies.
- Soles not stiff and offer less protection.

Wetsuit Boots/Trainers
- Offer a compromise between wellingtons and walking boots. They offer little protection when walking down rocky gorge beds.
- Wetsuit socks and trainers with a high ankle for protection are preferred for canyoning.

Climbing versus Helmets Water Sports
Helmets
- Consider the nature of potential falls.
- Assess danger from a possible debris collapse from above.
- If in the water all the time then canoe-style helmets are more appropriate.
- Best solution – a multi-sport helmet that meets climbing standards.

Wearing Buoyancy Aids
Whether it is necessary to wear bouyancy aids depends on:

- Depth of the water.
- Is body protection needed?
- Type of day expected – is there going to be a lot of swimming?
- Difficulty of combining with a rucksack.

Familiarity with a gorge is vital for an instructor's peace of mind. Ad-libbing with a group is awkward and undesirable. It is best to know and have practised escape routes before you need them. A knowledge of the specific hydrology of the chosen gorge is paramount. This activity is not a pure form of mountaineering and each year people drown from hazards such as rope entanglement in water, being swept downstream due to underestimation of water forces or during unexpected flash floods. Instructors need to acquire enough water-based skills to be able to make all important judgements on such hazards. Swift water rescue courses certainly highlight many of the issues, some of which are listed below, and instructors should try to ensure that they have access to the sort of information available on such course's.

- Hydroelectric and flood-management schemes can make water levels change extremely quickly.

- Each river basin has its own fingerprint for rate of rise and fall in response to rain.
- Doubling water velocity (volume) quadruples the force it exerts
- If someone is swept off their feet can you get to them fast enough to help them out? A stick thrown in the water for retrieval is useful to assess the situation in fast currents.
- Do you need a throw bag and can you use it effectively?
- Are you capable of using this equipment?
- Ropes and water do not mix. Beware of underwater snags, especially if using a non-floating rope.
- Take extreme care about the releasability of the student from both ends of the rope.
- Carry an easily accessible knife.
- If water levels are higher than normal, what criteria will you apply to the decision to turn around, adapt or continue with normal trip?
- Beware of foot entrapment dangers – these can be life threatening.
- Underwater tree projections, water flows leading to undercuts and submerged ledges are all potential life-threatening hazards, especially if jumping into pools.
- If water flows are high, dangerous situations develop when someone attached to a rope is creating a downstream 'V'.

Environmental Considerations

No section on gorge walking would be complete without some consideration of the ecological impact of multiple use on these fragile environments. Inaccessible sections of gorges may represent the only true fragments of primary ancient woodland left in the United Kingdom and as such are of massive importance, way beyond their geographical size. These uniquely rare habitats have been largely undisturbed since the last ice age and contain many rare plants, for example yellow mountain saxifrage and rose-root. These plants are usually confined to sungrazed mountain ledges, but here they are found in a more diverse woodland setting.

So should we enter? Will our presence alter and change these 'lost worlds' for ever? Conservationists may shout to remove human interference, but the wider question of environmentally educating the public, the very base of support for conservation bodies, cannot be ignored. Without letting people experience 'wilderness' first-hand we lose the opportunity to promote the protection of these special places in a real and long-lasting way. Clearly the instructor has a balance to achieve, but to back away from using a site might not always be the right solution. One should ask: 'What am I trying to achieve? Can it be achieved in another, less environmentally sensitive way? Is the environment sustainable for others to pass through in the future? Am I using a minimal impact approach?'

The good news is that very little damage is caused by sticking to stream beds and bare rocks, and new paths formed rarely expand due to the confined nature of these sites. Damage is caused by scrambling up the vegetated sides and by trampling flora. Extreme care should be exercised to minimize this, for example by using only existing paths and escape routes and by educating people about the uniqueness of this environment. Be bold in tackling green issues – when said in the right way and in the right quantity people are usually responsive. A spin-off for your boldness will be that people are very good in policing themselves about keeping on the bare rock if they understand why.

SPECIALIST TECHNIQUES FOR CANYONING

(Rob Spencer [Plas Y Brenin] and Phil Poole [Eclipse Outdoor Discovery])

Canyoning, as opposed to caving which tries to keep students out of the water, accepts the water for what it is and has adopted some specialist rope techniques. All ropes must be floating canyon ropes. A knife and a rescue rope is normally carried. This section is by Phil Poole, Eclipse Outdoor Discovery, and Robb Spencer, Plas y Brenin.

Abseiling

Abseiling is normally done using a figure-of-eight descender in a sports climbing mode; a rubber washer can hold the figure-of-eight in place. This avoids any chance of it jamming on the rope and it also stays on the krab when you take the rope off in a deep pool, which means there is less chance of losing the descender. Safety is provided by the person at the bottom holding the rope.

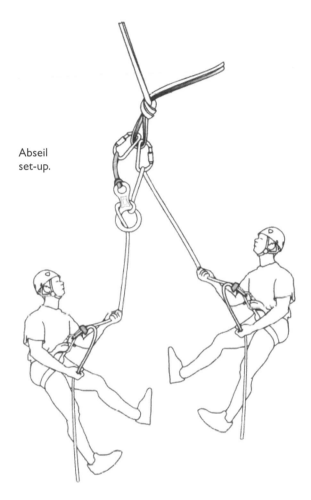

Abseil set-up.

Lowering is often done on an Italian Hitch or figure-of-eight descender.

Entering Pools

There are a number of ways of entering pools – slides or toboggans are rocky chutes and slabs up to 20m in length. Jumps are obvious and may require accuracy to avoid rocks or hazardous water features. Sometimes a flat landing is required when the pool is shallow. They can all be very serious.

Here are some points to consider before jumping, sliding or entering any pool:

- It is usual for an instructor to abseil into the pool to check it for depth and obstructions or to descend slides on a rope.
- Consider the size of the pool in case the student fluffs the take-off.
- Make sure the take-off is safe, not awkward or slippery and there are no irregularities in the slide.
- Brief everyone on how to jump, where to jump and to bend their legs on entering the water in case they bottom out.
- For high jumps do not have a rucksack on, keep arms in when entering the water and hold them to prevent your arms punching you in the face.
- On slides tuck the elbows in and keep knees flexed.
- Leave a rope in place until the last person has jumped or abseiled to give everyone the option of not jumping.

Rescues

The solutions to any problem will depend on the position of the leader and what equipment is available. The key to simple canyoning abseil rescues is to use a 'Fuse'. Some harnesses come with it fitted, although they can be retrofitted. If a regular harness is used, the belay loop can become the Fuse. Basically, the rescuer descends to the stuck student, attaches the student to the rescuer's descending device and cuts the fuse. It is a quick method, which is important when potential drowning is an issue, plus you do not have to cut ropes.

An alternative and quick method of rescuing a stuck abseiler is to attach a spare rope to the abseil rope using an ascender, then cut the abseil rope and lower using the spare. If there is no

The preferred method for attaching the rope to the abseil anchor is to thread the rope as for a retrievable abseil, then attach a spare figure-of-eight descender about half a metre from the anchor and clip this into the anchor. This allows two people to abseil simultaneously without having to worry about differences in weight. The last person removes the figure-of-eight descender and then abseils on two strands as per a regular retrievable abseil. It avoids placing knots in wet ropes. Safety is provided by holding the rope at the bottom of the abseil.

The philosophy behind using this method is that team members can safely install their figure-of-eight descender and understand the above system because the canyoning guide will be at the front of the party.

Safety ropes are an option for weaker members, but back-up prusiks are considered inappropriate because they increase the risk of someone getting stuck on a wet abseil.

spare rope, descend to the abseiler on a canyon prusik for protection, attach the student to you, cut his attachment to the rope and continue to the bottom.

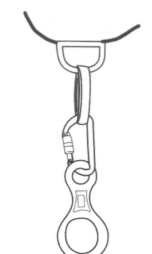

The Fuse.

The Canyon Prusik. Two-and-a-half metres of climbing rope. Remove half a metre of the core, tie an overhand knot on a bight at each end. Finished length should be 1.1m between knots. It will slide when you pull on it but lock if you sit on it. It works on all diameters of ropes, wet or dry, single or double.

APPENDIX

NATIONAL MOUNTAIN TRAINING AWARDS

(Adapted from National Mountain Training Awards leaflet of the UK Mountain Training Board.)

Who Organizes the Training?

The four home nation training boards, The United Kingdom Mountain Training Board and The British Mountain Guides administer seven awards that provide training and assessment for those who lead, instruct and guide others in the mountain environment.

What is Involved in Gaining an Award?

Although the detail of each award varies, there are a number of common elements in every scheme:

- **Registration:** Before attending any course you must be registered with the appropriate scheme.
- **Training Courses:** All the awards involve some practical training delivered by specially approved training staff. The relevant body monitors the standards of training. Experienced individuals can gain exemption from training.
- **Consolidation Period:** Training courses cannot turn people into effective leaders and for this reason it may take many months to consolidate the ideas put forward at training.
- **Assessment Courses:** All the awards have mandatory practical assessments delivered by specially approved assessors.
- **Continuing Personal and Professional Development:** Having gained an award candidates are expected to maintain their involvement in the activities as both an individual and as a leader. Opportunities for further training may be available through the relevant training boards.

Note

The awards remain valid only where the holder is deployed within the scope of the syllabus and has recent experience appropriate to the award. It is also a requirement that award holders have a current first-aid certificate.

Awards Relevant to this Book

Single Pitch Award (SPA)

This scheme trains and assesses people in the skills required for the supervision of single-pitch rock climbing and abseiling. Minimum age at registration is eighteen. Prior to registration, candidates should have led a minimum of fifteen outdoor routes of any grade, using leader-placed protection. Each course takes at least 20 hours and is often run over a weekend.

Mountain Leader Award (ML)

This is included because it is a step on the way to becoming a Mountain Instructor. This scheme trains and assesses people in the skills required for the leadership of hill walking arties in summer conditions. Minimum age at registration is 18 years. Prior to registration, candidates should have a minimum of 12 months' hill walking experience, and prior to training candidates should have undertaken a minimum of 20 quality mountain days. Each course takes at least 60 hours and candidates must be at least 24 years of age at the time of assessment.

Mountain Instructor Award (MIA)

This scheme trains and assesses people in the skills required for the instruction of mountaineering, including all aspects of rock climbing. Prior to registration, candidates should hold the ML award. Registration pre-requirements include extensive multi-pitch rock climbing experience at VS 4c or above and substantial group leading experience since passing the ML award. Candidates attend 9 days of training and 5 days of assessment.

IFMGA Mountain Guide

This scheme trains and assesses very experienced people in the skills required for the provision of instruction and guiding services in climbing, skiing and mountaineering on rock, ice and snow in all conditions and all seasons at BMG and IFMGA international standards. The award is administered by the British Mountain Guides and is valid worldwide. Candidates should register with the BMG and have gained substantial experience of United Kingdom and Alpine mountaineering. Pre-requirements for this scheme are broad and include fifty rock climbs at minimum E1 5b, winter climbs at minimum grade lV/V, alpine experience at minimum TD and skiing experience that includes off-piste and touring terrain.

USEFUL ADDRESSES

- British Mountaineering Council (BMC), 177–179 Burton Road, Manchester, M20 2BB
  0161 445 4747   Email: office@thebmc.co.uk   Website: www.thebmc.co.uk

- The Adventure Designs Project Co-ordinator
  Studio 26, Brunel University, Runnymede, Egham, Surrey TW20 0JZ
  01784 433262   Fax 01784 470880   Email: adventure-designs-dfl@brunel.ac.uk

- Mountaineering Council of Scotland (MCof S), 4a St Catherine's Road, Perth, PH1 5SE
  01738 638227   Email: see website   Website: www.mountaineering-scotland.org.uk

- Mountaineering Council of Ireland (MCofI), House of Sport, Longmile Road, Dublin 12, Ireland
  0035314507376   Email: mci@eircom.net   Website: www.mountaineering.ie

- United Kingdom Mountain Training Board, Siabod Cottage, Capel Curig, Gwynedd, LL24 OET
  01690 720272   Email: theukmtb@aol.com   Website: www.ukmtb.org

- Scottish Mountain Leader Training Board, Glenmore, Aviemore, Inverness-shire, PH22 1QU
  01479 861248   Email: smltb@aol.com

- Mountain Leader Training Board: as for BMC   Email: info@mltb.org

- Northern Ireland Mountain Training Board, Tollymore Mountain Centre, Brynasford, Newcastle, Co. Down, BT33 OPT
  0284 372 2158   Email: admin@tollymoremc.com

- Wales Mountain Leader Training Board, Plas y Brenin, Capel Curig, Gwynedd, LL24 OET
  01690 720361

- British Mountain Guides (BMG/IFMGA), Siabod Cottage, Capel Curig, Gwynedd, LL24 OET
  01690 720386   Email: bmg@mltb.org   Website: www.bmg.org.uk

- Association of Mountaineering Instructors (AMI), Siabod Cottage, Capel Curig, Gwynedd, LL24 OET
  Email: ami@mltb.org   Website: www.ami.org.uk

- DMM, Y Glyn, Caernarfon, Gwynedd
  01286 872222   Email: sue@dmm.wales.com   Website: www.dmm.wales.com

- Lowe Alpine UK, Ann Street, Kendal, Cumbria, LA9 6AB
  01539 740840   Web site: www.lowalpine.com

- Lyon Equipment, Rise Hill Mill, Dent, Sedbergh, Cumbria, LA10 5QL
  015396 25493   Email: info@lyon.co.uk   Web site: www.lyon.co.uk

- Scarpa, Unit 5, New York Way, New York Industrial Estate, Newcastle Upon Tyne, NE27 0QF
  0191 296 0212   Email: info@scarpa.co.uk   Web site: www.Scarpa.co.uk

- Wild Country Ltd, Meverill Road, Tideswell, Derbyshire, SK17 8PY
  01298 871010   Email: info@wild country.co.uk   Web site: www.wildcountry.co.uk

- Disability Information Trust, Nuffield Orthopaedic Centre, Headington, Oxford, OX3 7LD
  01865 227592   Email: ditrust@btconnect.com   Website: www.home.btconnect.com

- Disability Living Foundation
  020 7289 6111   Email: info@dlf.org.uk

- Radar, 250 City Road, London, EC1V 8AF
  020 7250 3222   Email: radar@ radar.org.uk   Web site: www.radar.org.uk

- Cheshire Shoe Repairs, 65 Folly Lane, Bewsey, Warrington, WA5 5ND
  01925 414945

- Base Camp Climbing School, North Lodge, Hundleton, Pembrokeshire, SA71 5QX
  01646 682007   Email: alunrichardson@cs.com

FURTHER READING

Performance Rock Climbing (1993), Dale Goddard and Udo Neumann, Stackpole Books.

Flash Training (1994), Eric J Horst, Chockstone Press, Colorado.

How to Rock Climb (1993), John Long, Chockstone Press, Colorado.

Self Rescue (1996), David J Fasulo, Chockstone Press, Colorado.

Outdoor Leadership (1997), John Graham, The Mountaineers, Seattle.

I Hate to Train (1994), Nancy Pritchard, Chockstone Press, Colorado.

Training for Rock Climbing (1994), Steve Bollen, Pelham Books, London.

Nutrition for Sport (1989), Steve Wooton, Simon and Schuster Ltd, London.

Learning to Rock Climb (1981), Michael Loughman, Sierra Club Books, San Francisco.

The Handbook of Climbing (1990), Allen Fyffe and Iain Peter, Pelham Books, London.

Mountaineering Freedom of the Hills (1992), The Mountaineers, Washington.

Further Modern Rope Techniques (1998), Nigel Sheperd, Constable, London.

Modern Rope Techniques (1987), Nigel Sheperd, Constable, London.

Rock and Ice Climbing (1983), Massimo Cappon, Orbis, London.

The Mountain Skills Training Handbook (2000), Pete Hill and Stuart Johnston, David & Charles, Devon.

INDEX